Professional's TV News Handbook

Charles Coates

Bonus Books, Inc., Chicago

98 97 96 95 94   5 4 3 2 1

Library of Congress Cataloging-in-Publication Data

Coates, Charles.
　　Professional's TV news handbook / Charles Coates.
　　　　p.　　cm.
　　Includes index.
　　　　1. Television broadcasting of news—Handbooks, manuals, etc.
I. Title.
PN4784.T4C55　　1994　　　　　070.1'95--dc20　　　　　94-9224
ISBN 1-56625-006-4　　　　　　　　　　　　　　　　　　　　　CIP

Bonus Books, Inc.
160 East Illinois Street
Chicago, Illinois 60611

Typesetting by Point West, Inc., Carol Stream, IL
Drawings by Gary Glasgow

Printed in the United States of America

To Elinor, Lindsay, Charlie and Nor, who put up with the learning years. Thank you.

Contents

Writing and Reporting News for Broadcast

Accuracy, brevity, clarity!

Keep it simple; viewers don't care how cleverly you write.

Make your story's main point twice.

Avoid the echo effect.

Select, rather than compress.

The statement you are about to read is *the* imperative of broadcast news writing. You've heard it before, you'll hear it again, and even if you're sure it's a cliché you still need to make it the beacon of your career: The ABCs of broadcast news writing are Accuracy, Brevity and Clarity.

It's risky to deal in absolutes, but accuracy and clarity are as close to absolutes in broadcast news writing as you can get. Brevity, while essential, isn't in the same league.

Accuracy, because there's no point writing and airing the story if it is wrong. Your stock in trade is your credibility. Mistakes made honestly can be just as damaging as deliberate misstatements. Accuracy is Number One.

Clarity, because your audience gets only one chance to understand what you've written and you get only that single chance to make yourself clear. Television isn't like a newspaper. The newspaper reader can re-read a troublesome paragraph, or look back to check information referred to a dozen paragraphs earlier. In broadcasting, the item is clear the first time or not at all. There's no going back over anything.

Brevity counts, of course, but for a reason that has nothing to do with journalistic integrity. In broadcasting, time is money. Time is what your station sells, and it can't manufacture more time. It allots just so much of the daily schedule to news programming; in turn, you must always try to make the best possible use of every second.

Ranking after accuracy, clarity and brevity is a fourth factor, interest. Interest attracts and holds attention. In news, interest should be inherent; otherwise, you wouldn't include the story in your program. Still, careful writing can make your story more interesting than your rival's, and that's what you should strive for. A word of caution: Don't let your writing destroy inherent interest. Another word of caution: If your writing calls attention to itself, it's probably not good writing.

Once properly written, the news must be broadcast with authority to create audience confidence. Nothing undermines authority like a stumbling, bumbling anchor. Nothing contributes to on-the-air flubs more than sloppy copy, strikeovers, carelessly penciled-in words, misspellings, etc. Professional copy must be neat.

So, be neat. And always—repeat, *always*—read your copy out loud. This is the sure way to find out how it will sound on the air. The best people in the business routinely edit copy by reading it out loud, regardless of how experienced they are. Does the copy make sense? Is it ambiguous? Is there a tongue twister or a double entendre? You find out by reading the copy out loud. This is also the most accurate way to time your copy—reading it out loud against a stop watch.

For the most part, broadcast news writers are re-write men and women, turning information from other sources into broadcast news copy. The original source may be the Associated Press, your local newspapers, a press release, notes from a reporter, a reporter's script, or copy from network and syndicated news services.

Newspaper reporters write their stories once and unless there are major developments between editions, that's it. The paper may print only two or three editions, and most stories run unchanged from the earliest to the final edition.

Television news departments typically present news in the morning, news at the dinner hour, news at bedtime, and, for some, news at noon and news after midnight. That's more demanding than getting out two or three editions of the same daily paper. It's like putting out entirely different papers for entirely different audiences, like being both the morning newspaper and the afternoon newspaper.

Radio has even more editions. A newscast every hour is common—and during "drive time" they may come even more frequently. It's not uncommon for radio stations to have upwards of 30 newscasts a day. A few stations around the country broadcast nothing but news, 24 hours a day.

Broadcast newspeople, unlike newspaper people, regularly update and/or revise their stories and coverage. Good radio stations don't keep reporting the same news in the same words, over and over again, every hour on the hour. Listeners would stop listening. TV stations don't present a story at 11 p.m. with the same pictures and same script they used at 6 p.m. Viewers, saying "I've already seen this," would click to a rival channel.

Suppose the story is that the local gas company's headquarters building blew up *this* morning and 31 people were killed. *Tomorrow* morning's newspaper typically would lead with that information—31 killed—because that is the news since the previous day's edition.

The radio station, on the other hand, couldn't keep reporting the same news, every hour on the hour:

"The Gas Company's headquarters blew up this morning and 31 people were killed."

"The Gas Company's headquarters blew up this morning and 31 people were killed."

"The Gas Company's headquarters blew up this morning and 31 people were killed."

Listeners would tune to other stations to get the latest news about the disaster.

Obviously, this explosion is the biggest local story of the day (possibly in the country, if it really happened, but let's overlook that). It will lead the local newspaper and probably every radio and television newscast for 24 hours.

The television station's position is somewhere between that of the radio station and the newspaper, but much more like the radio station's.

As a news writer at a radio station, your job would be to make each newscast sound fresh, either by keeping up with and reporting every new development, or by finding a way to revise old information so it sounds fresh. Keep that in mind: *to revise old information so it sounds fresh.*

Here are some hypothetical examples—so hypothetical they ignore the reality that any decent radio station would be interrupting its disk jockeys all day long with live, on the scene reports. For illustration, let's start with the first report on radio news.

9 a.m.: *"An explosion has ripped through the Gas Company's headquarters on 5th street in downtown Albuquerque. It happened about ten minutes ago. Fire and rescue units are on the scene. We will have more on the explosion at the Gas Company headquarters in downtown Albuquerque as it becomes available."*

10 a.m.: *"Police report that seven bodies have been recovered from the ruins of the New Mexico Gas Company building on 5th street at Chestnut in downtown Albuquerque. The building blew up little more than an hour ago...etc."*

11 a.m.: *"The death count in this morning's explosion at the New Mexico Gas Company headquarters is now 15, and rescue officials at the scene say they believe the toll will go higher...etc."*

As the story developed, you would keep leading with the latest information or, in the absence of fresh information of substance, you might stress different angles:

A) *"Fifth Street remains closed to traffic in downtown Albuquerque..."*

B) *"As bad as it was, with 31 people killed ...the explosion at New Mexico Gas Company headquarters this morning might have been worse... except for a flat tire. About 50 third graders from the Longfellow Elementary School were due to tour the building at 8:30, but their bus had a flat on Central Avenue. Otherwise, the pupils and their teachers would have been in the building when the explosion ripped through it just before 9 a.m...."*

C) *"Fire officials say they are sure there are no more bodies in the rubble of the Gas Company building...that the death toll will hold at 31..."*

A few times during the day, this same station might back up and recap the story—writing it as if listeners had not heard anything about the explosion. Television might compromise, writing stories that assume viewers already have heard about the tragedy but which parcel out the information in a fairly standard journalistic form. The 6 o'clock news might go like this:

"The tragedy is the worst in Albuquerque's history. Thirty-one people dead, 42 in hospitals. Fire officials say they have no idea what caused the explosion that leveled the New Mexico Gas Company's headquarters at 5th and Chestnut this morning. Reporter Carolyn Clancy is at the scene with this live report..."

Clancy then gives a full report. She may set the scene while she is "live on-camera" and then go into a chronological account of what happened, using videotape shot during the day.

Television reporter Clancy would be doing what a newspaper reporter would never do—starting with what in essence is a typical inverted pyramid lead (in the anchor's introduction to her) and following it with a chronological account. After the lead-in above, Clancy might start out: "The explosion occurred about ten minutes before nine this morning....." and finish with "....until investigators search through the wreckage a second time tomorrow morning. This is Carolyn Clancy reporting from downtown Albuquerque."

Back at the radio station, on this story or any other, you would be writing from information provided by your reporters or obtained by telephoning news sources, and from information on the wires or in the papers.

If you're lazy, what you write will sound just like what the wires and the papers wrote because you'll "borrow" key phrases from them. That's not good. Even worse, if you're not careful and your rivals at other stations are equally lazy, you'll all sound alike. That's very bad.

The proven way to avoid this is to learn to write without constantly referring to the source material. Read the wire's version of a terrible freeway accident. Then read the newspaper's version. Jot down salient facts on a piece of paper—names, ages, addresses, dates, sequence of events, attributions, etc. Think about the story for a moment. Make sure you understand what happened and how, at least so far as is known.

Don't write yet. Take time to decide on a general approach to the story and a lead. If you're writing a "long" story (30 to 60 seconds would be considered long) you should also try to figure out how you will end the story. Yes, half a minute to a minute might be long enough to require a beginning, middle and end. When you're ready, write from your notes, without consulting the source material. Lay out the information in an orderly, logical manner.

If you are given to analyzing news writing, you'll notice that new elements tend to raise new questions and that the best way to write is to answer new questions in the next sentence or two. Answer them or rewrite to eliminate them, but don't leave them hanging, unanswered.

As you write, make sure you *repeat* essential information: the name of the baseball player whose obit you are writing, or the name and location of the bank that was robbed, or the amount of the sales tax increase. Keep in mind that you seldom have the undivided attention of your audience. Their minds tune in and out, according to what interests them.

Your television viewer wasn't really listening until he heard something about a famous baseball player. A dead baseball player. Who was it? What happened to him? Give the viewer two shots at catching the name (even if there's a picture with a name under it on the screen, because viewers don't always have their eyes glued to the set). The viewer's mind was straying until he heard something about the sales tax increase. What increase? How much? How much? When? He can't go back and look, as he might with the newspaper. It's up to you to repeat key elements.

Another thing you must do is have a good idea of how long a story you are writing. Know what your goal is. "Long" is a misleading way to put it, because all broadcast stories are short— painfully short, until you get used to it. "There's nothing you can't say in 30 seconds—nothing." Or, "Take all the time you want—up to 30 seconds."

As a general rule, the more you work at anything the better you get at it. As you become an experienced broadcast news writer, you will begin to appreciate that you *can* cover a great deal of ground in 30 seconds, or 45 seconds, or a minute and 15 seconds. You can, if you're good, cover much more than most critics of broadcast news will concede.

It's a process of editing, of eliminating. You must learn to recognize what needs to go in and what doesn't, what is new and what people already know, what is essential background and what is superfluous. It takes practice, but if you have decent news sense and any facility with words, you can learn to strip a story to its essentials and provide a lot of information in just a few lines. It is far better to carefully choose the information you intend to impart, rather than try to squeeze it all in. The process is one of selecting—as much if not more than condensing.

And even as you are economizing in your writing, you may seem to be wasting some words. But only seeming to waste them. What you are really doing is skillfully separating one story from another, skillfully setting up a story, skillfully enabling your listener to understand—to make the most of the single opportunity you and your listener have to communicate.

That's why you will hear (or write) apparent "throwaway" lines like:

"There's trouble on the freeway tonight."

"Another breakout at the state prison."

"The legislature is still trying."

The line about the freeway might be followed by:

"A tractor-trailer jack-knifed during an emergency stop on Interstate 25, and skidded across the median into oncoming traffic. No one was seriously injured, but a massive chain-reaction, fender-bender brought traffic to a standstill about 10 p.m. State police advise staying off the eastbound side of I-25 between the Monterey and San Carlos exits for another hour. Again, that accident is on eastbound I-25 between Monterey and San Carlos."

Killing the line, "There's trouble on the freeway tonight" might save a couple of seconds, but it is more than worth using because it alerts the audience to the subject matter—like a headline—and it separates the accident story from the story that preceded it.

Let's assume the state legislature has been hung up for several days on abortion legislation. The lawmakers simply cannot agree, and while an emotional debate rages the legislature isn't getting anything else done.

This stalemate has been widely and frequently reported. It's in the news all the time. Gridlock in the legislature. Therefore, the throwaway line, "The legislature is still trying" immediately alerts your viewer, unless she's from Mars, that a story about the legislative impasse on abortion is coming up. Unconsciously, the viewer summons from memory what she knows about the situation. What you proceed to tell will make sense without a lot of background. It makes sense because that two-second throwaway line, "The legislature is still trying" gets the viewer ready.

What about the shortness of that sentence, "The legislature is still trying." That sentence is so short you could easily afford to follow it with a long sentence. After the long one, you might want another short one. After that, a long one, and so on. But not predictably rhythmic, of course, not short/long/short/long/short/long/etc. But you should make a conscious effort to vary the length of your sentences. And when doing so, keep in mind that short sentences usually have more impact than long ones.

And what about sentences? Must every "sentence" really be a complete, grammatical sentence? No, every sentence needn't be a sentence. But it must make sense. You can write fragments. You can drop words, skip phrases, get by without a verb. You can tell if you are getting away with it by reading the story out loud. Usually, that's all it takes. One 20-second reading of a 20-second story will tell you if it's an effective departure from the strictest rules of composition. If that reading tells you it isn't effective, then rewrite.

Many beginners are hesitant to rewrite their own work, as if they are ashamed or embarrassed to have to do something over again. They fear it may spotlight their presumed incompetence. They don't want to look like amateurs. And they don't yet know that seasoned pros think nothing of reworking their work, as many times as it takes. Pros rewrite because they believe writing is infinitely perfectible (which most of it is) and they rewrite because they lack the arrogance to believe the first way *they* write it must be the best way because *they* are so good. *Rewrite! Rewrite again!* Consider it proof that you demand the best of yourself, that you really care.

Verb Tenses

Broadcast writers make heavy use of the present tense, even when writing about past and future events. The goal is to project immediacy—broadcast news "is now."

When a story is important enough to be used over and over again, and when there are no new elements in it or no legitimate alternate approaches, broadcast writers will switch to the present tense, or the present perfect, or the present progressive to "freshen" stale news.

Let's say that venerable baseball manager "Twig" McGaw has worked wonders with the St. Louis Cardinals after being brought in at mid-season. The new manager rallied his charges and in September they swept a four-game series from the New York Mets to go back into first.

In the past tense, the story would have been written along these lines: "The St. Louis Cardinals *took* first place in the National League East, beating the New York Mets...etc..."

Let's say it was a night game and you reported the story on your late evening newscast. What are you going to do in the morning sports wrap-up, where the story continues to be important in the sports scene?

You'll write it in the present tense: "The St. Louis Cardinals are back in first place in the National League East, after beating the New York Mets....etc."

You might also have written in the present perfect tense: "The St. Louis Cardinals *have regained* first place in...etc." The present perfect clearly makes your lead appear fresher than the information is.

Another popular verb tense in broadcast writing is the present progressive, which in the example above wouldn't work with the verb "regain." You'd have to say the Cards "are sitting" in first place, or something like that.

But the present progressive would work nicely in a different story, like this: "Mayor Bunson *is sticking* to his decision not to resume negotiations with the police union."

This lead may follow a series of more conventional leads on the same story, that story being the news conference in which the mayor announced that he absolutely, positively won't change his mind on reopening wage negotiations with the police union. He would rather have a strike, he said, than give in to the threats of city employees who are responsible for the public safety.

The first time around, you might have been written:

"Mayor Bunson told a news conference he won't go back to the bargaining table with the police union. The mayor said he would rather have the police go on strike than yield to the union's threats. Etc...."

The next time, you might switch to the present perfect:

"Mayor Bunson has renewed his promise not to resume negotiations with the police union...etc."

Later, you might use the present tense of the verb "to say." This is the most common way to freshen an old story. You would write:

"Mayor Bunson says *he won't resume negotiations with the police union...etc."* Or:

"Mayor Bunson says *he'd rather have the police go on strike than...etc."*

This use of the present tense is so common that writers and listeners seldom question whether it is accurate. The mayor made the statement once and, technically, that's that. He isn't running around saying it and saying it and saying it. But it is a reasonable assumption that what he professed at four o'clock this afternoon he would profess at midnight or tomorrow morning or two days from now—it is a continuing condition. You can write "says."

That fact that something is a continuing condition is the foundation for the use of the present and present progressive tenses in broadcast news writing. You need only ask yourself whether what you are writing about is a continuing condition. If the answer is yes, use the present tense. If it's no, don't.

Suppose the police do go on strike. You would probably wind up writing dozens of leads on a story that might have only a few changes in it. When the strike begins, you would probably rather use the past tense than the present, because the past will suggest to the listener that the strike is new.

"Albuquerque police went *on strike tonight."*

Later, you might write: "Albuquerque policemen *have gone* on strike. They left their jobs at midnight..."

Still later: "Albuquerque police *are* on strike. The walkout began..."

As the strike wears on, you might have leads like these:

A. *"Albuquerque police* began *the 6th day of their strike..."*

B. *"The 6th day of the Albuquerque police strike* has begun..."*

C. *"Albuquerque police* are *in the 6th day of their strike..."*

Finally, agreement is reached, the union ratifies it, and the police go back to work.
Your leads?

A. *"The Albuquerque police strike* ended..."

B. *"The Albuquerque police strike* has ended..."

C. *"The Albuquerque police strike* is over..."

D. *"Albuquerque police* went *back to work..."*

E. *"Albuquerque police* are going *back to work..."*

F. *"Albuquerque police* are *back on the job..."*

G. *"Albuquerque police* are *pounding the pavement today..."*

All of these are acceptable, but they aren't all interchangeable. Probably the best is the "strike is over" followed (when it actually happens) by "are back on the job." Both "best" choices are in the simple present tense.

Voice: Active or Passive?

The examples we've just looked at are all written in the active voice—the preferred voice in news writing (and most other writing.) In some newsrooms, the injunction is to never use the passive voice. That may be going too far.

Let's say City Manager George Smith wants to visit his town's "sister city" in Africa. There's controversy over the expense and value of the trip, but not a big fuss. Smith works quietly behind the scenes and eventually the city council approves the expenditure.

A. *"The City Council* approved *George Smith's trip.....* "

B. *"City Council* says *it's OK for George Smith to..."*

C. *"George Smith* won *approval...."*

D. *"George Smith* gained *approval...."*

E. *"George Smith* has *the approval...."*

F. *"George Smith* has been given *approval by the City Council to..."*

Again, these aren't interchangeable. A and B are in the active voice, but the subject—the entity providing the action—is the City Council. In C, D, E and F, the subject is Mr. Smith but the emphasis varies. In C and D, it's on Smith's action rather than the Council's. C suggests a victory by Smith over the Council and D suggests a minor political struggle. E is so neutral it suggests nothing. But it may be that the circumstances of this case make the only entry in the passive voice—F—the best choice. It depends on where you want to put the emphasis. To make the trip, Smith needed the approval of the council. Would the council give it to him? Yes, it did. But is this a story about the council or Smith? It's really about Smith, so: "George Smith has been given approval..."

Consider the following, where your choice will depend on what you are writing about—on which information you are emphasizing—rather than the voice or tense. Are you writing about traffic accidents or people, murders or people, John Does or prominent people?

A. *"A pickup and a tractor-trailer collided on Route 33, killing three New Mexicans...."* (Active voice, emphasis on the accident.)

B. *"Three more New Mexicans died in highway accidents..."* (Active voice, emphasis on dead New Mexicans.)

C. *"New Mexico highways claimed three more lives..."* (Active, emphasis on highway carnage in New Mexico.)

D. *"Country music singer Tex Tyler and two other people were killed on Route 33 when..."* (Passive, emphasis on the prominent Tex Tyler.) .

E. *"Albuquerque's 39th murder of the year has taken the life of a 47-year-old truck driver..."* (Active, emphasis on the 39th murder being committed, makes little difference who the victim was.)

F. *A hitchhiker stabbed and then shot to death a 47-year-old truck driver..."* (Active, emphasis on what the hitchhiker did rather than who the victim may have been. This had better have solid attribution somewhere.)

G. *"Mayor Bob Bunson is Albuquerque's 40th murder victim..."* (Active, emphasis on the *mayor being* the 40th victim.)

H. *"Albuquerque's 40th murder victim of the year is Mayor Bunson..."* (Active, emphasis on the 40th victim, who just happens to be the mayor.)

I. *"Mayor Bob Bunson was shot and killed by an intruder in..."* (Passive, emphasis on the mayor being killed.)

All of the above are valid approaches to the news. It comes down to whether you intended a particular emphasis or whether your emphasis is the incidental result of trying to stay in the active voice. If you really meant the emphasis in "C" and "H", fine. If not, rewrite.

Would "D" and "I" be improved by switching them from passive to active—Tyler and two others "have died" and Mayor Bunson "is dead"? Probably not. In these cases, the passive voice gets to the point faster and is more conversational. Be careful about letting your quest for the active voice lead you to say things that aren't appropriate. Of course, in the Tyler accident you could have said "died" and been all right. Died would not have worked for the mayor's murder. You die when you are murdered, but being murdered is newsier than just dying. You could have written in the active voice that arch criminal John Dillinger "got his," but you wouldn't want to say that Mayor Bunson "got his."

Choosing Your Approach to a Story

It's very easy to color a story inadvertently by trying to make it a little different. Examine the three approaches to this innocent (and fictitious) news item.

> 1. *"The federal government is going to charge 30 percent more for the right to graze livestock on federal land, starting in June."*

That seems pretty straight forward, but not especially interesting. No conflict, no victim, no hero—no nothing. Let's try this:

> 2. *"It's going to cost New Mexico ranchers 30 percent more to graze livestock on federal lands, starting in June. That works out to about six thousand dollars a year for the average rancher."*

Isn't that more like it? Easier to understand, and it puts the news in personal terms. Poor ranchers! Wonder if I'll have to pay more for meat?

3. *"Starting in June, taxpayers will get 30 percent more money from ranchers who graze their cattle on federal lands in New Mexico. That works out to around six million dollars extra for the federal treasury."*

Hey, what's fair is fair! After all, I'm a taxpayer. I own that land just as much as some rancher. Who do those ranchers think they are? Go get'em, Feds! Just don't raise my taxes.

A pretty good case can be made that the dullest, most routine version of this story, the first, is also the best. This example is worth keeping in mind if you want to be a careful news writer.

Broadcast Style

The concept of writing "style"—in the sense of formal rules rather than graceful expression—is one thing in broadcasting and quite another in print. The print media are guided by two authorities, *The Associated Press Stylebook* and *The Chicago Manual of Style*. Each is a bible to its users. AP style is followed by most of America's newspapers and is used by all AP writers to keep the product consistent. It covers punctuation, capitalization, spelling, abbreviation, numbers, word usage and the meaning of terms frequently used in the news. It takes more than 300 pages to do this. The Chicago manual sets detailed standards in spelling, punctuation, capitalization, abbreviation, citations, bibliography and so on for trade and text books, and scholarly and scientific papers. It runs over 900 pages.

Broadcasting has no equivalents, no preeminent authorities. AP puts out a broadcast style book, but its use is largely confined to the AP itself, to keep AP's product consistent. The rest of broadcast news writers follow conventions and rules that are generally accepted everywhere but codified nowhere.

The purpose of broadcast style is to help writers produce copy the audience can understand and anchors can read without flubbing. What the copy looks like is immaterial because viewers will never see it, they'll only hear it. Broadcast writers write for the ear, not the eye, and not for comma cops.

The Basics of Broadcast Writing and Style

Attribution precedes statements 90-plus times out of 100, and always before statements of opinion—a criticism, attack, prediction, etc.

Names are used in their simplest complete form except in special cases, and should be repeated when they are important.

Titles are used in their simplest form, and sometimes much of the official title is dropped in the interest of clarity and brevity.

Ages generally precede the name or noun, as in "111-year-old elm tree." Note the hyphens.

Hyphens are used as above to help the announcer see and read the letters or phrases as units, as in P-T-A and "three-and-a-half-miles deeper."

Numbers are best rounded off when the exact number isn't important. They should be written in easy-to-grasp form. The following are OK:

7-million 300-thousand   half-a-million   230-thousand

939 (not 9-hundred 39)   three-tenths   3-tenths

four-and-a-quarter (rather than 4-point-25)

One through eleven are usually written out except in sports scores and time of day and compounds like "3-year-old dispute"— but the world would survive if you wrote "three-year-old dispute" or fourteen percent rather than 14 percent.

Symbols like $, %, @, +, =, #, etc. are not used. Write out the words—13 dollars each (rather than $13 @), Number One (rather than # 1).

Quotes should be clearly indicated when the words are important, with "quote....unquote" or "as she put it.....", etc.

Abbreviations like "Rd." and "Co." are not used. Spell the words out. Abbreviations like N-double-A-C-P and P-T-A are usually OK—but usually only on second reference after the full name. Obscure abbreviations are not used.

Capitalize all proper names and nouns, as in print style.

Spell correctly. Misspellings can lead to on-the-air mistakes.

Pronouncers. It is the writer's responsibility to include within the copy the pronunciation of unusual names.

Freshen old stories with the present tense, for the most part, or present perfect. Then be honest and put the time element in second or third sentence when it's important.

Avoid starting a story with an unfamiliar name or a number, although there are times when it's OK.

Be neat. Your copy must be easy to read; it shouldn't be a puzzle.

Be direct. Write simple, direct, straightforward English—Subject/Verb/Object. Almost any story that begins with a gerund, present participle, dependent clause, or "there is/there are" can be improved by killing the offender. Work hard to avoid backing into the news.

Read your copy out loud. This is the best way to spot tongue-twisters and double entendres like the pro golfer who is "playing a round with Nancy Niblick."

ACCURACY ACCURACY ACCURACY!!! (And, by the way, ACCURACY.)

PS: Get it right!

Attribution

The most striking difference between broadcast and print writing is the convention in broadcast writing that attribution goes first. That's not to say always first, because smooth and clear copy certainly can be written with interior attribution and—very rarely—attribution at the end. But the first thing you must learn is to "turn the sentence around."

Broadcasters do it for two reasons: first, to make clear the source of whatever is being reported, and, second, because people just don't talk the way newspapers write. (Although some papers are beginning to write the way people talk.)

A newspaper might report a fire this way, with a statement followed by its source or attribution:

"Fourteen people were killed today in a motel fire near Kingman, the Arizona State Police reported."

You would not tell it to a friend that way. You would turn the sentence around, and say to your friend: "I heard 14 people were killed today in a motel fire near Kingman."

"I heard" is an attribution. If your friend asked where you heard it, you might say, "On the radio." Pressed further, you'd say, if you remembered, "Arizona state police."

If you were writing the story for broadcast, you'd follow the pattern you used when telling your friend. You'd write: "Arizona state police say 14 people died in a motel fire near Kingman."

Or you could delay the attribution and hedge with "reported" in the first sentence, just in case there's a change in the number of fatalities: "Fourteen people were reported killed today in a motel fire near Kingman, Arizona. The Arizona state police said...

Later in the day, after the fire has been extinguished and all the bodies have been pulled from the rubble, the death toll has become fact. You could write that part of the story without attribution, although at some point you'd have to indicate some source for your information: "Fourteen people died today in a motel fire near Kingman, Arizona. The fire broke out at 5 a.m....etc. Arizona state police say they have detected possible signs of arson..."

Delaying attribution often works well, so long as the statement isn't controversial. Speculation about the cause, however, requires attribution, as written above. Otherwise, the speculation becomes yours or your news anchor's.

A day or two later you might follow up the story with this:

"Kingman Fire Chief Elio Sanchez said today his department is investigating the possibility of arson in last Sunday's fire at....etc."

That's fine, but a stronger way to write it puts the attribution in the second sentence: "The Kingman fire department is investigating the possibility of arson in last Sunday's fire at...etc. Fire Chief Elio Sanchez said today he ordered the probe....etc."

When the statement is an opinion, criticism or attack, everything changes. You must eliminate any possibility that the viewer will think the opinion, criticism or attack comes from the anchor. You do it by putting the attribution first.

Let's say the chairman of the state Republican party attacks the Democratic governor. Which would you write for broadcast, for the ear?

1) *"Horace Habble is the worst governor in the state's history. That's what Republican party chairman Morton Rogers told the ...."*

2) *"New Mexico's top Republican says Democrat Horace Habble is the worst governor in the state's history. Republican Party Chairman Morton Rogers told...."*

The difference is clear: The second version is better because there's no opportunity for a viewer to think even for a moment the anchor says Horace Habble is the worst governor in the state's history. The first version allows that interpretation, even if only for couple of seconds.

Now, let's look at an opinion or a prediction that is not an attack or criticism. First, in routine newspaper style:

"Gold prices will double in the next six weeks, billionaire speculator Midas King told a luncheon meeting of Albuquerque investment bankers...etc."

For broadcast, you would write this:

"Billionaire speculator Midas King says gold prices will double in the next six weeks. King says...."

Or you would write:

"Billionaire speculator Midas King predicted today that gold prices will double in the next six weeks. King told a luncheon meeting of Albuquerque investment bankers...etc."

Or another approach:

"Albuquerque investment bankers were told today that gold prices will double in the next six weeks. The bankers were addressed by billionaire speculator Midas King, who...etc."

Or:

"Albuquerque investment bankers heard a prediction today that gold prices will double in the next six weeks. The prediction was made by billionaire speculator Midas King, who...etc."

Incidentally, in these illustrations King has said, told and predicted. Predicted is by far the best verb because the wonderful neutrality of said in not an asset in this case—King did predict, and that's what you should write.

Punctuation

When you punctuate, you do so for yourself or another newscaster and not the viewer. No one is going to write a prissy letter to the editor about your misplaced comma or excessive reliance on ellipses. No viewer will see your script and know about your sins.

Although broadcast punctuation is basically the same as print, a number of modifications make the copy easier to read on the air.

- Use commas and periods and occasional colons, but not semicolons. What does a semi-colon signify,

anyway—especially when reading in front of a microphone?

- Use a dash—made with two hyphens—to indicate a
  pause slightly longer than a comma. A bit esoteric?
  Yes, but look:

  *"The government's expenditures—which some critics
  say are the real cause of inflation—are expected
  to rise next year by nearly nine percent."*

Some writers prefer to use a string of three periods (an el-
lipsis) rather than a dash. And some will say this means a slightly
longer pause than for the dash. Even more esoteric? Here's an example:

  *"Joyson predicted that Garcia...who has been aver-
  aging nearly 20 points the last four games...will hit
  for 30 in one of this weekend's games...probably Sat-
  urday night's contest with U-C-L-A."*

Whether you settle on dashes or ellipses, they clearly help
the announcer see and read the clauses as separate entities. The
clauses stand out far more than they would with commas, and that
helps the announcer make sense out of the copy.

- Use a single hyphen rather than periods or no punctuation in things like Y-M-C-A to indicate each letter should be read individually (clearer than
  Y.M.C.A and YMCA). Do the same for telephone
  numbers and similar constructions: "...that number
  again is 8-6-6 - 5-7-7-0."

- Do NOT use the following symbols and punctuation
  marks: # $ % & + = & * / @ and anything else like
  them that your keyboard might offer. Exceptions are
  sometimes made for $, & and %, but the risk of mis-

reading them is greater than the effort of typing out dollars, and, and percent.

- Make key words stand out by writing them in caps, setting them off with dots, or underlining them. Examples:

  "The jury found Edwards NOT guilty on four counts of..."

  "The jury found Edwards...not...guilty on four counts of..."

  "The jury found Edwards <u>not</u> guilty on four counts of..."

The idea, of course, is to reduce the chance of overlooking that tiny but essential word "not."

Names and Titles

Some do's and don'ts.

- Do use the simplest possible form of a name.

- Don't start an item with an unfamiliar name.

- Do repeat names. If the story is about a person and the viewer doesn't catch the name the only time you give it, then what is the story about for that viewer? It's a story about someone, just someone. Wonder who?

• Don't believe that a full-blown title is always necessary.

Compare the following:

1) *"Arthur Appleton, the owner of a home furnish-*
ings store in Albuquerque's Northeast Heights, was fa-
tally shot today while deer hunting near Belen. The
victim, 49, was pronounced dead on arrival at Belen
Hospital...etc."

2) *"An Albuquerque businessman was fatally shot*
today while deer hunting near Belen. Forty-nine
year old Arthur Appleton was pronounced dead on
arrival at Belen Hospital. Appleton, the owner
of...etc."

The second version is better for broadcast because it doesn't
lead off with the name of a person few people know or care about.
Viewer interest in "an Albuquerque businessman" may not be ram-
pant, either, but the term is a lot more inclusive than the name
"Arthur Appleton." Note also the handling of Appleton's age and
the repetition of his name in the second version.

Incidentally, here's the same story in the active voice. Is it
better?

"An Albuquerque businessman died today after
being shot while deer hunting near Belen. Doctors at
Belen Hospital pronounced 49-year-old Arthur Apple-
ton dead..."

The form of names and titles depends a great deal on who
your audience is. Examples:

"U-N-M Coach Gary Joyson says..." This is OK in New
Mexico but poor on a network broadcast because "U-N-M" is not as
well known as "U-C-L-A."

"The basketball coach at the University of New Mexico...Gary Joyson...says...etc...." This is better for network use. Note that it emphasizes the school rather than the coach.

"University of New Mexico Basketball Coach Gary Joyson says...etc...." This is an OK, all-purpose approach so long as it doesn't get too long—as would:

> *"University of New Mexico Valencia County Campus Assistant Basketball Coach and Adjunct Lecturer in Chemistry Norm Knight says...."*

Here are three forms of identification that are subtly different and not quite interchangeable because they place different emphases on the position, name and city.

> *"Albuquerque Chief of Police Wyatt Earp..."*

> *"Albuquerque's Chief of Police, Wyatt Earp..."*

> *"Police Chief Wyatt Earp of Albuquerque..."*

Here are three versions of a fire story. The first starts out with a name that's unfamiliar to most people, "The DeWitt Fulton Hotel..." The second version delays that name while suggesting it's an interesting fire story because a *landmark* burned down. The third version is a sort of compromise between the right approach, the second, and the wrong approach, the first.

> *1) "The DeWitt Fulton Hotel in Albany, New York, was destroyed by fire during the night. The 101-year-old landmark burned to the ground in about three hours."*

> *2) "An architectural landmark in Albany, New York, burned to the ground during the night. Fire destroyed the DeWitt Fulton Hotel in about three hours. The 101-year old...etc."*

3) "The DeWitt Fulton Hotel, a 19th century landmark
in Albany, New York, burned to the ground last night.
The DeWitt Fulton was destroyed in about three hours."

Names, even names of people or places or buildings unknown to the public, give authenticity to news stories. So can full
and correct titles. Still, you can omit names and otherwise abbrevi-
ate when the circumstances are right.

Are the circumstances right with the DeWitt Fulton Hotel?
Could you write that story without naming it—a nameless landmark
hotel in Albany burned down? You couldn't, or shouldn't. You need
the name.

Regarding titles, how about this?

"Howard Hund, Animal Control Officer for the
Milwaukee Environmental Health Department, says...
etc...."

Or,

"Howard Hund, a dog catcher in Milwaukee, says...
etc..."

The latter is better, so long as some peculiarity of the story
doesn't demand the official title. Of course, both of these examples
suffer from the flaw of starting with an unfamiliar name, Howard
Hund. If they were lead sentences they'd have to be rewritten.

Sometimes you can omit a name entirely. It's possible the
dog catcher story could be told without Howard Hund's name—not
in Milwaukee, of course, but certainly in Brownsville, Texas, because Hund would be a complete unknown. Carrying this a step farther, you probably would leave out the name of the chief of police
in Paris announcing a major development in the kidnapping of a
fashion designer. The name will be meaningless to American audiences, and it might also be unpronounceable. Leave it out. Write
"The chief of police in Paris says...: or even, "In Paris, police
say...." In the same vein, don't say "Mrs. Jane Smith of Corsicana,
Texas..." when "A Texas housewife..." will suffice.

It usually makes more sense to say "In a suburb of Pittsburgh..." than "In Sewickley, Pennsylvania..." But if a light plane were to crash into an elementary school in Sewickley, you'd have to use the name and you'd be remiss if you failed to make clear that Sewickley is a Pittsburgh suburb.

Finally, use the simplest form of a name that you can (unless you know the person prefers a more complicated form.) J. William Fulbright was a prominent senator from Arkansas for many years. Newspapers called him "Sen. J. William Fulbright." Broadcasters referred to him as "Senator William Fulbright..." leaving out the initial.

Newspapers often wrote of "President Richard M. Nixon" as if to distinguish him from some President Richard Nixon with a different middle name. Broadcasters wrote about "President Nixon" and left out not only the initial but the first name. Newspapers did not, however, write about "President George H. W. Bush." In fact, many reached the point of calling him "President Bush," just like broadcasters.

On the other hand, not many people wrote about plain old "F-B-I Director Edgar Hoover..." They wrote of "J. Edgar Hoover." No one would write about John P. Sousa if they meant John Philip Sousa. It is usually J. P. Morgan, not John Pierpont Morgan.

Ages & Addresses

Broadcasters tend to go light on the careful identification of people in the news—probably too light in the case of people in trouble with the law. If a man is arrested, most newspapers will try to include his age, occupation and address, so he won't be confused with another person with the same name.

But what newspapers do doesn't read well on the air:

"Police arrested Edmund Wilson, 53, 47 Easy St., a steam fitter...."

For broadcast, however, you could write:

"Police arrested 53-year-old Edmund Wilson, a
steam fitter who lives at 47 Easy Street..."

Using age as an adjective is the rule in broadcast, because it doesn't stop your sentence dead the way "Edmund Wilson, 53," does. Saying "Edmund Wilson, who is 53 years old,...etc." is better, but it still tends to slow things down. "Fifty-three-year old Edmund Wilson..." works best. In broadcast obituaries, however, the usual forms are: "She was 79 years old." or "....at the age of 79." One form that doesn't work well is, "Sixty-one-year-old Millicent Morgan is dead."

Quotes

The rule on quotes is to avoid them if you can, the rationale being that as a professional writer you can write better than most people speak. Therefore, for clarity and brevity you paraphrase news makers rather than quote them. But editorial considerations sometimes make a direct quote necessary.

When you must quote, you write the quotation marks into the copy by using words like "quote" and "as he put it" and "what Jones called" and "in her words." That's for your viewer to hear. For your anchor you should also place quotation marks around the quoted material. Sometimes you will need to indicate the end of a quote with "unquote." More often, it's not necessary.

Some examples:

POOR: *Mr. Nixon said "One year of Watergate is enough" and that others may "wallow" in it but he will be busy taking care of the country.*

GOOD: *Mr. Nixon said—and we quote him—"One year of Watergate is enough." The president added that other people may— as he put it—"wallow in Watergate"—but that he will be busy taking care of the country.*

It is important your audience knows the disdainful language was the president's, just as it should know that when Nixon said "I am not a crook," the word "crook," which we are not in the habit of applying to our presidents, was his. See the difference:

POOR: *President Nixon said today he is not a crook.*
GOOD: *President Nixon said today he is not, in his words, "a crook."*

Or:

" President Nixon said today, quote, "I am not a crook," unquote.

Some additional examples:

POOR: *The king told the ambassador this means war.*
GOOD: *The king told the ambassador—and these are the king's words—"This means war."*

The second version is stronger. It emphasizes the implication that war is imminent. Other examples:

POOR: *Coach Klinker said he plans to start fast and slippery Gary Gumbo at halfback tomorrow in spite of Gumbo's miserable attitude during practice this week.*
GOOD: *Coach Klinker said he plans to start Gary Gumbo—whom he described as "fast and slippery"—at halfback tomorrow, in spite of what he called, quote, "Gumbo's miserable attitude" during practice this week.*

The first version gives the impression the sportscaster says Gumbo is "fast and slippery" but has a "miserable" attitude. The second version pins the opinions on the coach, where they belong.

Sometimes it is necessary to quote a long passage. Then you should insert, as needed, phrases like "….and we are still quoting Senator Moynihan…" or "unquote" or "That's the end of Domenici's statement."

There are also occasions when you will use quote marks merely to guide the anchor, even though a speaker is not being quoted. The anchor will then give the word or phrase a little extra attention. Some examples:

- *A cornerstone of Reaganomics is the "trickle down" theory.*

- *The bank robber said he just wanted some money to "trickle down" to him.*

- *Among Mexican baseball fans, the only "numero uno" is Fernando Valenzuela.*

- *The French called it "le jazz hot" but Americans called it jazz.*

- *Evans said he was doing more than restating Lyndon Johnson's "Great Society."*

Time Elements

Most news stories need to have the time element expressed to show that the item is timely. However, there is an assumption in broadcasting, especially in radio, that the news being reported is "today" news. This means that one "today" can sometimes cover several news items.

Broadcasting stresses immediacy by using phrases like "within the hour" and "a few minutes ago."

As in all writing, avoid phrasing which requires translation. It's better to say yesterday, today and tomorrow rather than Wednesday, Thursday and Friday, which require the listener to remember what day today is.

Abbreviations

Use only abbreviations the anchor and viewer can grasp immediately. Otherwise, it's too late. P-T-A, N-double-A-C-P, Y-M-C-A, A-F-

L C-I-O, N-C-A-A, G-O-P, and U-N are among acceptable abbreviations. The abbreviation A-P-S, widely used in Albuquerque for Albuquerque Public Schools, is fine on second reference for Albuquerque TV but would never work for viewers in Durham, North Carolina, or Seattle, Washington. Some abbreviations are pronounced as words and should not be written with hyphens between the letters. Among these acronyms are NASA, UNESCO, OPEC, NATO, SEATO.

Avoid the trap of creating abbreviations that are not clear. You'll only confuse the viewer by writing about the National Society for Problems of the Aged, and thereafter referring to it as N-S-P-A. Who would remember what N-S-P-A means? Calling it "the organization" or "the society" is better than N-S-P-A because the vague words don't call attention to themselves the way a specific but meaningless abbreviation does. Likewise, the Public Transportation Association, thereafter called P-T-A, would be mightily confusing.

Do not use abbreviations such as No. for number or St. for street. Spell out words like senator and governor when standing alone. It's also best to spell them out when used with the officeholder's name..."Senator Jeff Bingaman...." Abbreviations like "St." and "Ft." used as part of St. Paul and Ft. Smith are OK. They are ridiculous standing alone, as in, "The cavalry returned to the Ft."

Capitals

Use them if your shop uses caps and lower-case typewriters. They can tip the anchor off to a proper name and improve her delivery by increasing her understanding. Examples :

"He quoted fish as saying..."
"He quoted Fish as saying..."

"...and chose leadville, colorado for their honeymoon."
"...and chose Leadville, Colorado for their honeymoon."

The capitals clearly make the copy easier for the anchor to grasp and read.

Spelling

Spell correctly. The attitude that "nobody will see it, they'll only hear it," can lead to trouble. Consider how your anchor could legitimately complain if you wrote these:

> *"He listed zinc, led and tin as major mineral products in…"*

> *"The beer was covered with flowers…"*

> *"Murphy makes frequent use of time-laspe photography…"* (This could make the announcer sound like he has a lisp.)

> *"The prosecutor said McCormick picked up the great and hit Spooner…"*

Pronouns

Use pronouns but remember that the listener can't look back over your copy to find out who is being referred to as he or she or her or him or its or they or them, etc. So be careful. Never write in terms of the former or latter. When in doubt, use the noun, name or title again.

Remember that an organization is usually referred to as "it" rather than "they" because organization is a singular noun. Likewise, association, league, company, university, team, group, police force, etc.

Pronouncers

The writer is responsible to the anchor for the pronunciation of unfamiliar words and names. There are two ways to do it. You can put the pronouncer directly after the word, or above it.

"...and lived in Bogota (Buh-GO-tah), New Jersey until 1957."
(Buh-GO-tah)
"...and lived in Bogota, New Jersey until 1957."

Wire services do it the first way, because their teletype machines can't do it the second way. Many newscasters prefer the second way because it gives them simultaneous display of the name and its pronunciation.

Numbers

These are tricky, and the trick is to make them clear so the anchor can read them without hesitation and the audience won't be overwhelmed. The general rule is to spell out numbers from one through eleven, and use numerals and combinations thereafter.

DO	DON'T
one	1
eleven	11
312 dollars	$312
400	4-hundred
400-thousand	400,000
12-million-617-thousand-208	12,617,208
6-dollars-and-12-cents	$6.12
6-and-3-tenths	6.3
6-point-3	6.3
one-fifth	⅕-th
one and a half	1.5
3 percent	3%
World War Two	World War II
World War One	World War I
October 20th, 1936	Oct. 20, 1936, or
	Oct. 20th, 1936
112th Street	112th St., or
	One Hundred and Twelfth Street

Some people (not many) write out the entire number: Twelve million three hundred and forty-eight thousand two hundred and ninety-one, but it's a lot of trouble and very hard to read. Don't do it, unless you love to type and don't care very much for your anchor, or maybe for your job.

Unless an exact figure is significant—for example, a record attendance or record gasoline price—it's usually better to round the number off. Say attendance was "nearly 18-thousand" or "about 18-thousand" or even "18-thousand" rather than "17-thousand-889." But if 17,889 is a record, it would be silly to report "a record crowd of close to 18-thousand."

As a rule, don't start a sentence with a number. When it's unavoidable, spell it out. Better to start the sentence, "Three hundred and twelve New Mexico businessmen..." than to start it, "312 New Mexico businessmen..."

Some writers like to play it safe with billions and trillions and millions by capitalizing Billion and Trillion and Million, or by doing this: 6 (b) billion, 300 (m) million.

Sports Scores

When giving scores, develop a pattern and stick with it. Some sportscasters take so many liberties with language, trying to be fancy or distinctive, that they fail to communicate the scores, even with the visual reinforcement of having them on the screen. The best approach is a pattern like:

Winner...verb meaning beat...Loser, number to number.

"The Dodgers beat the Padres, 7 to 4. The Giants clobbered the Cubs, 12 to 1. And the Braves shutout the Reds, 4 to nothing."

Don't try too hard to find substitutes for "beat" and "defeated." If you say "edged," it should be a one-run game. If you say "routed" it better be more like 11 to 2 than 4 to 2.

Avoid writing the scores in this form: "X beat Y 3-2; Z fell to B 9-5; and S defeated T 13-4."

That is, eschew the semicolon and dash. Use periods between games. Use "to" rather than the dash in scores. And don't break the pattern by naming a loser first. Establish and keep this pattern: "Winning Team/verb/Losing Team, number to number." You can't lose.

Note that numerals are used in scores. Exception is made for zero, which could be spelled out as "zero,""zip" or "nothing" or typed as "0."

Writing Television Reports

Newspaper and television reporting are the same in their basics— you collect as much pertinent information about the event or controversy as you can, use your experience and instinct to determine which of that information your audience needs, and then write it up accurately, fairly and clearly.

After that, they are different. The most obvious difference is that television reporters have videotape pictures to tell part of the story for them while newspaper reporters must work the descriptive material into their copy. A more important difference is in organization and writing.

Newspaper reporters write most of their stories in the "inverted pyramid" style, putting the freshest and most important information at the beginning of the story and the least important toward the end, so that editors can easily shorten the story to fit available space and readers can turn to another story confident they won't miss essential information by not reading to the very end.

Television reporters construct their stories so they have a beginning, middle and end—more like a novel (or maybe an anecdote) than a news report. They do this because their stories, once produced on videotape, are not easily shortened by producers or editors, and they must give the impression of coming to a logical conclusion rather than just stopping, bang, as most print stories stop.

Television reporters' stories are called "packages" or "spots." They are introduced by an anchor and played on the air as

"SOTs," or sound on tape segments. Editorially, the anchor's lead-in and the package are considered a unit; most or even all of the news will be related in the package but some of it may be in the lead-in.

Packages come in two varieties, depending on whether they are complete or whether they require some help from the anchor's lead-in. There's no official name for these two kinds of packages but they can be thought of as "self-standing" and "non-self-standing."

A self-standing package includes all journalistically necessary information and could be understood by a viewer even without an introduction from the anchor. A non-self-standing package lacks essential information and will not make sense to viewers unless that information is provided by the anchor.

Sometimes this is background information, which brings the viewer up to speed and enables the reporter to concentrate on what's new. Sometimes it is information not available when the reporter did the package. A reporter covering a plane crash would leave out the number of victims if bodies are going to be counted right up until air time. It's a simple matter to give the anchor the latest figure, but very difficult to change the package. Sometimes the missing information is carefully reserved for the anchor, so the anchor will appear to be doing more than handing the ball to reporters. Sometimes, unfortunately, it is information a careless reporter unwittingly failed to include in the package.

For several reasons, many producers prefer non-self-standing packages; they give the anchor a chance to deliver news and play a seemingly more important role in the program, they facilitate updating of information, and they cut down on repeat information that tends to slow down a program.

A lead-in like, "Our reporter Edna Quigley covered a big story today. Here's her report" would do the job for a self-standing package. Edna would follow, on tape, with everything—who, what, where, when, why and how, plus details.

If Edna's package was non-self-standing, the lead-in above wouldn't work. Suppose, for example, she started her package this way:

> *"Grogan said he was conducting his own investiga-*
> *tion when the F-B-I's cameras caught him stuffing the*

money into his pockets. He said Johnson's interpretation is all wrong and...."

Who is Grogan? What money? How much? What's the F-B-I up to? Who's Johnson? The package needs a lead-in that supplies the missing information, like this:

"Congressman George Grogan isn't denying the F-B-I's "Abscam" team videotaped him taking 25 thousand dollars in cash from a phony Arab sheik and putting it in his pockets. The South Dakota Republican defended that action at a news conference today. And he had harsh words for U-S Attorney Johnny Johnson. Our reporter Edna Quigley was at the congressman's news conference."

You, if you're Edna, start with, "Grogan said he was conducting his own investigation when the F-B-I's cameras...." and the viewer knows what's going on, thanks to the lead-in.

This approach also saves a little time and lends cohesiveness to the newscast. It doesn't happen accidentally. The reporter in the field and the writer in the newsroom must coordinate their efforts. If either of them fails, the viewer will be the loser.

Despite the risk and the extra work required to coordinate package and lead-in, many producers prefer non-self-standing packages.

The lead-in says: "It took three fire companies four hours to control a three-alarm blaze in an abandoned apartment building at North Fourth and Crickett Street this morning. Edna Quigley was there." That lead-in, many television writers would say, has too many numbers. Better, they would say, to write it loosely, like this: "A big fire in an old downtown building kept fire-men busy for a long time this morning. Edna Quigley was there." What do you think? Is it better without facts? Is it more journalistic?

Regardless, let's try a minimal revision of the original version for this illustration. "Three fire companies needed all morning to control a three-alarm blaze in an abandoned apartment building at North Fourth and Crickett Street. Edna Quigley was there." With that kind of lead-in, you (or Edna) can start out by saying:

"The fire broke out in the basement of the 70-year-old building about 6 a.m. and...."

You don't have to include "what" and "where" and can devote more of your air time to fresher, more interesting information. You are also leaving the anchor with the opportunity to deliver some news rather than merely introduce you (or Edna).

Suppose you hadn't done that? Suppose you included the time and location and three alarms and four hours and three fire companies? What would be left for the anchor? Nothing, and the producer would have had to choose between having the anchor do nothing more than introduce you, or repeat some of the information in your package.

Few things sound as bad as pointless repetition of information ("pointless" because at other times information is so unusual or so difficult to grasp that repetition is desirable). Under the pointless repetition heading, the anchor may say: "Two armed men held up the Central Avenue branch of the Cactus Savings and Loan Association at noontime today and got away with an estimated 47-thousand dollars in cash. Edna Quigley covered the story:"

And you, as Edna, may lead your package with: "Two armed men got an estimated 47-thousand dollars in cash from the Central Avenue branch of the Cactus Savings and Loan Association in a noon-hour robbery."

That "echo" sounds terrible, and permits the ready inference that your station's news team doesn't know what it's doing, or who's doing what. It also tends to stop a newscast dead.

One kind of "echo" is good rather than bad, so good that in many shops your are required to do it. That is, you must write a lead-in that echoes the *point* of the story being introduced, that tells the audience what the report is going to tell them, that gives the audience a reason for paying attention. Then the reporter tells the story. The trick here is to find a different way to say it, to avoid echoing words.

There is another sense in which packages come in two varieties, again without standard names. In radio, they are "voicers" and "wraparounds." A voicer is the reporter only, telling about the event. A wraparound is the reporter wrapping his voice around the recorded voice of a news maker, from a speech, news conference, trial or interview.

These terms don't quite work for television because pictures complicate definitions. Voicers are called "standuppers," meaning the reporter is standing somewhere, or sitting somewhere, or walking around somewhere, and reporting the story (or analyzing it) with no pictures of the event or subject matter. All the viewer sees is the reporter.

Many stories are done with pictures but no sound bite, leaving them somewhere between the standupper and the wraparound. Some television wraparounds are done with the reporter on camera bridging sound bites, but without pictures illustrating the event or subject matter. Most packages, however, are illustrated wraparounds—pictures and sound bites and, more often than not, the reporter in a brief standupper.

In the most general way, television people refer to reporters' stories that have pictures of the event and/or sound bites as "packages" and those with neither—with nothing but the reporter—as "standuppers." This serves to tell everyone involved, producers in particular, whether the story has visual value that might affect where it is placed in the program. Standuppers don't have visual value; the other varieties do.

When you are preparing to write your story, it helps immeasurably to know whether a self-standing or non-self-standing story is wanted. If you can't find out beforehand, you're better off doing a self-standing version because, even though it opens the door to repetition, it assures that the viewer won't miss out on essential information.

Most television news packages are wraparounds. Sound bites give television reports reality and credibility. Viewers prefer to *see and hear* the sheriff call the police chief a "bum" than be told he did. They prefer to *see and hear* the pickets calling for passage of abortion legislation than be told they chanted that message.

The basic television news package follows this pattern:

REPORTER/SOUND BITE/REPORTER, in which you voice over scenes telling what it's all about, use a bite from a principal in the story, and voice over additional scenes to a conclusion of some sort. This could be a news conference, a speech, a fatal accident, just about any straightforward, uncomplicated story.

The most common variations on this theme are:

REPORTER/SOUND BITE/REPORTER/SOUND BITE/ REPORTER, typically used to present two sides of a controversy or two aspects of an event. You set up the controversy or event in the first reporter portion, let one person say his or her piece in the first sound bite, bridge to the other sound bite with the second reporter portion, let the other side have his or her say, and then summarize in the concluding reporter section. This structure can go on and on and on as you introduce more sound bites.

REPORTER/SOUND BITE/SOUND BITE/REPORTER, often used when sampling opinion or getting two (or more) comments about something that doesn't involve setting out two sides of a story—for example, in a story about a charity auction you would voice over some of the auction action, get two or more comments on what a worthy cause it is, and then voice over something about how much the auction earned for the charity.

As a rule, you start your report with a line or two of the hard news of the story, regardless of which structure you are following, and then set up the sound bite. After the sound bite, you add some information and close with a "signature," your name and news organization and sometimes the dateline—"Edna Quigley, KJD News, in Tijeras, New Mexico."

As the reporter, you bear primary responsibility for getting the essentials of your story into the program. If you have not arranged with your anchor or producer to prepare a non-self-standing report, you should drop the 5 W's into the story a couple at a time, rather than cramming them into the first sentence or two the way a newspaper reporter does. It is much easier on the viewer when you parcel them out.

You also bear primary responsibility for making sure viewers know who is talking in sound bites and understand what they are saying. You must set up the sound bite with a "lead-in" that prepares the viewer for what's going to be said.

Let's suppose the mayor has refused to spend money appropriated by the city council to begin design of a proposed sewer system for the south side of town. People there are very upset. Here's a sound bite, from the mayor's press aide Arthur Simpson:

"It's the right thing because spending the design money without knowing whether the council will appropriate additional funds to actually build the sewers could create a real mess. If this means the people who live in that area have to wait a little longer to get what all the rest of our citizens have, why it's the council's fault,

not Mayor Bunsen's. The mayor is in favor of this improvement, but he insists council members go all the way, not part way."

There are many ways to lead into this bite. Let's look at five possibilities.

1. *"City Hall said this about that."*

Well, at least it's not inaccurate. But all this cliché tells the viewer is that here comes someone saying something on behalf of the administration, City Hall. Who? What? The viewer is given no idea. Of course, Mr. Simpson can be identified with a super—his name across his chest as he talks. And what he says is clear as soon as he says it. Many newsrooms accept this approach, on grounds that it saves a few seconds. But if the super is not inserted or if the viewer happens to be looking away from the set, important information is lost.

2. *"At City Hall, the mayor's spokesman said this."*

A slight improvement. At least it indicates the position held by the person who is going to talk.

3. *"At City Hall, mayor's spokesman Arthur Simpson defended the decision."*

Not bad. It identifies by name and position the person who's going to speak and it hints at what he's going to say ("defended the decision.")

4. *"At City Hall, spokesman Arthur Simpson said the mayor had done the right thing."*

Like number three, except it's a step backwards because it produces what is called "the echo effect." The lead-in says "the right thing" and the sound bite echoes the phrase instantly. The echo effect sounds silly. Your best defense against the echo is a simple one: *never* use a noticeable word (other than a proper noun) from the first part of a sound bite in your lead-in.

5. *"At City Hall, mayor's spokesman Arthur Simpson told reporters to blame the city council."*

This one is best. It identifies the person by name and position and points to what he's going to say—"blame the city council." It also makes clear Simpson is talking about *city* council, even though he doesn't use the word "city" in the bite.

This lead-in (or set-up) would be less good if it said, "At City Hall, mayor's spokesman Arthur Simpson told reporters it's the council's fault" because that phrase produces a minor echo.

All sound bites must be set up so they make sense. When they're not, bites add nothing to the story except confusion. In the case of Mr. Simpson, it's assumed that the controversy has been laid out in voice-over or set out in an immediately preceding sound bite from another figure in the story. Sometimes, it takes more. Sometimes, because you must edit interviews and speeches to save time, you cut out the context of the person's remarks. Then you must restore it your lead-in. Ordinarily, you'll find the material you need in the few sentences just before the pickup of the bite.

Sometimes the person in a sound bite can be re-identified. This is standard practice in many radio newsrooms (where sound bites are ordinarily called "actualities") because radio can't provide a super and a face for a listener to look at and recognize. It can be overkill in television, and if it's poorly done it can stall the story, as would re-identifications like, "Mayor Haig" or "That was Mayor Haig."

A little better re-identification would be this: "Mayor Haig, addressing the city's Italian-American Club tonight." At least it adds information. Here's one that would be even better, because it re-identifies and contributes substantial additional information:

"Mayor Haig also told the Italian-American Club he expects City Council will unanimously approve the money for a proposed City Hall statue of the club's founder, the late Mayor Alphonse Amico."

Oddly, although it's poor practice to use words from a sound bite when introducing it—because you'll produce the echo effect—it's good practice to lift a word or a phrase from a sound bite to write out of it.

SOUND BITE: *"When we decided to raid the compound, we relied heavily on informants who told us the commune members were non-violent and, in fact, had no weapons of any kind. On that basis, we knew we'd be safe going in there, that it wouldn't be life-threatening. We'd complete the raid and have them all arrested in minutes."*

YOU: *"Minutes was all it took, just minutes...before a barrage of gunfire from the compound left four federal agents dead..."*

Every now and then you will butt together bites from two or more people. When you do this, the conventional way to introduce them is to name them in reverse order, so that the last name you give is the first bite heard and seen.

Example: "After the vote several members of the council talked with reporters. We got these opinions from Karla Curley and Ross Tweed." The first bite should be Tweed, the second Curley, not the other way around.

It's also easier on the audience if the story gives the impression (at least) of being complete. Completeness can be a journalistic impossibility in 45 seconds or a minute and a half. But writing a story that leaves no glaring loose ends is feasible.

It helps if you think of a broadcast news story as having a beginning, a middle and an end. The end is where you give the impression of completeness, by wrapping up loose ends, by summarizing, or, sometimes, by looking ahead. That's why you'll often hear packages ending with material like:

A) *"The City Council will vote on the question next Tuesday. Edna Quigley, KJD News at City Hall."*

B) *"The demonstrators said they'll keep picketing outside City Hall until the mayor meets with them—no matter how long it takes. Edna Quigley...etc..."*

C) *"Crenshaw was booked into the county jail on an open charge of murder. He'll be arraigned in Criminal Court tomorrow morning. Edna Quigley, etc..."*

D) *"The 64-year old school teacher said the currents were too strong and the water too cold. He said he'll never try the English Channel swim again. Edna Quigley, etc.."*

E) *"Steinbrenner said despite his failures so far, he remains determined to improve the Yankees' pitching staff. Edna Quigley, etc..."*

F) *"The union last struck Widget International in 1969. The walkout lasted 91 days and produced a better contract for the workers. Edna Quigley, etc..."*

G) *"Residents say there have been no burglaries since they started their neighborhood patrols six weeks ago. So far, it's working. Edna Quigley, etc..."*

H) *"Until then, it's anybody's guess. Only time will tell. Edna Quigley, etc..."*

Yes, you do hear these clichés on the air. Just make sure they aren't coming from your mouth or your typewriter.

These endings bring the stories to an apparent conclusion, even though some of them are clearly temporary. For the most part, you get to an ending by figuring it out in advance. That gives you a target to write at and can make stories seem to write themselves.

The key to making the "wraparound" work is choosing a good sound bite. It can't be too short. It can't be too long. And it must add more than a mere respite from the reporter's voice.

Length of the sound bite? The simplest guideline is 10 to 30 seconds, but every case is different. Occasionally you'll hear a sound bite that's only one word long. If it's done *very* carefully, a one-word sound bite can work—but it's really more a trick than a way to communicate. Usually you do better with a minimum length of one or two complete sentences, and a maximum of what might be considered one short paragraph.

Contents of a sound bite? Your viewers want to see and hear the sheriff calling the police chief a "criminal type." They want to see and hear the father thanking the fireman for saving his child. They want to see and hear the all-pro cornerback agonizing over the fact that the man he was guarding caught the game-winning pass.

You choose a bite because it lends color to your report or because it provides expert knowledge or a newsworthy opinion. You avoid using sound bites for the mundane parts of a news story, because most of the time you can write that part better than someone else can say it.

You may get all your information about the worst car crash in the county's history from a state trooper, and get it all on tape. He'll tell you when and where it happened and who was driving and who killed and who was hospitalized. This part of your interview may be laden with "policese" and move at a snail's pace. You can write it better than the trooper said it. But when the trooper describes the horror of the crash scene, he may talk like a real person and give you a sound bite you can use, while you write the routine material.

The state fire marshal holds a news conference to report on his investigation of the explosion at the Gas Company. He gives all the background—when and where, how many were killed, how long he investigated, what it cost, and so on. He offers his opinion on the cause. He makes recommendations for the future.

The news is in his findings—what caused the explosion and what he thinks should be done to prevent occurrence of similar disasters. You use a sound bite of the fire marshal on one or both of those subjects, and write the background yourself.

A different example. The mayor comes up with yet another plan for testing auto emissions. He outlines it at a news conference, tells why he's for it, and answers questions. Again, the course is clear. *You* outline the provisions of the proposal and use a sound bite of the mayor defending the new plan, or promising that it won't cost much money, or will only take 10 minutes of a citizen's time. Your listeners may remember those comments. They won't remember the mayor listing points A, B, C, and D of the new proposal.

When you pick a sound bite your primary concern is whether it will add to the story, but you also take into account technical and ethical considerations. On the technical side, is the bite going to sound as though it was edited or will it be smooth? On the ethical side, have you done anything that might distort what the person said or appeared to mean?

Often, the person's voice will be "up" or high at the point you want to edit. This can happen at the pickup and the out cue, although it is more noticeable at the out cue. It is frequently much better to take a slightly longer sound bite than to cut while the voice is up and leave viewers wondering what they weren't allowed to hear.

The risk of altering someone's meaning by taking a bite out of context is ever present. That is why many reporters try to take their lead-ins from the words spoken by the individual just before the bite, trying to recreate the original context.

Writing to Picture

Because television is a visual medium, you can't be a television news writer if you can't "write to picture." To do it, you must learn:

1. When picture and script *must* coincide.

2. When they *don't have to* coincide.

3. When they *should not* coincide (so the script doesn't "fight" the picture.)

4. How to work into the script essential information that isn't illustrated by your pictures.

5. How to make use of "natural sound" from the photographed event.

One of the axioms of the business is "let the pictures tell the story." The pictures should, but in practice television news is more like "news *illustrated* with pictures that move" than it is "news *told* by pictures that move."

Why? Sometimes you have some of the pictures you need but not all; you can't let pictures tell the story because some of the story is missing. More often—in fact, most of the time—the story isn't worth the significant air time and effort it takes to let the pictures tell it alone.

What viewers see is the product of a series of compromises made all along the line—by the photographer, the reporter, the writer, the videotape editor, and the program producer.

If the only consideration were letting the pictures tell the story, here's how it might be done. You'll immediately recognize why it's impractical.

1. The photographer would get all the time and all the special equipment and all the assistance needed to properly cover the story.

2. An editorial person or team—writer, reporter, field producer—would accompany the photographer.

3. After covering the story, the editorial person or team would screen the footage with a videotape editor. They would share their impressions and reach agreement on how to open the story, how to end it and the major shots to put in between.

4. The tape editor would assemble the story according to the group's agreement, letting the individual scenes and the entire piece run as long as the editor feels is pictorially necessary and desirable. Will it wind up a one-minute piece? A four-minute piece? It's up to the editor.

5. The writer or reporter would screen the edited story and write a script that conforms to it. The pictures would tell the story, with the script offering some guidance and details.

6. The producer would put the story in the program at whatever length it turns out to run, regardless of news value or other considerations.

This never happens. Stations don't have the money and personnel to lavish on routine news events this way. Nor do they have the air time necessary to present them at whatever length they turn out to run. Nor is it likely there'd be much audience for stories that take longer to tell (in pictures) than they are worth.

Still, pictures can be allowed to tell important parts of the story without wasting time. Look for examples and you'll see them every time you watch the news.

One of the networks ran a little story about Britain's Princess Diana presiding at the dedication of London's first hospital ward exclusively for AIDS patients. A male nurse on the ward was HIV-positive, and the princess had been told about him. Would she shake his hand, ungloved, as she moved down the receiving line? Would she treat him the way she treated everyone else?

The reporter framed the story that way and let the pictures tell what happened. As Princess Diana moved down the receiving line, viewers saw the male nurse's anxious expression. The reporter did not point it out. In a tight shot, thanks to an alert photographer, viewers saw the nurse unconsciously crossing his fingers as Diana drew closer. The reporter did not point it out. The princess reached the infected male nurse, unhesitatingly extended her ungloved hand and greeted him as she had everyone in the receiving line. Viewers saw the pleasure on his face. The reporter had no need to point it out and did not.

After that, in a interview, the male nurse explained how concerned he had been and what it meant, he thought, for the public to see the princess was not afraid, for her to make the statement that people who are HIV-positive with the AIDS virus need not be shunned.

If the script had given viewers a play-by-play description, this tiny drama would have been ruined. Television may not be able to tell the entire story in pictures, but it can let pictures tell important parts. In this case, television allowed viewers to feel they were right there, watching to see what would happen.

In local television, reporters often cover two or three stories a day. They must frequently write and record their narrations at the scene, without seeing the tape or hearing the sound. They rush to the next story while their footage and narration are sent to the station to be put together by a tape editor, who makes the pictures conform to the script.

In somewhat better circumstances, when there's time, the reporter might be able to hastily view the pictures and sound bites in the field, watching playback on the camera's viewfinder and listening to sound with an ear piece. He will then write and record a narration that takes into account what he has seen in his quick review of the tape.

In cases when the reporter is able to get back to the station to view the tape, in color with good sound reproduction, he'll "index" it—that is, make a written inventory of the scenes, referencing them by minutes and seconds on a stop watch or by time code on the tape. He will write and record a narration, based on the pictures he knows are available, and provide the tape editor with script notations on which scenes to use where, and where the sound bites are and how they start and end.

Another approach, when time permits, is for a writer (or the reporter) to screen the footage with the editor. They'll agree on how to approach the story, which scenes must be in it and how long it should run. The editor then edits it and gives the writer a "spot sheet"—a list of edited scenes, in order, describing them and giving the duration of each. The writer writes a script that conforms to the spot sheet, and the story is aired with live narration by an anchor or the reporter. Because the pictures are edited before the script is written, this may be as close as television gets to letting the pictures tell the story.

In the broadest outlines, and to grossly oversimplify, there are two approaches to writing a television news script—the tight way and the loose way, or the radio way and the television way. (The script about the male nurse was loose.)

Let's assume we are doing a baseball story that's easy to understand and visualize. The St. Louis Cardinals and the Chicago Cubs come to the last game of the season tied for first place in their division. They are playing in Chicago and the Cardinals carry a one to nothing lead into the last of the ninth inning.

The Cubs are down to their final out when veteran Stan Hack beats out a bunt on a close play. Cardinal manager "Twig" McGaw argues the call with umpire Sal Maglie and gets thrown out of the game.

Ernie Banks comes to the plate. The count goes to three balls and two strikes. Banks hits a home run over the center field wall off Mort Cooper. The Cubs win 2 to 1, and are champions.

The editor cuts a story for the writer. The major scenes will be Hack beating out the bunt, McGaw being thrown out of the game, Banks hitting his homer, and Cubs players mobbing Ernie after he crosses home plate. Other people involved in the action are Cardinal third baseman Kenny Boyer and Cardinal center fielder Terry Moore.

Here are two possible scripts, each acceptable in its own right but quite different in approach. Running down the middle of the page in this example is a brief description of the scenes. Don't worry about how long they run. Assume each narration is for the same scenes at the same length. Also assume the scripts are set up adequately by the same lead-in.

It would be difficult to do otherwise in this case —but you must be sure your narration (or lead-in) makes clear what the situation is when Hack bunts. If you fail to do this, the drama is lost.

TIGHT ("Radio")		LOOSE ("TV")
Cub third baseman Stan Hack called on 15 years of big league savvy to push a perfect bunt down the third base line. Only a strong-armed fielder like Kenny Boyer could make it close. Umpire Sal Maglie called Hack safe at first and the Cubs were still alive.	SCENE 1 HACK BUNTS, IS SAFE ON CLOSE PLAY	Stan Hack caught the whole stadium by surprise. (HOLD NATURAL SOUND) Only Kenny Boyer's strong throw made it close. (HOLD NAT SOT)

Chicago fans were on their feet ... cheering the Cubs on.	SCENE 2 FANS CHEER	Cub fans loved it, but Cardinal manager "Twig" McGaw didn't.
And Cardinal manager "Twig" McGaw was on his feet, roaring from the dugout to argue with Maglie. The furious manager bumped Maglie with his chest. He kicked dirt at the umpire. He shook an angry finger right in Maglie's face. And he must have said something bad...because Maglie ejected McGaw from the biggest game of the season.	SCENE 3 MCGAW ARGUES, UMPIRE MAGLIE THROWS HIM OUT OF GAME	McGaw let umpire Sal Maglie know how he felt about Sal's call. He made it very clear. (HOLD NAT SOT) Maglie let McGaw know how he felt...bringing Twig's season to an early end.
Cub fans were on their feet again, as Mort Cooper quickly got a 3 and 2 count on Ernie Banks.	SCENE 4 FANS CHEER	It was classic baseball. The pennant on the line...and Mort Cooper with a 3-2 count on Ernie Banks
When the big pitch came, Banks was ready, He powered the ball to center field with such force that Terry Moore seemed to know immediately that the ball game was over. Moore just watched it fly.	SCENE 5 BANKS CLUBS HOME RUN	(HOLD NAT SOT) Terry Moore could only watch...and listen. (HOLD NAT SOT)

Jubilant Cub players streamed onto the field to greet their longtime leader as he crossed the plate. Ernie's 39th homer of the season gave the Cubs a 2 to 1 win and their first division title in four years. The playoffs start Thursday in Cincinnati. Vern Bickford is expected to start for Chicago, against Ewell Blackwell.	SCENE 6 CUB PLAYERS MOB BANKS AT PLATE	A 2 to 1 victory...and the Cubs' biggest celebration of the season. (HOLD NAT SOT) The Cubs go against the Reds Thursday in Cincinnati...with Vern Bickford expected to start the playoffs against the Reds' Ewell Blackwell.

What we have here is an exaggerated example of the difference between a television script and a radio script accompanied by pictures. The "loose" script on the right is the "TV" script. The "tight" script on the left is the "radio" script.

Both scripts meet the basic test of telling what's happening and who's doing it—Hack bunting, Maglie throwing McGaw out of the game, Banks hitting his home run and the Cubs congratulating Banks. Both do this properly—as the viewer sees it, not beforehand and not afterwards.

In this respect, both are appropriate examples of the script coinciding with the pictures. The "radio" script, however, goes too far, and includes examples of when the script and the picture *should not* coincide.

For example, in scene 1 the "radio" script tells us that the batter bunts toward third base. That's true enough, and you would not leave it out of a radio or newspaper report. But the television audience sees the ball go down the third base line, and pointing it out is like telling baseball fans the ball is round.

In scene 3, the "radio" script describes action-by-action what is perfectly obvious to viewers—that McGaw bumps Maglie with his chest, kicks dirt at him, and shakes a finger in his face. This approach to scripting results in a dull, sophomoric presentation. It's TV from the "see Spot run" school.

The "radio" script also offers examples of script and picture coinciding when it's entirely *optional*.

In scene 1, it gives us the name of the umpire who calls the runner safe. That's OK, but the name clutters the script at that point. Maglie's name can be worked in later, during the argument scene, where it's going to have to be used anyway.

In scene 2, the "radio" script tells us the people we see standing and cheering are Cub fans standing and cheering. Would they be Cardinal fans cheering a Cub safe at first base? Can we make better use of the time devoted to the words we are using here?

In scene 3, the "radio" script tells us that McGaw comes "roaring" out of the dugout. If he does, do we need to point it out? If he doesn't really "roar," is it hype?

In scene 5, we are told that the home run was hit to center field. That's OK, but baseball fans will see it and know it, and non-fans won't care.

The "radio" script on the whole is too literal, too specific. It matches the action too closely, in too much detail—rather than letting the picture carry the action. The "radio" script distracts from the pictures and disregards the important concept that television news should give viewers the sense of being there.

On the other hand, the television script makes good use of the pictures. With "holds" for "natural sound," it catches the drama and excitement that is generated by the cheering crowd. It gives the viewer a better sense of attending the game, or at least watching it live on TV.

In scene 6, both scripts demonstrate how to work in information that isn't illustrated by the pictures. They do it by "writing away" from the pictures, by explaining the action first and following it with information for which there are no pictures.

This works because viewers won't be confused—they've been told what they're seeing—and so long as that action continues and the information isn't in conflict with the pictures and doesn't sound as though it was written to go with different pictures, it will continue to work. In other words, it works so long as the words don't "fight" the pictures.

In scene 4, both scripts include the name of the pitcher even though he is not shown. There's no problem, however, because the scripts have made clear what is being seen. Had they started with the pitcher's name many viewers might expect to see the pitcher, and might be distracted when they did not.

If you hadn't named the pitcher in scene 4 and wanted to do it in scene 5, the worst way would be to start with his name. That would make viewers think they should be seeing Mort Cooper pitching when they are seeing Ernie Banks batting. The solution is to cast the script in terms of what viewers are seeing: "Ernie Banks dug in for the 3-2 pitch from Mort Cooper...." The viewer knows what he's seeing, and he doesn't necessarily have to see Cooper.

Suppose in scene 5 a fan ran out on the field and thumbed his nose at center fielder Terry Moore as Moore watched Banks' home run sail over the wall? You couldn't ignore it in your script. People would wonder if they really saw that and, if so, what happened? If you couldn't edit the incident out of the story, you would have to write about it.

This introduces another rule of television scripting: Never leave unexplained something that is pictorially arresting. Explain it or get it out of the picture.

Example: A police detective who solved a major crime is honored in a public ceremony. He scoots across the platform in a wheelchair, à la TV's "Ironsides." It would be mandatory to explain this—if only to say that "Jones was allowed to stay on the force after being crippled by a gunman's bullet four years ago." Not a long explanation, but enough.

Another way in which our "radio" and television scripts differ is that the television script gives the viewer a chance to absorb the action without being pestered by narration that isn't essential. Viewers need time to absorb what they are seeing. Sometimes that means running a story longer than you might otherwise do.

There's a prolonged labor strike in an essential industry. A blue ribbon panel is appointed to seek a solution. The panel meets for the first time and you have tape of the meeting. The key members are all well known—financier Merrill Smith, economist Maynard Laugher, mediator Theodore Hull, unionist Walter Debs, and Senator Hartley Taft.

It takes eight or nine seconds to read those five names the way they're written. That's under two seconds per face—barely giving the viewer time to examine the faces. You need at least three seconds per face, more than half again as much time as it takes to identify them.

You could say nothing, letting the picture continue silently for an extra second or two between identifications. That would give the viewer time, but the silence makes your story drag. There's no interesting natural sound with which to fill the silence, so it must be done with additional words about each person. The added information may not be editorially necessary, but you'll have better television if you change the copy to: "Investment company president Merrill Smith, University of Chicago economist Maynard Laugher, New York City mediator Theodore Hull, retired Machinists union leader Walter Debs, and labor-law author Senator Hartley Taft. Possibly better, in order to put the names on the faces sooner, would be:

"Merrill Smith, president of an investment firm ... Maynard Laugher, University of Chicago economist ... Theodore Hull, New York city mediator ... Walter Debs, retired Machinists union president ... and Senator Hartley Taft, labor law author."

The problem comes up frequently. You are doing a piece about the zoo. You may want to write that there are lions, tigers, walruses, kangaroos, polar bears, camels, seals, giraffes and elephants. A picture of each thrown over each identification would be dizzying—about nine animals in four or five seconds, unless you spaced the words out abnormally.

Don't write it that way. Run the scenes longer and pad the script with information, so the viewer can absorb each picture, or with good natural sound. Or, put together a montage in which you assume viewers will recognize the animals without having them named. Your script can be about something else, so long as it isn't about something that "fights" the film—like listing the zoo's board of directors while showing the various animals.

One of the "hits" that comes up most frequently in television news writing is the identification of a person shown in the tape. You can name the person before she's seen, exactly as she is seen, or after she's been seen. Right on the mark is best.

Early is second best, and late is worst. So long as you are only a couple of seconds early, you will have set the viewer up for that person by using the name (unless, of course, you used the name while a different person was being seen and produced a misidentification.) Late is worst because you run the risk of having already irritated the viewer by showing something, or a person, without explanation or identification.

Organizing and Reporting a Story

The key to good reporting is knowing exactly what story you want to report—what you want to tell your audience. It's that simple, but not always that easy—especially for broadcast reporters, who cannot, as print reporters often do, cover all bases by shoveling additional points into the bottom of their stories, one paragraph per item of information.

Many news events provide material for more than one story. Every public issue can be examined from a dozen perspectives. Step One, therefore, is figuring out what your story is; only after doing that can you start thinking about how you are going to tell it.

With breaking news, hard news, it's relatively easy to decide what the news is: police catch a bank robber after a six-block chase; the city's first high school, a long-abandoned building, burns down; the mayor announces he has heart disease and won't stand for re-election.

In the first instance, the assignment desk picked up the bank robbery from the radio scanner and alerted you and your crew, who were in the area. You got the end of the chase and the arrest, did some interviews with police, then went to the bank to get eyewitnesses, the teller who was robbed, and so on.

In the second instance, two photographers got a lot of good fire footage. You went to the school for interviews and found out the fire captain on the scene had been a member of the school's last graduating class and his grandfather a member of the first. He knew the entire history of the school and gave you a fine, very personal interview.

Another day, you attended the mayor's news conference, not knowing what the topic would be, and were just as surprised as anyone when your city's 38-year old political star said doctors told him he'd be taking a grave risk if he didn't get out of politics and into a stressless 9-to-5 occupation. End of political career. His wife was there. She said they were both disappointed; they'd looked forward to running for governor, but dropping out was better than dropping dead during a ribbon-cutting ceremony.

These are straightforward stories. The first one could be done with the footage you got at the arrest and back at the bank. The other two could be embellished with file footage—for a sequence on failed efforts to preserve the old high school by converting it to offices, and to provide a retrospective of the mayor's brief but spectacular political career.

Time permitting, you'd be able to screen the footage and pick sound bites before having to write a script for any of these stories. Before screening, you'd have blocked out the story in your head if not on paper, very likely in the car on the way back to the station. (Some reporters give themselves a head start by recording their interviews with a small cassette recorder as well as on videotape, so they can choose and time bites in the car or at lunch. You can do this by taking a line out from your photographer's deck, or by wearing a little mic on your jacket or shirt to pick up audio good enough for review purposes.)

After screening, you'd block the story out again, more than likely making revisions. Try it one way, then another. Then maybe another. Do it until you are comfortable with the result. You might come up with this outline for the bank robbery:

Set-up VO, Bank exteriors	:12 secs
Standup bridge to cover the chase	:12
Arrest scenes, suspect in custody in cuffs, being put in paddy wagon	:15
Bite, Cop #1, who started chase	:16
Bite, Cop #2, who cut robber off and stopped him	:18
VO return to bank to set up teller bite	:06

Bite, w/teller who was so scared by
robber she fainted after giving him
money. Bank's video monitor shows it
in layover, she faints, gunman flees   :23

VO paddy wagon takes suspect to   :10
county jail

Then you rethink it and come up with this:

Set-up VO, Bank exteriors, add intro to teller :15 secs

Bite, of teller who fainted, with bank's
video monitor as layover   :23

Standup bridge to cover the chase   :12

Arrest scenes, suspect in custody in cuffs,
being put in paddy wagon   :15

Bite, Cop #1, who started chase   :16

Bite, Cop #2, who cut robber off and
stopped him   :18

VO paddy wagon takes suspect to   :10
county jail

You rethink it again and make more changes. Now it's going to be:

Set-up VO, Bank exteriors and teller intro   :15 secs

Bite, of teller who fainted with bank's
video monitor as layover   :23

Standup bridge to cover the chase   :12

Bite, Cop #1, who started chase   :16

Bite, Cop #2, who cut robber off
off and stopped him   :18

Arrest scenes, suspect in custody
in cuffs, being put in paddy wagon   :15

A good writer could tell this story well all three ways. The three versions share one strength: major elements are being told by people who were part of the story, by the teller who fainted and the two officers responsible for catching the suspect. They are much better choices than the bank manager or the police watch comman- der would be, because these two "officials" could only talk about the story whereas the other three were key players, participants. Your narration provides the basic facts (which you might get from the "officials") as a framework for the color in the sound bites; you are doing the objective part of the story and the teller and the two police officers the subjective part.

The revisions accomplish two things, the second revision doing so better than the first. Both make the story a little tighter, and both make it less choppy and therefore easier to follow because they minimize the number of shifts in location and thought.

Now it's time to write. You probably have saved consider- able time by stopping to think about your story and experimenting with your plan, rather than charging ahead with the writing to see how it will come out. Substantial revision of a written story is much more work than reordering a plan or map. And psychologically it's easier to reorganize a story before you've invested time and effort writing a first version; it's only human to tell yourself your first ver- sion "is good enough, just fine —no need to write it all over."

After you've written your narration, if there's time you should read it aloud to someone else, to another reporter or the edi- tor or photographer, or your producer. Does it make sense to them? Does it flow, is it easy to follow? Some people are more willing to try to help than others, but if you make a practice of seeking help you'll find it.

More difficult stories—news features, series, documen- taries—are, of course, more difficult to prepare even though the basic principles are the same—namely:

1. Figure out what your story is. Work hard at this. It *is* hard.

2. Then, block or map out the way you are going to tell your story, before writing it. Put down the order of events as specifically as possible and the number of seconds you plan to devote to each section. Revise this outline as necessary.

3. Strive to let the people *in* your story *tell* the story. You do the objective part, let them do the subjective. Build a framework that allows them to tell what it was really like, what they really did, how they really felt.

4. Keep the organization simple. Try to stay with visual sequences and editorial components as long as possible rather than bouncing around, leaving things and returning to them as if you were writing a movie. In television news you should seldom say "meanwhile, back at the ranch..."

5. Write as tight as you can—be accurate, clear and tight. Kill every paragraph, sentence—even clause—you don't really need. (This is very hard to do.) Try to get someone else to listen to your script before you record it.

On breaking stories, such as the bank robbery, you seldom need research or have time to do it. News features and series are a different matter. Their quality depends on the quality of the research that resulted in the decision to do them. Some of this research can come out of a reporter's head—from memory of related stories. But more of it comes from newspapers, magazines, even books, and from interviews (usually on the telephone) with experts on the issue and people involved in it.

The better your research, the better the story you'll produce. That's axiomatic. Your story, however, will include only a part of what you've learned in your research, the merest fraction. You've got to be prepared for that, prepared and smart enough to know that it wasn't wasted work, that the information you don't use gives depth and perspective to your choice of the information you do use. It enables you to make sound decisions about the story. And, often, it provides material and ideas for later stories.

Step One, figuring out what your story is, can become a tough chore when you know you have more information than you can ever use. Which information is pertinent? Whom will I interview? What locations will I cover? You can answer these questions only after you've decided what you are trying to say, what the point of your story is. Write it down in a single sentence, or two at the most—"The point of this story is: ...."

More than likely you'll revise and refine this statement several times before the result really suits you. And it is far better to actually commit to writing the statement than to hold it in your head. Another reporter or your producer can generally give much more useful reaction to a concise, written statement than they can to something you tell them.

Now you have a target, something to aim at, to focus on. You can go to Step Two, making an outline or plan or map of how you are going to tell this story, or series or documentary. Make it as detailed as possible in terms of content and the time you plan to allot to the various sequences. From this you can figure out how to shoot the story—where to go, what to shoot, whom to interview, etc.

Then shoot. As you shoot you'll know how your plan is holding up. You'll recognize changes and improvements, and disappointments, as you go along. After you've shot and screened your footage, go back to Step Two, the plan. Do it again. Do it as many times as necessary, always focusing on the statement you developed in Step One.

Apply the principles of Steps Three, Four and Five. Let the people involved tell the story, rather than you. Keep it as simple and direct as possible, sticking with sequences as long as possible. And write as tight a script as you can, a script that is to the point, and a script that makes that point several times rather than once. Invoke the old chestnut: "First, tell them what you are going to tell them; second, tell it to them; and third, tell them what you told them."

Finally, try to end your piece, or each segment in your series, with strong elements—a memorable picture that represents your point, an evocative sound bite that makes the point, a pithy piece of narration that makes your point. Frequently, the best thing you can do is look for your ending as soon as you settle on your statement. This gives you something to aim at and practically eliminates the risk of a flat finish. Make it your practice to start strong and end strong.

Working with the Desk and Producers

Reporters are hardly autonomous beings. For the most part, rather than picking stories themselves, they are given stories to cover. That's the general practice everywhere, and the reporter who won't accept unwanted assignments with a smile and do a good job with them is a reporter in trouble.

Not only are reporters told what to cover, they often are told how to do it. That's because someone—the assignment editor or a producer—has decided the story warrants coverage and probably will be used in a program. Otherwise, why cover? And why make that decision without a preconceived notion of what the story is?

Reporters often complain about assignment editors and producers with their "preconceived" ideas about stories. Why don't they leave it up the reporter on the scene, the complaint goes. (Why don't they leave it to *me*?) The jerks can't sit in the office and know what's going on out here! Back in the newsroom, meanwhile, they're wondering why they have to put up with reporters who won't do what they're told.

One of the three rules you need to follow in your dealings with producers and the desk is this: Do your dead-level best to understand what they expect from the story (and therefore, from you). The second rule is to keep in touch with the desk or producer when you are in the field. The third is to know as much as you can about a story idea *before* you pitch it to the desk or a producer.

Finding out what's expected can require more than just asking that simple question. You frequently need to look behind the answer for the underlying assumptions. Just as you need to work up a focus statement for yourself before organizing and writing a story, or before starting to cover it, you need to try to reduce what the desk or producer tells you to a single focus statement. When you can, test the accuracy of your understanding by bouncing that statement back at them. Then go cover the story. If it turns out to be what was expected, fine. If not, your understanding puts you in position for intelligent discussion of the problem. This can save you from being forced to report in a manner you believe is wrong (which is bad for you) or from appearing to be defiant and bullheaded (which is bad for you).

Producers and deskmen want and need to know what's going on in the field. Some give the appearance of being paranoid about how the troops are doing. That's because their concern is filling a program rather than covering a single story. You can help by informing them of good news ("The story's in the can, it came out fine. What do you want us to do next?") and of glitches, especially glitches ("The guy wasn't here and nobody knows where he is," or, "They say approval to shoot inside the factory never came from the Phoenix office, and right now the boss in Phoenix is out to lunch. They don't think it's going to be a problem, except that he's got a big meeting right after lunch and we might not hear until 3:30, maybe 4 o'clock. What do you think?").

News of either type, and many categories in between, can have a profound effect on the plans of the people receiving it. Put yourself in their place, and remember to use the telephone, be it mobile, pay or borrowed. You'll get to be known as a reliable team player (which is very good for you).

Reporters need to generate stories on their own. That ability distingishes reporters from mere recorders of events. If you are assigned to a beat, you are entrusted with everything relating to that beat. If your beat is city hall, you must try to know more about city hall than anyone else in town. If it's the environment, you must become *the* expert—and so on. It's not easy to know everything about your beat, but at least you are dealing with the subject every day, focusing on it, and when it comes to generating stories it's likely to be easier than if you were a general assignment reporter.

Most television reporters are on general assignment. They may have one or two areas of specialty, but on any given day they can expect to cover any kind of story—police, politics, pretty babies, campus clowning, the state economy, a cooking contest. On general assignment, you make your reputation in two ways—how well you do the stories you cover, and how good you are at coming up with story ideas. Ideas can seem to be a dime a dozen. Ideas that turn into stories are another matter; the difference is in how carefully you have thought them through before proposing them. Compare the following:

You say to the assignment editor, "Mae, I wuz thinkin' about doing a story on those people out on Nine Mile hill. You know the ones who're squatting on the land, or something. I don't know if they're really squatting or if they have some right to be there, but you know—the ones who live in those houses they built themselves, and they don't have utilities and so on. I thought I'd grab a photog and drive out there tomorrow. There ought be a story in that, don't you think?"

Indeed, there may be a story out there but you might never get to cover it with that approach. If you had done a little research you might be able to say, "Mae, I found out the county is trying to enforce the building and zoning codes in that area off Nine Mile Hill where people are living in houses they built themselves. They have no sanitary facilities, no water, no electricity, no roads. Different county inspectors are going to go out there, starting next week. Maybe we could do something in advance tomorrow or the next day. Here's a memo you can read when you get a chance. I'll check with you tomorrow."

Now there's little question it's a story. Your memo will provide editorial details and possibly some logistical information. It will also give Mae a piece of paper with facts and proposals she can consider at her convenience, when she won't be harried or hurried into rejecting your idea. This is far better than the vague musings of the first approach.

Working in the Field

In the field, you deal with the people involved in your story and with your photographer. You want them on your side and usually you can win them to it, with the exception of people who don't want to be in the news, people about whom you are doing a negative story.

As in so much of life, the first thing to be is polite. Your station may be number one, a powerhouse. You may be the best-known reporter in town, on the verge of landing a job in a Top 10 market. The folks in your story may clearly be wimps. Be polite anyway. Be self-effacing, modest, not pushy. Let them see you know what you are doing, that you're competent. But be as pleasant as you can. Say please and thank you. If something you want to do might inconvenience the people in your story, try to explain why you want to do it and why it will result in a better story. The right attitude works wonders. The wrong wreaks havoc.

Your photographer is automatically on your side, or should be, even if there's no bonding between you. Bring him or her into every phase of the coverage if you can, from the planning to the wrap. Explain what you are trying to do with the story, how you envision it will look, how long it will run. Photographers have lots of good ideas and experience, and you should take advantage of that by soliciting their suggestions. Try to develop the kind of relationship that allows you to do leg work, talk with people, gather information, set up interviews, while the photographer, knowing what you need, shoots independently.

Finally, being in the field doesn't mean you've cut the umbilical with the desk. Stay in touch, without being a pest. Be prompt to report when something seems to be going wrong, or when you know you'll need file footage from the library, or that you'll have to do a second interview across town, or that the story is much better than it looked on paper. The more you can help your colleagues, the more they'll help you.

Ethics in Reporting

If you are accurate with the facts and honest with yourself and your viewers, you won't run into many ethical dilemmas.

One network did a reaction story in a city that was going to lose a major military installation. The closing, announced a day or two earlier, meant the loss of civilian jobs on base, the loss of business for military suppliers and contractors, the loss of customers for restaurants, supermarkets, shopping malls, auto dealerships, apartment owners, carpet cleaners, etc., the loss of jobs at all those places, and the loss of relatively secure futures for the town's young people.

The network's reporter painted a gloomy picture. He didn't have hard figures on how many people would be out of work or when. He didn't have hard figures on the economic importance of the base to the city. He glossed over these deficiencies and instead presented a parade of unhappy citizens. He cast them more as authorities than as legitimately worried laypeople. Making no distinction, he generously used footage of already closed businesses as cover—even though the just-announced base closing had nothing to do with their demise. Again making no distinction, he peppered his piece with "for sale"and "for rent" signs on local real estate. And someone—the reporter, his producer, his tape editor—found music to run behind the voice-overs and even some of the interviews, with the effect of a dirge.

The city and its people clearly faced an uncertain future. Their reaction, including their fears, constituted a valid news story, one being repeated all over the country as Congress approved a long list of base closings. But the network reporter all but killed this 200-year-old city in three and a half minutes. He did it by ignoring his lack of facts, by using only pessimistic sound bites, and by adding music which had nothing to do with the story. He produced a piece his bosses may well have called "powerful."

But was it honest? Was it ethical? Is it even in a murky area? The answers should pop right out at any reporter or producer determined to be accurate with the facts and honest with themselves.

A local reporter covered a preliminary hearing for a man charged with a heinous crime against a child. A mean-looking man he was, with a record. He pled not guilty. Outside the courtroom, the reporter interviewed friends of the victim's family. They called the accused a "criminal," which was technically correct for an ex-convict, even though it was clear they were talking about the new charge, not the past. In courtroom voice-over, the tape editor divided a close-up shot of the accused, turning his head toward the camera while looking shiftily to his right, into a series of quick freeze frames. Snap: Good lord, what a monster! Snap: Evil personified! Snap: Look at that criminal! Snap: He did it; just look!

Was this an accurate report? Well, the people actually said what they said. And the accused really did turn his head with a shifty look. And there's certainly nothing sweet about his appearance. A murderous Mexican if ever we saw one. Was this an ethical report? Again, the answers should pop right out at any reporter or producer determined to be accurate with the facts and honest with themselves. But of one thing there is no question: it made arresting television.

A station's investigative reporter comes on with information about happenings at the state capitol "that are sure to shock you." He attributes his information to unidentified "confidential sources" and gives the impression the story is the product of hard digging by a tough-minded reporter. The investigative team, he says, "has learned..." and "is able to confirm..." when, in fact, the information was volunteered by a person with an axe to grind and all that "source" really did was show the reporter where in public records the information was, had anyone had the good sense to look for it.

This could be regarded as the standard hype of television's investigative reporters—benign stuff. The case also can be made that this hype actually deprives the viewer of essential information, namely that the story (however valid it may be) was handed to the reporter by a person out to get someone else through the media. If that's the fact, hasn't the viewer been deceived? Is it ethical to deceive the viewer?

The best investigative reporting—the best reporting of any genre—relies on "sources" only as a *last* resort and is as forthcoming as possible about where information comes from. That's the way it should be, although in real life insistence on such a standard can add days to the time it takes to get a story in shape to use. It can even kill a story. It always pits practicality, convenience and ratings pressure against ethics. These days, in the eyes of many, ethics is losing the battle.

Performing as Part of Reporting

In the early days, television reporters were heard a lot more than they were seen. They needed to be able to read out loud distinctly and intelligently, but they didn't have to be on-camera performers with actors' presence. Now they do. You do. Standuppers and live shots are standard fare. Some reporters are more skilled than others, but employers expect all their reporters to perform creditably in front of the camera, on tape as well as live.

That means you must develop an aura of authority and unflappability. You don't need to be commanding, but viewers should feel you know what you are talking about. You must learn to treat the camera as your best friend or lover or mother or father, and look at it always. When you need to look at your notes (which is only human), do it forthrightly. Don't let viewers think they've caught you sneaking a peek. Do it unmistakably, then go back to telling that lens your story.

Standuppers

Standuppers serve many purposes in television journalism, not the least of which is to prove to the audience (even though it could be faked) that the reporter actually did cover the story. For that reason alone, some stations require reporters to appear in every story doing a standupper, sitdowner, lie-downer, kneeler or walk through, or, to really be cool, doing a jog by, a skate past, a swim by, and even a take-a-pie-in-the-facer.

The trick is making the standupper contribute to your story. Among many situations that call for a standupper are these:

1. When you have no pictures to illustrate an editorial point. Something is amiss if you are frequently in

this bind, but it does come up. When it comes up, standup, or sit down, etc.

2. When you need to make a transition between people, sound bites, ideas, thoughts, locations, etc., your appearance on camera is often cleaner and more satisfactory than routine set-up footage, and you can write without being tied to pictures.

3. When you need to establish yourself in some unusual place. If you've been sent a thousand miles to cover a story, don't do your standupper in front of a brick wall that looks like your station's parking lot.

4. When you need to provide history or context. Even if pictures are available for this, you can often do a more effective job with the information if you're talking directly to the audience.

5. When you are analyzing a situation or speculating on what may happen (but please, don't editorialize).

6. When you must describe intangibles like attitudes, emotions, sensations, flavors, aromas, etc. "Survivors said the smoke was heavy, acrid, like an insecticide. They said it started coming out of this vent, right here (pointing), about two in the afternoon."

7. When you must demonstrate something. For example, "The thingamabobs (while holding one in your hand) are so small most people can't get their pinkie through them" or "The problem was how to move the two-ton statue from there (pointing) to here, 300 yards away, without a vehicle."

You can get into a standupper in a number of ways. Chief among them:

1. You simply are in the shot, bang, delivering the material. You may stand, sit or lie still and finish it, and resume voice-over or take a sound bite. You may do it in an unchanging frame, or the camera may pullback or zoom in—more often the latter. Or you may start walking, come to a stop and go to voice-over or a bite. Or you may walk out of frame. Or you may have the camera pan away from you or push past you to the next part of your report.

2. You may start the standupper narration while the camera is on something else and have it pan to you, or pullback to reveal you, or, when you've got a really long lens, zoom in and find you in a scene in which you weren't noticeable at the outset. Then finish in any of the ways above.

3. You may start by walking (swimming, rowing, jogging, etc.) into frame and finish in any of the above ways.

A point to keep in mind is that there's almost always a noticeable difference between standup audio from the field and narration audio recorded in a booth at the station. If you can, try to work in a little natural sound before the standup audio. At a minimum, let the camera run so there are a few seconds of spare audio at the head and tail of the standupper to pick up the presence of the standup location.

Another point to keep in mind is the need to look neutral in a standupper and, as you finish your signature, to manage the slightest start of a very modest smile (except in stories of death and disaster).

Live Shots

To do these you need two things: confidence and notes.

Some people are born supremely confident. Others must develop confidence over time. Some of the latter retard the process by refusing to call themselves competent and confident until they can consistently turn in near-perfect performances. Try to avoid placing such an unreasonable demand on yourself. Just remember that to the people in the audience, you are a professional by virtue of being on the air. You are doing it and they are not, and they are not going to notice minor missteps nor be in a position to criticize you for them. So just get out there and do it! It's akin to "I'm Chevy Chase and you're not."

But make sure you get it right. Draw up a short list of talking points, the things you need to include in your report. (Because they're stiff, index cards are nifty for the purpose.) If the order of the items is important, list them in order. A word or two or three, plus names and figures, are all you need. (You might try putting the talking points on one side of your card and figures on the other, with a line down the middle.) In most cases, you'll have time to go over these talking points with a producer so everyone will know what to expect. If it's a question format, you'll know in advance what the first question will be.

There are times when you should use a formal, written script. One is when you are doing a remote voice-over and "hits" are required. Another is when precision of language is essential, so much so that viewers often find it reassuring to see you reading. Otherwise, most reporters say they do better ad-libbing from notes. They prefer to rely on notes to kindle the information in their heads rather than attempt word-by-word memorization. With a formal script and a human memory, you may never get back on track if you foul up.

Last in your notes—maybe with a circle around it—should be a reminder of a fact or facet of the story that's interesting but not necessary. Hold it back, in case you finish your live report and still have time to fill.

Before you go on the air, warm up. Not mentally but physically. Try it, anyway, because a lot of reporters do it. Stretch. Put your arms straight up and strrretch. Get on your tiptoes and stretch. Put your hands on your hips and throw back your elbows and shoulders. Move your head around to relax your neck. Take some very deep breaths. Yawn, yawn big. Exercise your voice in its lower ranges. You'll be amazed what 20 or 30 seconds of this can do to help you get ready for a live shot. Some reporters develop a regular set of exercises they always follow. You might do the same.

Shooting News Stories

Fill the frame.

The higher the gain, the greater the grain.

Pros use tripods, only amateurs don't.

Shoot with one eye, watch with the other.

Don't cut out without a cutaway.

Television is a visual medium. No craft is more important to the visual side of television news than photography (which is the very same craft as the one described by the high fallutin' term "videography"). Making television news visual requires much more than pointing the camera at the news and rolling. You must understand how the camera operates, what the lens and electronics do, which buttons to push, which settings to set. Learning is not a daunting task; most students can master the basics of camera operation with a few hours of instruction and several good practice sessions.

In addition to this moderate amount of technical knowledge, you also need to know about composition; how to frame a shot, how to balance a picture. A natural eye is an asset, but study and practice will get you there, too.

Once you are shooting, you need to take pictures that can be edited into a smoothly flowing story. Doing this requires mastering the basic techniques, the self-discipline to develop good work habits, and practice, practice, practice.

If there's any shortcut to learning, it is to dissect television news stories according to the principles in this chapter. Record programs while you're watching them, then use slow motion playback for a close look at individual shots and edited sequences, in routine stories as well as challenging. Frequently look two or three times. Put yourself in the shooter's place. Examine the framing. Look for balance. Try to figure out the distance and angle the photographer shot from, whether the lens was at wide or closeup. Was the camera on a tripod or hand-held? Was the shot done with lens movement or camera movement, or both? In your practice, emulate what you analyzed. If you approach this TV viewing as serious and purposeful work you'll get a big payoff: You'll learn fast.

Finally, you must understand which pictures among the countless choices available at a news event will tell the news story you are trying to tell. Some students think they've got it after a few months. Some professionals say they are still learning after 20 years. They're the best professionals.

Operating the Camera

ENG cameras are automatic. A fool can run them. A bright and interested broadcast journalism student can do much better than a fool. There are a lot of things to know about cameras, but the number of major variables is only two—the amount of light you let into the camera, and the way you focus the lens.

The "speed" factors that are so important to still photography don't apply to videotape. Regular videotape comes in one degree of sensitivity. The speed of the video shutter is constant (except for special cameras that provide a shutter speed adjustment for slow motion and other purposes), and the tape moves through the video cassette recorder at a fixed speed.

LIGHT: The camera gives you two choices, automatic and manual.

Automatic, in which the electronics of the camera gauge the intensity of the light in the scene and adjust the lens aperture accordingly.

Manual, in which you set the f-stop for the amount of light you want to let in.

Ordinarily, you use automatic. It's easy and helpful. It permits the camera to re-adjust itself if light conditions vary while you are shooting. If the variation isn't abrupt, your tape won't show that the light changed at all. If you were in manual, the change could show—perhaps enough to ruin some scenes.

You can see the automatic aperture work by putting a camera in a room and watching the f-stop ring on the lens move as you increase and decrease the light in the room, or simply move your hand back and forth a few inches in front of the lens.

You use manual when you want to override the automatic setting. This is most often done when you there's a big difference in the light that's on your subject and the light that surrounds it, or when you expect the light may change quickly and frequently.

A simple example is an interview of a person standing on a covered porch with the street to the rear on a sunny day. The person will be in the porch shade, and the background will be in the sunlight. If the camera is in automatic, it will set its aperture for the brighter light and you'll get little or no idea what the person's face looks like because it will be too dark. (This is fine if you're interviewing a source who doesn't want to be identified, but otherwise it's an unusable shot.)

One solution is to put artificial light on the face. The other is to set the lens on automatic aperture, zoom tight on the face so the camera isn't seeing the brighter light, and then push the button that switches the lens from automatic to manual. When you pull back, the aperture will hold at its setting for the face, and you'll have a usable picture if the brighter light isn't overwhelmingly "hot." If that happens, you'll have to do the interview in another location, or add artificial light.

You might also choose manual when shooting around automobile traffic in bright sun. Chrome and light-color cars will reflect the sunlight, dark cars will absorb it and a lens on automatic could go crazy—so manual is better.

Most of the time, however, use automatic aperture.

LENS: ENG cameras come with variable zoom lenses. When focused on a close scene, the lens works as a wide angle lens. Focused on a distant scene, it works as a telephoto lens.

When using the lens, you have two considerations—getting the subject in focus, and then controlling how much of the rest of the scene before the camera is in focus.

Getting the subject in focus is easy. You zoom in as tight as possible and adjust the focus ring on the lens until your subject is in focus. (Try to focus on something well defined; the lettering on the side of a bus is better than the door of the bus.) When you pull back, the subject and everything else in the same plane as the subject will be in focus and stay in focus no matter how wide or tight your framing is, so long as you don't move the camera or change the f-stop appreciably.

Controlling how much of a scene is in focus—your "depth of field"—is more challenging. The variables are three: how far the camera is from the subject, the focal length you have set the lens at, and the f-stop.

Sometimes you may want the subject in focus but not the background, because it may be distracting or inappropriate, or because you want a special feel or mood in the shot. To do it, you need to zoom in *less* than all the way, maybe only two-thirds of the way, and focus on your subject with the focus ring.

If you get what you want, fine. You're either skilled or lucky. If you don't have what you want, try it all over again with the zoom a little closer or a little further out. If you do this a few times and still don't have what you want, try moving the camera closer or farther from the subject and focus again. Eventually, you'll get what you want. And in time, with practice, you'll be able to get what you want the first time.

Depth of field is detectable, if you make a point of looking for examples while watching television. When the president addresses a joint session of Congress, the camera's subject is the president, but sitting right behind him are the vice president and the speaker of the house. The president is kept in focus, but the veep and speaker are often intentionally "soft" or blurred so they won't distract from the president. This is accomplished by controlling the depth of field. Depth of field is a constant consideration in expensive commercials. A pretty girl delivers the spiel in intimate tones, and the carefully chosen background is deliberately blurred into ephemeral, out-of-focus pastel patches so the viewer will concentrate on the girl making the pitch. The scene resembles a painting as much as a photograph.

An example of depth of field coming into play in a news story might be this: You want to shoot cars running a stop sign and need the sign and the cars in focus. You get off to the side at an appropriate angle, then zoom on the sign and focus. Then you pull back to the framing you want and wait for some cars, but when they get there they are out of focus because you don't have enough depth of field in front of the sign.

What to do? It'll be easier if you can remember these difficult-to-recall rules:

1) Your depth of field decreases as you increase your focal length. Or, it's shallower the more you have zoomed in.

2) Your depth of field increases as you decrease your focal length. Or, it's greater the less you have zoomed in.

3) Your depth of field increases as you move the camera away from the subject. Or, the farther away you are, the deeper the depth of field.

4) Wherever you are focused, there's always more in-focus area behind your focus point than in front of it. This may be the most important rule to remember.

So, what to do to get your stop sign and the cars in focus? Find something closer than the sign to focus on so you can take advantage of the fact that there's more depth behind the focus point than in front. That should work. If it doesn't, move the camera farther away to take advantage of the fact that depth is greater from a greater distance.

The size of the lens opening—the f-stop or aperture—is another factor in depth of field. The higher the f-stop, the deeper the depth. This is very useful in still photography, where you can govern the f-stop by changing shutter speed—the slower the shutter speed, the higher the f-stop. But with a video camera, you have no choice about f-stop because the cameras's equivalent of shutter speed is fixed. Still, it's good to keep aperture in mind as a factor because you can change the lighting in some circumstances. Add light and you can raise the f-stop and increase depth of field.

Other than the aperture, the only "automatic" feature of the lens is whether it's on power zoom or manual. Power zoom is much easier to use. It gives smoother lens movement in your photography. But it gobbles up battery power faster than any other function on the camera. If you have the time and patience, you can conserve battery power by framing manually and using the power zoom for when you are rolling, or when practicing a camera or lens movement.

Other Camera Controls

The features of professional video cameras are practically universal. The difference in cameras is how well the features work.

Viewfinder: Central to using the controls of an ENG camera is the viewfinder, the tiny black and white television screen that shows you what you are shooting. The viewfinder is packed with indicator lights that tell you when you are recording, when the light level is too low, when you have raised the gain setting, when you have succeeded in "white-balancing," when the battery is running low, and when you are nearing the end of your tape. Some viewfinders even display VU meters for monitoring sound levels.

The brightness and contrast of the viewfinder's picture are adjustable, and it's a very good idea to check the adjustments regularly. To do it, flip the camera switch marked "bars" or "color bars." The viewfinder will show vertical color bars in gray tones rather than colors. Then adjust brightness and contrast if necessary to make the gray tones look "right," which is a matter of judgment you develop quickly. This gives you a benchmark, so that if scenes you are shooting look "off" in black and white they probably are off and you need to double-check your white balance, lens opening and filter.

The viewfinder shows you what you are shooting, but not exactly. Most show you more around the edges of the picture than will be in the picture that viewers see. To compensate for this "TV cut off" many viewfinders are marked at the corners and you are supposed to keep within those marks the picture you want viewers to see. That's fine, and you do it, but it's still no guarantee of what you will actually get because cameras seldom are perfectly adjusted. If your station assigns you a camera for your regular use, you'll soon learn how to use its viewfinder. If you use several different cameras, be prepared to sometimes have more or less picture than you thought you were getting.

Filters: Most cameras have four, in a rotating disk located about where the lens and camera body join. They're numbered 1, 2, 3 and 4. A legend on the camera body tells you when to use which one—what kind of light they are for. Use the wrong one and you're apt to throw your color off. So don't forget the filter.

The hard part is knowing which one to use, because the legend doesn't always describe the "heat" of the light in clear or comprehensive terms. Typical filter choices are these:

1. 3200K, for indoor shooting with a lot of light from ordinary incandescent or tungsten bulbs—your living room, your kitchen, at night. The "K" stands for the Kelvin scale of color temperature, about which you need to know nothing.

2. 4300K, for fluorescent light or a mix of fluorescent, tungsten and daylight.

3. 5400K, for bright sunlight (indoor as well as outdoor.)

4. 6600K, for natural light in the shade, in or outdoors.

Choosing your filter is the first step before shooting. Next is white balancing.

White Balance: All modern cameras have automatic white balance. In the light in which you are going to shoot, hold a piece of white cardboard a few feet from the lens. Zoom in until the white cardboard is all the lens sees. Press or hold the camera's "white balance" button or switch until the WB light or "WB OK" comes on in your viewfinder. The camera is "white balanced." This gives it a reference to reproduce all whites the same, so that the rest of the colors will fall into line. Whether you set this reference with a sheet of white cardboard, a piece of white paper (unlined), a white wall or a white T-shirt, be sure you use the same white item all the way through a shoot. Don't use anything very shiny. (In a pinch, shooters have white balanced against a white cloud in the sky; just don't point the camera at the sun because that can damage your pickup tubes.)

White balancing is essential every time you change shooting locations or the light changes noticeably—when the sun goes behind a cloud, when you step from the sun-drenched sidewalk to the shade of a lawn tree, or when you move outdoors from the kitchen of a fast-food restaurant to the line of cars at the drive-up window. Some cameras have circuitry allowing you to preset an indoor and outdoor white balance, so you can adjust by flipping a switch rather than stopping to get out your white-balance card and reset. If you have such a camera, use this feature for fast-moving events—such as when you are chasing a prisoner from a squad car at the curb into the booking room at the police station. But under ordinary circumstances, white balance normally.

The need to white balance is familiar to people who are regularly in the news; more than one U.S. senator has been known to happily hold up a sheet of white paper for the benefit of photographers just before a news conference.

Black Balance: Most professional cameras also require you to set the camera's "pedestal" or black balance. All you do is push the right button. The lens then closes and the camera's electronics automatically balance on the black produced by the total lack of light.

Gain Control: This control enables you to record pictures in lower than optimal light levels—to get pictures you couldn't otherwise get without adding artificial light. The problem is, the more you turn up the gain, the coarser or grainier the pictures become. The control is on the camera body, with settings ordinarily at zero, six, nine, 12 and 18 decibels. Keep it at zero in normal conditions. Graininess begins to become noticeable above six decibels. It fairly screams at you, and at the viewer of your news story, at 18 decibels.

Most cameras have two indicator lights in the viewfinder that relate to the use of the gain control. One is a "low light" indicator that tells you the camera isn't seeing enough light for a good picture. When it comes on, you can take one of three steps—add artificial light, move to better light, or turn up the gain. The other indicator light comes on as a warning that you've got the gain cranked up (some cameras do it at 6 db, others won't until you get to 18 db), and you can expect graininess in your picture—moderate graininess at low settings but severe at 12 and 18 db.

Macro Lens: This mechanism allows you to do super close-up work—subjects like the text in a book, a photograph, the temperature gauge on a boiler, or a bee buzzing around a flower. It's right where the lens assembly fits into the camera body. Bring it into play and you shorten the focal length of the lens so you can move very close to subjects and tape them in focus. Always remember to restore the lens to normal after you've used the macro. If you don't, you'll have focusing problems.

Here's how to use the macro. First, make sure you're on the tripod. This isn't shoulder work because every tremor will be exaggerated. Then:

1. Set the focus ring at the closest setting on your lens.

2. Move the camera closer or farther from the subject until you get the framing you want.

3. Move the camera's macro lever as far as it will go toward "macro on."

4. Adjust the focus with the zoom lens, not the focus ring.

Shooting with Lights

Today's ENG cameras record good, broadcast-quality pictures in remarkably low light levels. They get dramatically better pictures than 16 mm film ever did in low light, and far better results than the ENG cameras of only a decade ago. Consequently, artificial lighting is used much less than it once was. But it still is needed, sometimes because without it you'll have an unusable or marginal picture, and also because it will improve an otherwise acceptable picture by adding detail and texture to the scene.

News photographers' lighting kits commonly include three light heads and light stands (sometimes just two of each), a selection of bulbs ranging from 500 to 750 watts, a number of plastic or polyester filters, scrims, barn doors, reflecting umbrellas, extension cords, three-prong adapters, cloth or sheet foam for handling bulbs (so you won't get body oil from your fingers on the bulbs and cause them to explode), clamps for mounting light heads, and a roll of gaffer's tape. In addition, photographers carry a battery-powered portable light, which can be camera-mounted or hand-held. These are often called "portalights," as well as "sun guns" and frezzis" from the trade names Sun-Gun and Frezzolini.

The bulbs are tungsten-halogen. They produce light at 3200 degrees on the Kelvin scale, somewhat higher than the ordinary bulb in your reading lamp. The filters—still called "gels" because originally they were made from gelatin—are used to alter the color temperature of the tungsten-halogen bulbs. The most important one is the dichroic or blue gel filter which changes tungsten-halogen light from 3200 degrees Kelvin to 5400 degrees Kelvin, the same as bright sunlight. The blue gel is used when artificial light supplements natural light—that is, when you are mixing artificial light with daylight.

Many light heads can be focused as spotlights or floodlights. The scrims and barn doors attach to the light heads—the scrims to diffuse or soften the light and the barn doors to further refine where the light falls. Most portable light stands have three legs, and by telescoping they enable you to mount lights from as low as two feet to as high as eight feet above the floor—or higher if the ceiling is high and you put the stand on a desk or table.

You use artificial illumination in arrangements commonly referred to as single-light, two-point, and three-point lighting.

The most frequently used single-light set-up is the battery-powered portable light, usually 200 or 250 watts. You use this light for general illumination at night, covering fires, accidents, arrests, and so on. Most of the time, you simply turn on the light and let the camera's automatic aperture adjust to it. There's nothing subtle about the results: you get a picture, often with shadows and powerful hot spots, but you do get an image satisfactory for spot news when otherwise you might get no picture at all.

You also use this same portalight around dawn and dusk, when natural light is too low for a usable picture without boosting the camera's gain and risking a grainy picture. You also use it indoors to supplement existing light, in which case you often can soften the effect by tilting the light upwards and bouncing the beam off the ceiling, or by tilting it up so only the outer edge of the light pattern falls on the subject, "feathering" it. In other situations, the light can be hand-held by another member of the crew and bounced off walls or ceilings, to soften it, or it can be shone from an angle rather than straight-on (as when it is camera-mounted) to provide shadow and depth in a face.

Different situations demand different techniques. If you are shooting a standupper outdoors at night with a portable light, you should use as little of its light as you can while still getting a usable picture. This improves your chances of having at least some of the background show in the shot and minimizes the flat "black hole" effect you may get when the reporter, thanks to the sun gun, is far brighter than anything else in the scene. You reduce the amount of light falling on the reporter by moving back, and increase it by moving closer. The rule on this, which you use in all lighting situations, is that the intensity of light is inversely proportional to the square of its distance from the subject. That means at four feet away you get four times as much light as you get at eight feet, or at three feet you get five times as much light as at seven feet.

For safety's sake, to avoid the risk of causing retinal damage to the person being photographed, you should stay at least two and a half or three feet away with any of these powerful tungsten-halogen lights. This is easy enough to remember in controlled situations, but more difficult when you're one of several cameras covering an event "gang-bang" style.

A step up in sophistication with a single artificial light is a light head powered by household AC current and mounted on a light stand. Try to get the light as high as possible so it shines down on the subject (from seven or eight feet) and place it about 45 degrees from the camera. This is called a "key light" and it is commonly used for interviews. You control the intensity by moving the light closer or farther from the subject. It's about right when you fix it so your camera's automatic iris settles on about f-8.

The need for a key light in interviews and standuppers sometimes is dictated by the color of the person's skin. A dark-complected person may need the light to bring out facial features, whereas a fair-skinned blonde's features may be washed out by added light. This happens because dark skin reflects less light to the camera than light skin. You also need to watch the background when shooting dark-skinned people; a background that's generally dark in tone works better than one that is far lighter than the person.

A variation on the key light, when you are seeking general improvement in the illumination of a scene or interviewee, is to use a reflecting umbrella to soften the light. These are white or silvery umbrellas with short handles that attach to the light stand with the concave side in front of the light head. You set the system up with the light head pointing *away* from the subject so the light is reflected from the umbrella. When an umbrella is unavailable, you can try softening the light by bouncing it off a wall or ceiling, or, if you have such, a large sheet of white pasteboard or even a large white towel.

Next is two-point light, using a key light as the main light and a second "fill light" to cut down on the shadows created by the key light. The fill light goes off to the other side of the camera, usually at a slightly wider angle than the key light, and always a little further away so the key light remains the more intense light. As a rule of thumb, you'll get the right intensity ratio if you put the fill light a third to half again as far from the subject as the key light.

Next after the two-point set-up is three-point lighting in which a "back light" is added to the key light and fill light to separate the subject from the background. You put the back light behind and above the subject, so it shines down at 30 or 45 degrees and lights the edges of the subject—in the case of a person being interviewed, the head and shoulders. You want the back light to be nearly as intense as the key light.

Lighting is at once easy and extremely difficult. You can get a handle on the basics for routine news work with a little attention and practice. It becomes difficult when you move from the regular run of the news to documentary work where, if you're going to be taking 30 or 60 minutes of a viewer's time, you want your pictures to look as good as they possibly can. Then the subtleties of lighting come into play. Where it may not have mattered much whether the background of a scene was clearly visible, now it does. Where you didn't care how palpable the texture of brick or velvet appeared, now you do. Where normal color fidelity was adequate, now it must be as perfect as the camera can reproduce. Proper lighting then requires exceptional care and experience, just as it does in the finest art and documentary still photography.

Composition

A well-composed shot is "balanced." A poorly-composed shot is not. You have two kinds of balance to consider, mass and color.

Mass is the greater concern, because in news coverage you have lots of control over how you frame your subjects but very little over their color.

A good place to start is the "rule of thirds." In your mind's eye, draw two vertical and two horizontal lines to cut your television screen or viewfinder into nine equal parts.

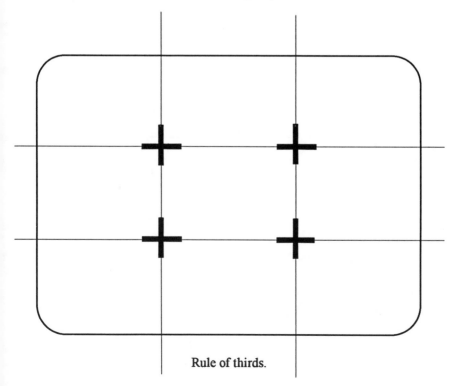

Rule of thirds.

What counts when you balance your composition are the four intersections and the two horizontal and two vertical lines. You want the center of interest of your scene at one of the four intersections, with the elements of your composition running along the lines. Easier read than grasped? Some examples may help.

Unbalanced.   Balanced.

Unbalanced.   Balanced.

A number of the examples below are heads—the heads of people being interviewed. A shot can be perfectly balanced in terms of mass, but still upsetting to the viewer because the central feature is a head, a face. For some reason, except for straight-on shots, viewers prefer to have more space or "lead" in front of a face than behind it, and they don't like profile shots, or anything else, dead center.

Not good: more space
behind than in front.

Not too good: equal space
in front and behind.

Good: more space
in front than behind.

Not too good. Dead center.

Not good. No lead space.

Good. Plenty of lead space.

Two more considerations need to be added to this mix. One is color balance. The other is the importance of the angle you're shooting from.

The thing to remember about color is that bright colors attract the eye. When all other factors of balance are equal the viewer will look at white, yellow, orange or red masses before black, brown, navy, purple, or olive drab. If the bright masses are large enough they can throw the composition out of balance.

As much as possible, you want a three-dimensional feel to your scenes rather than flatness. A good shooting angle is essential to getting the depth needed for this three-dimensional look.

Flat. No depth.

Good. Angle and height show more of car.

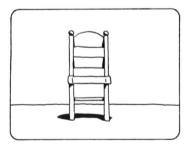

Flat. No depth.

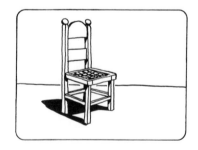

Good. Angle and height show more of chair.

O.K. Camera at normal angle.

Distorted. Camera too high.

Distorted. Camera too low.

As a general rule, you want to shoot only from "normal" angles. Angles that depart from what the viewer might see while walking around the scene of the news story tend to call attention to themselves, usually at the expense of what you're trying to show. Shoot the basic sequence from "normal" angles. If there's time after that—only after—try for supplementary unusual angles. They can strengthen your piece, especially in feature work, but get the basic shots first.

Basic Types of Shots

Movement makes moving pictures. Without it, you've got a still. It may be a splendid image, but it won't have the life that moving pictures depend on. When you shoot an establisher at a shopping mall, it's better with people going in and out the door. The jammed parking lot scene looks better with a few cars moving. The flag atop the entrance has more interest when the breeze disturbs it. Your general goal should be to have movement in all your shots—remembering, of course, there are many instances in which movement can interfere with showing viewers what you want them to see (or read), or destroy the mood of a piece.

At the risk of oversimplifying, let's say television news photographers shoot four kinds of shots:

1. Static—scenes without movement.

2. Real Movement—scenes in which something moves.

3. Created Movement—where the camera or lens moves.

4. Combination Movement—combining real and created movement.

The scene is a painting hanging on a wall at a museum. The camera can record it in a wide shot, a *static* shot, just hanging there. Then a museum-goer walks between the painting and the camera, which is still rolling. This is *real movement*, with part of the scene, the person, moving. When the person has passed by, the photographer zooms tighter on the painting. This is *created movement*, with the lens creating the movement. Then a woman steps into the scene. She plucks the painting from the wall and walks off, and the camera follows her. This is *combination movement*, combining movement within the scene with movement of the camera.

You should always try to shoot your scenes longer than you expect to use them, for two reasons. You need control track for editing (read more about control track in the editing chapter), and you want flexibility. A good general rule is to shoot nothing shorter than 15 seconds, with the "extra" ordinarily at the beginning of the scene.

Another general rule about static scenes is to shoot at least two angles or framings of the majority of them, so you will have variety and flexibility when you get to editing. Shooting three versions is even better. And it doesn't take a lot of time.

Making Camera and Lens Movements

The zoom lens is fun to play with, so much fun that beginners seem unable to resist. In the process, they waste a lot of time. Once you've overcome the novelty, you need to plan your use of pans and tilts, which are *camera* movements, and zooms and pullbacks, which are *lens* movements.

In a pan (from panorama), you move the camera horizontally, from a beginning scene to an ending scene. In a tilt you move the camera up or down from a beginning scene to an ending scene.

In a zoom, you start out on a wide shot of something and zoom tight to a detail of the scene. A pullback is just the reverse.

The execution of these shots is simple, so long as you use the tripod to keep the movement steady, and take the trouble to rehearse before you record. If you don't rehearse, you may move too fast or too slow and you may not finish where you want to finish. Then you'll have to do it again, and maybe again and again. Later, the tape editor will have to waste time going through them all to find a good take.

The trick with movement shots is, first, knowing when it will be useful to make one, and second, picking the right beginning and ending scenes.

The first rule, therefore, is that both the beginning and ending scenes must be shots that can contribute to telling the story as static shots. If only one is germane, your pan or zoom is wasted because there's no point in going from a pertinent scene to one of no value, or vice versa.

The second rule is to be aware of how long the whole pan or zoom runs. If you're putting together a routine minute and a half news story, there's simply no point recording a moving shot that runs 45 seconds, or half the anticipated length of the story.

The third rule is to shoot *enough* of the beginning and ending shots that they can be used alone. A good rule of thumb is 20 seconds of the first scene before the movement begins, the movement itself, and 15 seconds of the ending scene.

This gives you three things: flexibility in the length of the two static scenes, if you use them alone; flexibility with the overall time of the pan or zoom; and enough uninterrupted control track to roll back on to edit the first scene.

You could decide to use ten seconds of the opening shot all by itself, or five, or three, without the movement. Ditto for the closing shot. Or, if your movement between the opening and closing shots took 15 seconds, you would have a pan that could be used from as long as 45 seconds (15 of the first 20, + 15 for the pan, + 15 of the ending shot = 45) down to half that (3 + 15 + 3 = 21), or anything in between.

The same considerations hold for tilts, zooms and pullbacks. Make the beginning and ending scenes meaningful, and shoot enough so you can use them in their own right, without the movement.

Finally, you can combine camera and lens movements very effectively. A "pullback pan," for example, can make a nice transition. Under the right circumstances, so might a "pullback tilt zoom." (How's that again?) Watch television carefully and you'll see these shots. They're good, and fun to try, but they're not for beginners. In fact, even pros usually treat these fancy shots as supplements to straightforward basic photography; they make sure they get the story before they get fancy.

Moving In and Out of Frame

Here you have a scene into which you let your subject move, or out of which you let your subject move, or through which you let it move.

Suppose you are shooting a feature about a museum curator and you need to show him and some of his domain. You could do it very smoothly with these shots. Try to visualize them:

1. Backshot of the curator looking at a painting on the wall, then turning and walking out of the scene while you keep taping the painting on the wall. The subject, the curator, has moved out of frame, out of the picture, and you are now free to pick him up anywhere else in the museum (or in the world, for that matter).

2. High shot (you're on a staircase or a ladder) of a gallery, through which the curator walks—into the frame, then out of it. You can now pick up the curator anywhere.

3. Shot of a statue, and after 10 or 15 seconds (for editing control track) the curator walks into the frame, past the sculpture and out of the frame while you stay on the sculpture. Again you are free to pick the curator up wherever you wish.

4. Shot of an open door with a sign on the wall reading "curator." The curator walks into the scene, through the door and out of view.

5. Shot of the corner of a desk with a telephone on it. A
hand moves in and takes the handpiece off the phone
as the camera widens to show the curator seated at his
desk talking on the phone. Or Alternative 5. Instead
of the phone on the desk, you could shoot the curator
sitting at his desk, being interviewed by your reporter.

Obviously, you need the curator's cooperation to shoot
these scenes and just as obviously, in the strictest sense these
scenes are "staged," but there's no breach of ethics so long as
you don't pretend you were desperately chasing through the
museum to keep up with the curator on his typical whirlwind day.

Match Cuts

The effect here is to shoot with one camera a sequence that
looks like it was shot with two cameras in simultaneous operation.
Like the in-and-out-of-frame example above, match cuts require a
degree of "staging" that is generally regarded as acceptable so long
as it isn't misrepresented.

What you do is shoot the same action twice, from radically
different angles. You get two scenes when otherwise you'd have
had only one in the same number of seconds, and you end up with a
visually superior piece. Here's an example:

First shot: Close-up of a parking ticket on your subject's
windshield.

Second shot: Wider, your subject and the car, ticket on
the windshield. Your subject steps closer, removes the
ticket, steps back and looks at it.

Third shot: A repeat of the second, but shot from a significantly different angle (perhaps 90 degrees or more

from the other location.) Your subject moves closer, removes ticket from windshield, steps back and looks at it.

When you edit, you establish the ticket with the first shot, use the
second shot to the point that your subject touches the ticket, and cut
to the third shot at the point where the subject removes the
ticket. Stay with the third shot as the subject steps back and looks at
the ticket.

If you do it right you'll have "matched" the action, and
this routine sequence will be a bit more interesting because viewers
will see it from two perspectives in what looks like uninterrupted
action. Real movie making.

Inserts and Cutaways

These are sometimes quite the same and sometimes quite different. In
fact, at times the same shot can be called an insert or a cutaway. As a
general rule, however, an insert is a close-up of something that you
"insert" so the viewer gets a good look, while a cutaway is a shot you
use to "cut away" from and condense the action you are showing, most
commonly synch sound from an interview, speech or news conference.

If you were to continue the parking ticket sequence, you
might have your subject examine the ticket, make a few faces, and
tear the ticket up.

In the first three shots, the ticket is the central element.

Your next shot could be the subject's frowning face, shot
from a little below and showing the shoulders, so the subject appears to be looking down at the ticket. This shot would be a cutaway, taking the viewer away from what is now the real subject, the
confounded parking ticket.

The next shot could be a close-up of the front of the ticket in
the subject's hand, shot so it looks like the viewer and the subject are
looking down at it. This would be an insert, a close look at the ticket.

Next, a fiendishly smiling face (used as a cutaway) followed by a relatively tight shot of the ticket and the hands, which
begin to tear the ticket up (an insert).

Next, perhaps, a wide shot from the side as the subject finishes tearing up the ticket, drops the pieces to the ground, and turns and walks out of frame. If you do this right, you'll have made another match cut with the hands tearing the ticket.

Here are other examples of inserts:

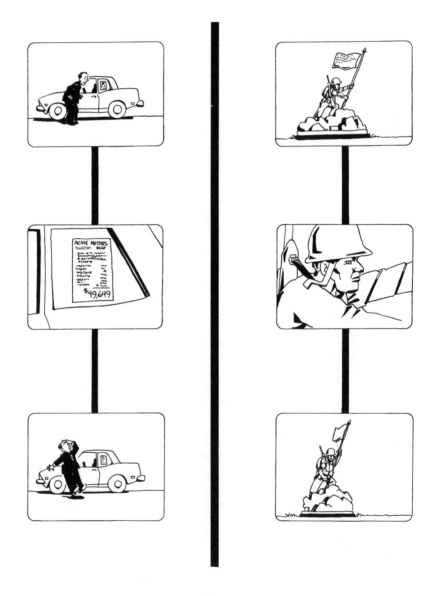

Some cutaways:

Interview subject

Reporter listening

Interview subject

Early action

Crowd as cutaway

Later action

Building a Sequence

A few years back, a student shot a story about the training of K-9 police dogs. The student used many of the techniques we've been discussing to build a professional sequence that looked as though it had been shot with two cameras.

It opens with a man firing a pistol (blanks) as if he were a "bad guy." As the firing continues, viewers see a second man restraining a police dog before letting it go. They see the "bad guy" still firing as the dog reaches him, seizes his shooting arm (padded) in its jaws and struggles to disarm the man.

Next, the dog negotiates an obstacle course. First it jumps a series of hurdles. Then it squeezes into the mouth of a long concrete culvert, crawls through and pops out the other end. Then the dog climbs up a seven-foot high wooden barrier, like an A-frame, goes over the top, down the other side and runs out of view.

The following pages illustrate how the photographer shot the sequence and made it look like the work of two cameras.

What Photographer Does	What Is Seen On Air

SHOT A: The photographer shoots the "bad guy" trainer as the trainer fires a blank pistol. The photographer is in front of the man at about 45 degrees and shoots wide enough to show his full body. As the man fires, another trainer, not in the picture, releases a police dog. The dog runs into the scene and seizes the trainer's shooting arm in its jaws. The photographer zooms in a little as dog and man struggle.

SCENE 1: Shows the "bad guy" firing blanks. Taken from the top of Shot A.

SHOT B: The photographer stays put as the action is repeated, but this time the photographer shoots in the other direction to get the second trainer, who restrains and then releases the dog as the "bad guy," not in the picture, fires more blanks. The dog takes off for the "bad guy" and runs out of frame, whereupon the photographer pivots and zooms in on the dog and "bad guy" struggling.

SCENE 2: Shows the dog held and then released by a second trainer and running out of frame. Taken from beginning of Shot B.

What Photographer Does	What Is Seen On Air

SCENE 3: Shows the dog rushing the "bad guy," seizing his arm in its jaws and struggling with him. Taken from the end of Shot A or end of Shot B, or possibly some of both, depending on what works.

SHOT C: The photographer moves to the obstacle course and shoots a very wide side view of a series of hurdles. The dog is released from out of the frame on the left, runs into the picture and jumps over the hurdles, one after the other, moving from left to right and out of frame.

SCENE 4: Shows the dog entering the frame from the left and jumping over several hurdles in the series. Taken from the beginning of Shot C, the edit is made when the dog is on the ground between jumps, a match cut.

SHOT D: The photographer moves to his right to a position in front of the hurdles, gets his camera as high as he can on the tripod to "stack" the hurdles full-frame. From out of the frame, the trainer releases the dog. The dog, moving towards the camera, jumps over the hurdles again. The photographer

What Photographer Does	What Is Seen On Air

shoots this and lets the dog run past him and out of frame.

SCENE 5: Shows the row of hurdles from the front, momentarily without the dog until it comes up and over a hurdle, then jumps the remaining hurdles and runs towards the camera and out of frame. Taken from Shot D, the edit was made when dog was between hurdles and couldn't be seen.

SHOT E: The photographer moves to the next obstacle, a concrete pipe, or culvert, through which the dog is going to crawl. The photographer gets behind the pipe about 30 degrees from head on, framing a wide shot of the mouth of the pipe and about a quarter of its length. The dog runs into the picture from the left and disappears into the culvert. The photographer tilts up and pans along the top of the pipe as if following the dog with X-ray vision, stopping at the end of the pipe.

SCENE 6: Shows the dog entering the frame from the left, running to the mouth of the pipe, entering it and disappearing from view as the camera appears to follow its progress. Uses Shot E from when the dog enters the

What Photographer Does	What Is Seen On Air

frame until the photographer pans to the end of the pipe.

SHOT F: The photographer moves to the other end of the pipe, framing the opening in the lower left corner. The dog, meanwhile, crawls through the pipe a second time. The photographer is rolling as the dog emerges from the pipe and keeps running out of frame.

SCENE 7: Shows the dog coming out of the pipe and running out of frame. Taken from the end of Shot F.

SHOT G: The photographer moves to the next obstacle, a 7-foot high, up-and-down wooden ramp like an A-frame, and he frames it just left of center in a wide side shot. The photographer is rolling as the dog enters the frame from the right, runs to, up and over the structure and out of sight.

SCENE 8: Shows the A-frame ramp and the dog running toward it and part way up it. Taken from the beginning of Shot G.

SHOT H: The photographer moves so that the "up" side of the ramp is directly in front of him, a little more than full

What Photographer Does	What Is Seen On Air

frame. The photographer is rolling as the dog runs to and climbs the barrier again. The photographer shoots the dog from behind, as it goes up and over and out of view.

SCENE 9: Shows the dog, from behind, going up the ramp. The edit is made as from part way up the ramp to the point where the dog's ears are silhouetted above the top of the ramp. Taken from Shot H.

SHOT I: The photographer moves to the "down" side of the ramp. He frames it as he did the other side, and he is rolling as the dog's ears appear, followed by its head and body as it comes over the top again and runs down and out of frame.

SCENE 10: Shows the down side of the ramp, starting just as the dog's ears appear over the top in a match cut. Following the ears comes the dog, over the top, down the ramp and out of frame. Taken from Shot I. End of sequence.

This relatively simple sequence required a lot of work on the photographer's part—and also the police dog's, because, in fact, more than one take of each shot was needed to get the framing and timing right and give the editor some choices. Good photography means work—work, work, work!

Shooting an Interview

The interviews you do in the course of routine news work can be classified in a number of ways: they can be brief or longer, on-the-fly or relaxed, and gang-bang or exclusive. You'll approach them differently, according to the circumstances, but the basics are always the same:

1. Shoot set-up footage—that is, scenes to be used to introduce the person being interviewed.

2. Choose a location for the interview that adds visual information to the story (when you can choose).

3. Frame the subject pleasingly.

4. Vary the framing of the subject during the interview. Use at least two basic framings.

5. Get cutaways.

6. If a hand-held mic is used, try to keep it out of the shot—unless, of course, you work for a station that insists on showing its mic and logo for self promotion.

Set-up footage means a few scenes you can use to talk about the person being interviewed, to set up the interview. The biggest cliché in this area is the two-shot, showing the interviewee and the reporter at the interviewee's desk, or in facing chairs or sitting on a couch or park bench.

Something better would be the subject and reporter walking in and out of frame before a cut to the interviewee answering a question. Or the subject going about regular activities—such as our museum director going in and out of frame, or a chef working in the kitchen.

You can shoot set-up footage at the interview location or elsewhere, before or after the interview. The only difference is that when you decide to shoot set-up after the interview, make sure in advance that your interviewee will stick around and cooperate. Otherwise, you may find yourself out of luck.

The location of the interview should be related to the story. But keep in mind that merely being in the subject's element doesn't mean viewers will know it. You may interview a world-famous surgeon in the operating room, but if the background is nothing but a blank wall, viewers won't see "hospital" any more than "bus station" or "men's room." Make sure you are in the right place and that it shows.

When framing the subject, make sure you always have more room in front of the person's face than behind. Try to stay away from a full profile or a head-on shot; three-quarters profile is always good. As a rule, save close-ups and extreme close-ups for special interviews, the long, probing ones that may have emotional impact that will be enhanced by framings that emphasize the features of the face or give the illusion of intimacy.

Make "medium-tight" your basic frame. That could be defined as a shot of a man from the top of his shirt pocket upwards. The second frame should be wider, enough so that you could smoothly cut from one to the other without a cutaway. Try to change the frame while your reporter is asking a question; that way, you won't have a good sound bite start or end in mid-zoom or mid-pullback.

Basic interview framing: between profile and full face, shot from shirt pocket upward.

Wider, but not enough difference to edit without a cutaway.

Will edit without a cutaway.

Poor interview framing: full profile, too tight.

Poor interview framing: too tight and dramatic for a routine information interview.

Cutaways are needed so the interview can be edited—so the tape editor can cover any visual problem that develops when getting out of one sound bite and into another.

The most common cutaway is the reporter listening to the subject. Shoot this cutaway in frames that match the framing of the subject, so you'll have the reporter's head the same size as the subject's or smaller when the story is edited. Regardless of what some reporters think, the interviewee is more important than the reporter so don't shoot the reporter any tighter than you shoot the interviewee.

Next is the two-person cutaway from behind the subject, showing the reporter listening while the interviewee speaks, as evidenced by the interviewee's moving cheek. This cutaway is more often used with sit-down interviews than standing interviews. You must, of course, ask the interviewee to talk while you shoot and you must take care that the moving cheek shows. Otherwise, you have a cutaway giving the impression that the words continue even though both people have their mouths shut. (A seldom-used variation on the two-shot cutaway can be taken from behind the reporter, with the interviewee listening to a question.)

You can, of course, shoot both the reporter cutaways and the two-shot cutaways from the same location. If the interviewee is in a time bind, do the two-shot first and let the subject leave. Then do the reporter only.

Keep a close eye on your reporter during cutaways. Maybe it's OK if he or she smiles or laughs or nods, or scowls, but remember that these expressions can easily be taken for what they are—editorial comments. They show that the reporter agrees or disagrees, likes or doesn't like what's being said. Watch for the proverbial raised eyebrow. Make sure you always get the reporter doing nothing but listening, no matter how blank or uncomprehending he or she looks. Cutaways that show the reporter comprehending or being amused are fine, but get the neutral, non-editorial, just plain listening shot first because it's the one most often used, the one you can't do without.

Among less common but still very satisfactory cutaways are high shots of the subject and interviewee, perhaps taken while you stand on a table and they are at a desk, or a long shot of the knot of reporters around the subject in a gang interview.

Sometimes, you might shoot the interviewee's nervous hands tapping the desk top, or you might find photos on the wall or items around the room that add to a sense of the person or the subject. These work when the presence of such items has been established in previous shots. If it hasn't, they become disembodied items that could be in another county, and they don't work as cutaways.

Up to this point, we've been talking only about silent cutaways. An entirely different kind is the "sound reverse" in which the reporter repeats questions from the interview. These are usually shot only in sit-down interviews. You should shoot some showing the reporter only, and some as two-shots from behind the interviewee.

An experienced reporter usually can remember the questions. If he or she can't, sometimes an experienced photographer can remember at least some of them. It's a good idea to do all of your sound reverses in the presence of the interviewee. That way, the interviewee can point out a subtle change in phrasing between the original question and the reverse, or scream like a stuck pig if your reporter throws out a question that was never asked, or alters one so that it could alter the subject's answer, or misrepresent it.

Here is an example—a ridiculous one that makes the point.

Original Question: "Have you ever beaten your wife?
A. "Never... why would I want to do that?"
Reverse Question: "When did you stop beating your wife?
A. "Never ...why would I want to do that?"

If the interviewee spots a discrepancy, do the reverse again just as the interviewee wants it, even when you think the interviewee is mistaken. In the editing room, you can find out who was right by comparing the original question with both versions of the reverse, and act accordingly.

Beginning photographers often get in trouble with cutaways because they "cross the line" and end up with a reporter who appears to be looking away from the subject and paying no attention to the interview.

The "line" or "axis" is imaginary. It runs from the interview subject to the interviewer. As the photographer, you are on the left side or the right side of that line, pointing the camera toward the interviewee, when you shoot the interview. To shoot the reporter in cutaways, you are going to move the camera so you are facing the reporter. When you move the camera, don't "cross the line."

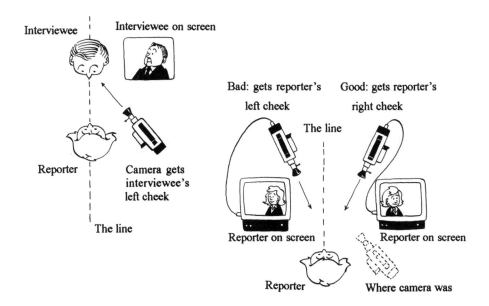

If you do, you'll shoot both persons from the same general angle and when the shots are edited together it will look as though the reporter was looking *away* from the subject. A rule of thumb on this is to remember that if you shoot the left cheek of the subject you want the right cheek of the reporter, or vice versa. (If you can't remember what you did, roll back the tape and take a look before you leave the scene, or shoot the cutaway both ways.)

Interview subject.

Backwards cutaway.
Reporter looking *away*
from subject.

Interview subject.

| Interview subject. | Good cutaway. Reporter looking *at* subject. | Interview subject. |

Long Interviews

Every now and then you'll be assigned to interviews you know will run long on the air. A single interview sometimes constitutes an entire program. You should pick your location with great care. If possible, you want it to reinforce the subject matter and add to the viewer's understanding of the person being interviewed. At the same time, you do not want the location and background to compete with the interviewee for the viewer's attention.

Most of the time you are going to show the subject talking, not the interviewer listening, so you need to pay greatest attention to what is behind the subject. If you are interviewing a veteran but still active sailor, you need a nautical background if it's available. But if the old sailor is retired to a home for old sailors, you want a setting that suggests "old sailors' home." If you are talking to a migrant farm worker, a background that shows fruit trees or green plants is appropriate. The wide shot might include other people working, but not to the point of distracting the viewer. And if you are going to start out with people in the background, make sure they'll be around for the duration. Otherwise, editing may be difficult: the people are there, now they've disappeared, now they're back, oops, they're gone! What's going on here?

Location can be irrelevant. If you are interviewing a poet, you may want to focus all your attention—and that of the viewer—on the poet's words and intriguing face. To do so, you throw the background out of focus, into a soft blur. If it's a soft blur of pretty colors, so much the better if it's a romantic poet. Then let your cutaways of the interviewer and an occasional wide two-shot remind the viewer of the surroundings.

Long interviews, especially those intended to be program length, are usually shot with two cameras, one on the interviewee and one on the reporter. This way, your cutaways will show the reporter's real, contemporaneous reaction to an answer, every sound reverse will be real, and the subject's expression while listening to a question and considering an answer will be real. The two photographers need to agree on procedures and framings, so nothing bizarre happens, and they need to decide who (maybe both) is going to shoot the wide shots. Also, both cameras should be recording with synchronized time codes.

Shooting a Speech

Just like an interview, you need set-up footage, a couple of framings of the speaker and some cutaways.

Frequently the sponsors of speeches confine cameras to a particular area—their goal being to keep you from obstructing the audience's view of the speaker, or from banging into a table and spilling everyone's soup.

You're better off if the sponsors allow freedom of movement, because you can get better cutaways and better set-up footage. But if you're stuck in one spot you can still do the story. Here's how.

1. Shoot the speaker in three frames—medium tight (maybe from six inches below the adam's apple), medium wide (from the waist area up), and wide or very wide (if this is not so wide that the viewer loses the speaker, but wide enough so lip movement isn't distinct, you've also got a cheap cutaway).

Make your frame changes during applause. This minimizes the chance of camera movement getting in the edited story because you zoomed or widened while something important was being said.

2. From your restricted position, you still can isolate other people who are on the stage or dais for cutaways. Get them both listening and applauding— both, not just one. Try to catch them looking up toward the speaker.

If the room or auditorium is large enough, often there will be people behind your camera position. If the lighting is adequate, you can turn the camera and shoot them listening and applauding. Getting them listening and breaking into applause makes a nice cutaway.

It's best to shoot your cutaways during the speech of the person you are covering rather than during another person's speech. The best time is usually during the opening remarks, when speakers seldom say anything worth using so you won't miss anything while shooting the audience.

You should, however, also shoot cutaways while someone else is speaking—perhaps during the convocation or the introduction of the main speaker. These scenes can serve as set-up footage and provide you with cutaways if you are unable to get them during the speech. (You never know what's going to happen: the speaker may be so strong you don't want to take the camera off him or her, or the audience lights may be dimmed after the speaker begins.) The problem with these cutaways is they put you at risk of showing someone applauding remarks they might not have applauded. Also, if you shoot cutaways while another speaker is speaking, be sure your featured speaker isn't in your cutaway. Can't have the speaker in two places at once, or applauding herself.

The best cutaways are available to the photographer who can roam around a bit. If that's permitted, take your camera off the tripod and go portable. Wide side shots at a right angle to the speaker make good cutaways. So do backshots if you can get behind the speaker and show his or her back and some of the audience. Be patient and try to get the audience listening and the audience applauding.

You can also shoot audience reaction head-on. Shots with several people are better than just one person (the viewer may wonder who *was* that person and why was he or she singled out?). If you are shooting the speaker head-on, you can shoot audience cutaways from almost any angle. But if your position for shooting the speaker is off to the side, take care that you don't cross the line and get cutaways of people who seem not to be watching the speaker, or even to have their backs to the speaker.

Shooting a News Conference

This is very much like shooting a speech, except on a smaller scale. The news conference is the birthplace of the biggest visual clichés in the business, the battery of photographers covering the news, the reporters busily taking notes. But clichés are always better than no cutaways. A very effective cutaway in news conferences is the backshot, showing the news maker full length or from about the waist up, from behind with the reporters in front of him or her. When you are back there, you can also zoom in on other camerapersons and on note-taking reporters (be sure to get a good close shot of your own reporter). Of course, unless you've got the news maker on a wireless set-up, you disconnect and forget the sound while shooting backshots, so choose the moment with care. When you're shooting from the front, remember to get at least two different frames of the news maker, changing frames during questions.

And remember, unless you are unionized, your reporter can be helpful by holding a microphone, preferably a shotgun, to pick up other reporters' questions while you are shooting sound of the news maker.

Courtrooms

Most state and local courts allow photography and recording devices during trials, so long as neither side objects. The federal courts allow no photography, not even in the hallways of federal court buildings.

Many courtrooms are wired for sound, with microphones for the judge, witnesses and lead attorneys. Photographers shoot from a fixed location and take audio on a line feed from the court's sound system. This minimizes distractions that the presence of television news crews might cause. To cut down even further on distractions, many judges allow only one camera inside the courtroom and require stations to pool their footage. In cases where time is not a factor, the pool may be accomplished by dubbing. When time is tight, the one camera may feed several VCRs simultaneously.

As the cameraperson, you need to do two things: Get the major testimony and get cutaways so the testimony can be edited. Depending on camera angles and distances, you may be able to get cutaways from wide shots with lip movement that's too indistinct to read. If that's possible, do it for every witness. Also shoot plenty of listening shots of the judge, some jurors (when allowed), the defendant, the attorneys, and possibly the court reporter (who, of course, is the most neutral cutaway you could get). These can be used as cutaways and talk-over footage.

Your footage will be almost exclusively people talking. It's a good time to use time code and, if no reporter is with you, to keep timed notes on testimony that sounds significant. You can jot down what you heard and the approximate time it was said during lulls in the action, of which there always are plenty. Rough notes are far better than none, and can really help editors and writers who are working with your tape under severe deadline pressure. It's also a good idea to get the swearing in of each witness, to give the tape editor an easy way of identifying witnesses.

Hearings and Meetings

Hearings and meetings tend to be boring to shoot and boring to watch on the news—to the point that many news departments simply will not shoot them. But there are exciting, electric exceptions.

You need to know the protocol at a hearing—what the rules are, who will talk, where questions will come from, whether the cameras will be allowed to move around or whether they'll be confined to one area.

The typical arrangement at hearings is that witnesses (and their colleagues and attorneys) sit at a table facing the people holding the hearing, who themselves are seated at tables or a rostrum. If you're not allowed to move around, your best bet at a hearing is a side location that enables you to get testimony as well as questions by panning. But favor the angle for witnesses because they are usually more important than the panel of questioners.

If a mult box is provided, use it for the sound. Otherwise, use a standing mic for witnesses and one or two more (depending on how many your camera will take) for questioners. If you have an assistant to run sound, you will probably wind up with a mixer and four mics—one for witnesses, a couple for the panel, and a shotgun. If you're on your own, improvise and use as many mics as your camera has audio channels—two in the case of some professional cameras, four in the case of Sony Beta.

If you are allowed to move around the room, try to get very wide shots of the hearing room, including the audience, if possible from the back of the room towards the panel and from behind the panel towards the audience and witnesses. If you can get to those positions, shoot a variety of shots rather than just one. If conditions permit, get down between the witness table and the panel and shoot listening shots of panel members. If you can't move around, do the best you can from your fixed location, aiming for listening cutaways of the panel and audience ("spraying the scene," it's sometimes called). Another listening cutaway is another person at the witness table—a lawyer, a second witness. The shot will work only if you shoot that person with the witness and the editor uses the shot. Otherwise, it's a cutaway of a person from nowhere. Also, always shoot the witnesses listening, not talking. Shoot just enough to use as a cutaway in case you get and want to edit a question being asked by one of the group holding the hearing.

The same general principles apply to covering meetings. The key again is finding out what's going to happen, what the rules are, and what the physical set-up is. Then you can figure out what to do.

Group Interviews and Discussions

These can be hard to shoot because you never know which member of the group is going to talk when. It's axiomatic, or so it seems, that while you are on Jack, Jill will interrupt with the best comments of the session. If you have the set-up correctly miked, you'll get the sound of everything Jill says—but she will have said much of it before you find her with the camera.

Sometimes your editor can use your pan from Jack to Jill, but it's more likely the pan will be too fast and blurred, or you'll overshoot Jill and have to back up and reframe, or maybe even refocus. You need plenty of cutaway listening shots to fill in—shots of each individual, shots of groups of two or three, plus a variety of wide shots (from several positions) or high shots of the group (stand on a chair or table). Shoot plenty, because you can also use these shots for talk-over footage.

Usually you can control the set-up for group interviews. Try to keep the participants relatively close to one another and all about the same distance from your camera so everyone (or almost everyone) will be in focus. Check before you start that you're not going to have a lighting problem—some folks in dim light, others in a backlight situation, etc. Work from the tripod for the interview and wide shots (if the location permits) and from the shoulder for high shots.

If you work for a station that wants to spend the money, the job is better done by two photographers. One will shoot a base shot of the entire group, so that when Jill interrupts with the best quotes of the session, you'll have her in synch sound in a wide shot and can use it until the second camera gets to her closer-up. This base shot will also give you the spontaneity of the group's reaction to what members say—laughter, tears, approval, dissent. An alert second cameraperson will, of course, shoot a variety of tighter shots and look for revealing expressions, especially, when it happens, tears.

As an alternative to two photographers, if you work in a non-union shop and don't mind doing it, you can set up a second camera for the base shot and let it roll without a photographer. If you get anything that's technically usable—and you will—you'll be much better off than if you had nothing. This is a good time to use time code to help the editor. And because it will probably be a multi-mic set-up, it would be convenient to feed both cameras from a mult box or mixer.

If group interviews are extra trouble, why do them? Sometimes because the individuals in the group insist on it—all of us or none of us, they say, and you comply even though you know you care only about what one or two of them have to say. But more often you do group interviews because they can be extremely productive. You're way ahead when you get the spontaneous interplay, affection and emotion of three generations recounting a family ordeal, or the mix of pride and fear generated by a fast-food kitchen crew telling how they outsmarted and overcame two gunmen after being held hostage six hours.

Shooting Continuous Action

Coverage of continuous action like open heart surgery, where you are trying to catch the drama or skill or teamwork involved, can be a challenge. Two conditions probably apply: one, you don't know exactly what's going to happen, and two, you are going to be confined by rules or physical circumstances to one location or area.

You need to determine where the center of activity will be and how far from the center the rest of the action and people will be. Do your best to assure your location (and the lighting and your lens) gives you enough depth of field that everything, or most of it, will be in focus at all times and you can work the lens in and out without losing focus.

When ready, work from the tripod. You can pan and tilt from person to person and activity to activity, zooming and widening as necessary, often for minutes at a time without stopping. Include framing changes and even focus changes, if any. Just make sure you hold scenes long enough that they'll be usable in editing. This way you'll have static scenes, movement scenes and uninterrupted control track ahead of anything you want to use.

Layover or Cover Footage

Layover or cover footage is supposed to illustrate what a person in a sound bite (usually from an interview) is talking about. At its best, when carefully shot and edited, it enhances the story admirably. But far too often it is used merely to replace the talking head—to put some pictures up rather than a face. In such cases, the footage serves a production purpose rather than editorial.

Layover runs from general to specific. In theory, it is shot specifically for a particular interview. That's when it's more likely to be good and to improve the television version of the story. But all too often, it's just pulled from file footage. If the subject is roses, a tape editor finds shots of roses and uses them regardless of how well they fit the sound bite or whether they are even the kind of roses being talked about.

To shoot good layover, you need to know what the interviewee actually said. You can try to remember main points you heard while you were taping the interview. Or you can re-rack the cassette, listen to the interview and take notes on subjects and timings, and then go out and shoot. You need to know what you are looking for if you are to do it right.

Throw or Rack Focus

These are arty shots used as transitions. You start with only part of the scene in focus—the part you are highlighting—with the rest out of focus. Then a quick lens move throws the first highlight out of focus and brings a second highlight into focus. For example, you may start with a sign in focus reading, "Silence: Study Room," against a blurred background of people sitting at large tables. Then the sign goes out of focus and the Rhodes Scholar who is the subject of your story comes into focus, sitting at a library table hitting the books.

You do this by controlling the depth of field and focus so that the two features will not be in focus at the same time. To get the framing you want, you may have to fool around a bit with your distance from the scene and the zoom lens. This done, you focus on the first highlight and practice moving the focus ring (not the zoom) so that the second highlight comes into focus. You make note of the two appropriate distance readings on the focus ring, and then execute the shot. Hold on the first scene for about 15 seconds, then turn the focus ring quickly to the second distance you have noted and hold the scene for about 10 seconds.

A variation might go like this. The last shot in one sequence may be a close-up of a diner sinking a knife into a T-bone steak. The next sequence may start with a blur—an out-of-focus blur that comes into focus as the barb on a barbed wire fence as you push through the fence to see a steer (many potential steaks) peacefully grazing. The whole sequence could also be used in reverse, from steer to blurred barbed wire to steak on a plate.

Screen Direction

You need to be mindful of the direction in which your subjects move because you'll have problems if you don't. Visualize a parade, for example. If the parade is heading north and you shoot everything from the east side of the street, the marchers will move from left to right regardless of the angle you are shooting at (except, of course, straight head-on). When you edit, you'll be OK. But if you jump across to the west side the parade will move from right to left, just the opposite of your other shots. When you edit, you'll have no flexibility because you will need a cutaway between parade scenes each time you change screen direction—and even then your parade will have a helter-skelter look. A better bet would probably be to group your scenes by running a number of scenes from one side, throwing in a cutaway, and running scenes from the other side. The best bet is to stay on one side.

Angles

The saying goes that you shoot a news story the way viewers would have seen it if they had been there themselves. That's a good approach to take, the best, in fact, but don't make it a hard and fast rule because it isn't true. The man in the street doesn't see a political demonstration from the roof of a tall building or a helicopter; only the police and news photographers do. But that high shot can be indispensable to telling the story.

If a model railroad is set up and exhibited on the floor, few adults will lie down to watch the trains go by. They'll stand and look down at an angle. You might establish the exhibit with a shot looking down from that angle, but from there on you'll get better results if you get the camera on the floor, or close to it on a flat box or some books, or, in some circumstances, even if you let it hang low from your hand. Most ENG viewfinders pivot upwards, so you can see what you're doing without lying on the floor yourself.

When you get very close to things and above or below them, you run the risk of distorting the scene with a sharp angle. So keep an eye on what you're doing. This is especially true if you're using the macro. For example, if you are taping the text in a document, you can get all the text by slowly moving the document in front of the camera without changing its distance from the lens. If you try to tilt down to get the bottom of the document you run the risk of distortion and loss of focus.

Riding Shots

Riding shots provide a very effective way to give viewers the feeling of "being there" while combining an interview with visual information. Ride with a cop on patrol and see the beat while hearing about being a cop. Jump in a pickup and see the farm as the farmer tells about the rigors of farm life, or the difficulty of making ends meet, or of losing the spread.

There are at least four keys to success with riding shots. One, shoot with the lens as wide as possible. This minimizes shakiness from the ride and shows more of the area you're passing through. Two, vary your shooting angle. From the back seat, this is easy. You can shoot almost directly behind the driver and then move to the right for two more angles. You can shoot a little up and a little down. You can also stop, move to the front seat and shoot from there, too. This provides variety for editing. Three, shoot cutaways. Yes, you can get cutaways. From the back seat you can get the driver in the foreground while concentrating on what's out the window or through the windshield. You can shoot the driver's hands turning the wheel. You can shoot out a window without the driver in the frame at all. And four, stick your lens as close to the subject as possible without sacrificing focus or safety—the subject's safety, your safety and the equipment's.

Non-interview riding shots that don't include the driver are, of course, entirely different. It's better to do them from a pickup bed than a car, because you won't have windows and door posts getting in the way. Naturally, you are hand-held, usually on the shoulder, and you are sitting down or kneeling. Do not risk standing. Shoot with the lens as wide-angle as possible consistent with the scene you want, and remember that the combination of speed and proximity to a stationary subject can result in a blur rather than usable footage when the subject is only a few feet away.

With care, if you match their speed you can interview joggers and cyclists to the side or behind your pickup. Add wireless microphones and you can record an interview or conversation with two people in the front seat of a vehicle following yours, or you can shoot a jogging or bicycling standupper.

Covering Sports

A dream for some photographers, a nightmare for others. Knowing the sport makes all the difference in the world. Otherwise, what would you do when the batter drives one off the left-center field wall with two out and a man on base in the bottom of the ninth with the score 2 to 2?

You would have started with a nice wide shot of the pitcher's windup and delivery and the batter hitting the ball. You'd have followed the ball (in ball games, always follow the ball) until it hit the fence, but then what? Do you stay with the ball and the outfielder until he gets the ball and throws it in? Or do you leave the ball as soon as it bounces off the fence and go check the runner with your camera?

If you know baseball, you know what to do and you know it depends on whether the runner was at first, second or third base. If you don't know baseball, you're in a quandary. Good luck.

The major ball games—baseball, football and basketball— are played differently, but two can be shot according to the same principles and one can't. That's baseball. Because the ball is in play anywhere on the field—fair territory or foul—photographers are restricted to the stands, usually to a press box or other area behind home plate. They have to stay out of the way, along with the fans. In the other sports, photographers can shoot from the stands or the press box and from the out-of-bounds areas around the field or court.

If you are sent with a reporter to shoot a package, make it a rule to get an exterior of the stadium or arena, a sign saying who's playing, fans buying tickets and going in. Go in yourself and get a high shot and other scene-setters. These are clichés, but unless you work at a station that never, ever uses these shots, don't get caught short. They can help a reporter set the stage before the game action.

Otherwise, your job is to shoot highlights. You never know when one is coming, so you must shoot, shoot, shoot—almost all the action, from beginning to end. Use time code. Try to keep notes of the highlights by the time on your watch—all scoring plays (except basketball) and exceptional and exciting non-scoring plays. This habit can make an incredible difference in the editing bay.

If you're diligent, you will get most of the highlights, but it's unreasonable to expect yourself to get them all. In any game, you must stop shooting to change tapes, and while you try to do this between innings or during time-outs, you can't always foresee the precise moment when you can change without missing a key play. You can minimize the chance of getting caught by making it your habit to change tapes when you're still a few minutes from the end rather than waiting until there's no choice.

Football presents a special problem because the field is so large. When a team completes a 50-yard pass play, you've got to scamper down field 50 yards to catch up with the action. Another play could run in that time and you might miss it. The only way to be sure of getting all the plays in football or basketball is to have a second camera shooting from high—in the press box or from a live camera position. Those are bad spots for covering an entire game, because the angle will bore viewers and you'll necessarily be shooting a lot of the action from behind. But it's a great place for a second "protection" camera if your station thinks the game is worth the extra money and editing effort, but that's a big if.

In football, as mentioned, you have to keep up with the plays, moving up and down the field with the ball. You should try to set yourself about 10 yards down field from the line of scrimmage at the start of each play, so you can get the action coming towards you (unless, of course, you're a genius who can predict every sack and backfield fumble.) Remember, of course, that you can work the lens to your advantage. You can start tight on the center for the snap and pull back to capture the play. You can zoom in on a player who has just scored a touchdown. You can try to pan and zoom tight on the kicker after you've followed his crucial field goal through the uprights.

In basketball, you can shoot some high shots but generally you get the best footage from court level. Generally speaking, you'll be shooting from your knees because fans won't stand for you blocking their view. Start at mid-court and stay there until you get a play that looks like a highlight. Then move to the right corner. Get a highlight and go back to mid-court. Get a highlight and go to the left corner. Stay at each position until you get a potential highlight. The purpose of moving is to get a variety of angles that will make your coverage interesting and the editing easier. Since you'll only edit highlights, there's no point moving until you get one.

In any game, shoot game action for two or three minutes of tape and then shoot some cutaways. An editor working under deadline will really appreciate having cutaways near every shot, rather than having to hunt, or roll way back or way ahead. Standard cutaways are the fans, the scoreboard, the bench, the coach. (In basketball, some photographers try to get the scoreboard after every highlight so the reporter or writer will be able to say, "and that put the Blue Devils 20 points ahead," or "that closed the gap to a point" and so on.)

In any game, shoot all natural sound. Let the tape run a bit after every exciting play, to get the natural sound and to give the reporter or sports anchor a little talking-over footage for commentary without having to make a disrupting edit.

Always stay on the same side of the field or court. Let the teams change direction at halftime, but you stay where you are. If you move to the other side, the teams won't change camera direction (as they will for fans in the stands), your second-half shots will look the same as your first-half shots, and alert members of your television audience will have reason to wonder if you know the first half from the second.

Shoot your court-level shots hand-held and your high shots from the tripod. The movement of the players will offset normal shakiness in the hand-held footage, but up top you'll be zooming in on the action and that will exaggerate shakiness, so stay on the tripod.

Bracing the Camera

The very best way to get steady shots is to put your camera on a tripod. Nothing beats the tripod, nothing. When you're experienced, you can set the tripod up in less than a minute because you'll instinctively know how high you want the camera off the ground or floor, you'll instinctively judge how far out to pull the telescoping legs to get that height, and you'll level it in a flash.

When you're working on a nice, level floor, you pull the three leg extenders out, line them up and tighten them at the same length, then spread them out and check to see if you need to refine the set-up. You check by looking at the bull's-eye level on the top of the tripod. Adjust the legs if necessary to get the bubble in the center of the bull's-eye.

Tripod assemblies are made up of two parts, the three-legged tripod itself and the "head" to which the camera adapter is attached (and to which you attach the camera). The head has a handle for panning and tilting. You get control over the range and speed of these movements by adjusting the resistance the head offers to movements. The "fluid heads," operating on ball bearings encased in oil or silicone, work far better than "friction heads" where resistance is supplied by surfaces rubbing against each other.

Obviously, there are times when you can't use the tripod and must go "portable" with the camera on your shoulder. You can work with or without a camera brace. Two types of braces are commonly used. Both have shoulder pieces to which you attach the camera. These extend about a foot forward from the shoulder. In one style, a leg with a curved "tee" at the bottom pivots down from the front and rests on the abdomen. In the other style, a fixed, V-shaped piece cuts down from the front toward the rib cage, and goes back up to the shoulder piece.

With or without a brace, here are some ways of steadying yourself when shooting portable:

1. Lean against a wall or tree or car or light post; straddle a chair backwards so you use the chair back for a brace; or lean against another person (one who's willing of course).

2. Try to cradle the camera between your shoulder and the side of your head, tilting your head to keep the camera in place.

3. Try to keep the elbow of your camera-holding arm against your body.

4. Breathe normally; don't take deep breaths unless you are going to hold your breath during a relatively short shot.

Another approach, without a brace, is to place the camera snugly between your rib cage and upper arm and get as much of your forearm and hand under the camera as possible. If you are a right-hander, do this on the right side. Then pivot the viewfinder up so you can see, and operate the camera controls with your left hand.

The wider the angle you can shoot at, the easier it is to minimize shakiness. Conversely, it's just about impossible to get a steady shot from the shoulder when the lens is in telephoto. The same is true in macro.

Also, make a point of carefully watching your viewfinder for any sign that you are failing to hold the camera level. This can be hard to detect on a tiny two-inch screen, but is the top of that table really tilted? Is that really the leaning telephone pole of Pisa? Maintain a level horizon.

If you need to shoot a pan from the shoulder, start by pointing your feet in the direction of the final scene. Then twist your torso to the starting scene and shoot while twisting back to the first position.

Watching with the Other Eye

You're in a crowd shooting. Maybe it's even a melee between rioters and police. Or you're out in a tranquil forest, shooting a walking shot down a narrow hiking trail. Nothing can guarantee that you won't get shoved or pushed or hit by a flying object in the crowd, or trip over a rock or root in the forest, but you can reduce the chances by learning to concentrate on your scene in the viewfinder with one eye while peeking at what's going on outside the scene with the other eye.

Being able to do this can also help you when shooting action in a sports event. If you're following a receiver in a football game in the viewfinder and see the defensive back moving in for an interception with the "other" eye, you might have time to widen and get a better shot of the upcoming action.

Filling the Frame

This is so fundamental it shouldn't need to be pointed out, but many beginning photographers fail to fill the frame—that is, they give the viewer much less to look at than the viewer can absorb and less than is needed to make a scene visually interesting. This is often the result of concentrating so much on the subject of the shot that you forget the perimeter of the frame and shoot the subject with nothing around it, against a blank wall, as the only object on a table, or in some other grand isolation. The cure is to be alert and look not only at what is in your viewfinder but also at what else might be in it if you were to change your shooting angle (vertically as well as horizontally) or get a little closer or move the object or person to another location. It's easier said than done but if you apply yourself it becomes habit, a professional habit—filling the frame.

Where's the Photographer???

That's the question, the real question. When U.S. troops were falling to Viet Cong machine gun and mortar fire and the American people saw it all in their living rooms—where was the photographer? Right there with the troops.

When the 6 o'clock news shows heroic firemen risking their lives to rescue people from a flaming rooming house—where's the photographer? Right there with the firemen, or at least as close he or she can get without being chased or arrested for being in the way.

When we are looking straight into the eyeballs of a spread-eagled sky diver plummeting earthward —— where's the photographer?

When the air on Mt. Everest is getting thin and even Sherpa guides are wheezing—where's the photographer?

The question and its answer are at the heart of television news. The photographer is wherever he or she needs to be to get the story, sharing every labor and every risk—while viewers (and too many employers) seldom notice.

Editing News Tape

Pad going in, pad coming out.

Edit on phrases.

Don't repeat scenes.

Take a beat, then stop.

If you must miss a hit, show the picture late, not early.

Videotape editors take the work of photographers and reporters and turn it into the news that viewers see. Good editing can salvage inadequate shooting and writing, just as poor editing can undo otherwise brilliant work. In a perfect world, all shooting, writing and editing would be—at the minimum—above average. In the real world, the importance of editing is sometimes overlooked. It should not be.

Editing is fun, great fun. From your chair in the editing bay you can push buttons, turn knobs and make magic with pictures and sounds. Should you make a mistake, you can magically and instantly correct it. What a happier world it would be if all our mistakes could be fixed on the spot, like a bad edit.

The most important technical matter to understand about videotape editing is the role of control track—what it is, what it does, and what happens when you lose it. Next, you need to know the difference between "insert" editing and "assemble" editing. After that, you need to master the buttons and knobs on the machines. You are then ready for the hard part—developing speed and confidence to work under deadline pressure, and developing a good sense of the aesthetics of editing.

Control track is a series of electronic pulses, recorded along the upper edge of the videotape in most systems. They can be likened to the sprocket holes in a piece of film. They are as regular as sprocket holes and serve comparable although more complicated purposes.

Videotape recorders—whether field units or those in an editing system—take control track from a video source and put it on the tapes. In field recorders, the video source is the camera. In an editing bank, it is color bars or "black" (which can be changed to any color at the turn of a knob) fed to the recorder from a video switcher.

When ENG (electronic news gathering) began, the U-Matic format using ¾-inch-wide videotape was all but universal. Now broadcasters have switched to lighter and more compact half-inch formats, or are in the process doing so. Sony Betamax is the most popular and most expensive half-inch format. The S-VHS format (Super Video Home System), manufactured by Panasonic, Hitachi, JVC and others, is finding its way into news work because it is less expensive than Sony Beta and its quality is so much better than its predecessor, VHS format. Panasonic is also marketing camera and editing equipment it designates as "M-2" and places between Beta and S-VHS in quality and cost. In addition, a few stations make use of even smaller formats like Hi-8, especially as cameras for stringers.

Although they're not universal, the major formats tend to have two things in common: the broad middle portion of the tape carries picture signals in what's called a "helical scan" arrangement, and the edges are devoted to recording control track pulses and audio, in horizontal tracks.

Tapes carry one control track pulse for each "field" of picture. There are two fields per frame of picture, and 30 frames of picture per second.

Videotape editing relies on these control track pulses to synchronize the transfer of material between tapes, from the source tape to the editing or "package" tape.

When you are editing, you pick edit points ("ins" and "outs") on the source tape and the edit tape. When you command the editing system to edit, both tapes rewind to a "cued" position and stop. Then, as they automatically move forward, their electronics synchronize or "lock up," and when they get back to where they started, back to the original edit points, the transfer of signals from the source machine to the editor takes place and the edit is performed.

In order to rewind and return to the original editing points simultaneously, the machines count control track pulses. If control track on either of the tapes is intermittent, the edits will be imprecise because more tape will move on one machine than on the other and they won't return to the starting point at the same time. If track is missing entirely, editing will be impossible.

In assemble editing, new material from the source machine erases and replaces whatever signals may already be on the package tape—all of it, including control track. And even though the edit lays down new control track, a bit of track is lost between edits, leaving you with irregular track.

In insert editing, control track on the editing tape is used but not altered in the editing process, with the result that you can edit audio only, video only, or both together.

Insert editing, therefore, is always used for editing reporter packages because you can put the narration on the package tape and go back and add or change picture without erasing the narration, and you can lay "cover" footage over sound bites.

The typical editing system in a news operation is made up of a videotape cassette recorder called the source (or player or slave machine), a VCR called the editor (or editing machine or package machine), a controller (either stand-alone or incorporated in the editing machine), an audio mixer, and a television monitor for each VCR. Systems typically include an audio cassette deck and a microphone. Many older systems include a time base corrector as an add-on to clean up and stabilize the video signal. Newer systems have built-in TBCs.

Many newer systems are also set up for A/B-roll editing. They have two source VCRs rather than one and a switcher (or a controller with built-in switcher), making it possible to introduce special effects. Visuals from the "A-roll" VCR and the "B-roll" VCR are fed simultaneously to the switcher, and an edit is made with a wipe, dissolve or other effect. The result is fed to the package VCR, where it is recorded. Words and other graphics can be edited into the package in a similar manner.

The difference between a source machine and an editing machine is a thousand dollars or more of extra electronics that turn a basic "player" or source machine to one that performs insert edits. Some stations opt to save money and buy a "player" and an "editor" for each system while others choose flexibility and buy all editors. That way, any machine can replace any other machine in case of a breakdown. As a practical matter, when you're editing it makes no difference whether you are using a player and an editor or two editors.

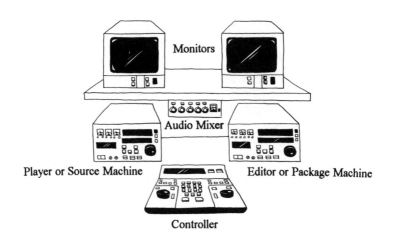

Player/Source Machine

You play tape from the player/source machine to the editor, controlling what you do with the controller and the audio mixer.

Before you put a tape in a machine, you need to take up any slack in the cassette. Tape that is slack can jam up during threading. You eliminate slack by putting your fingers in the open hubs of the reels on the underside of the cassette and holding one reel still while turning the other reel against it until the tape inside is taut.

Push "eject" to remove any tape that may be in the machine or, if your machine has one, to raise the tape basket. Insert your cassette and press "play" or "forward."

As the tape plays, you can check two things: the tracking and the audio. If the tracking needle isn't in the safe range, which is clearly indicated on the dial, usually by a green or "go" area, adjust with the tracking knob.

Check audio to determine where the audio is recorded and what its level is. VCRs have a VU meter for each audio channel. If the needle rises, there's audio of some kind on that track. If not, there's no audio. A switch next to the meters allows you to monitor or listen to Channel One alone, Channel Two alone, or both together, usually designated as "mix." (Some Sony Beta machines have four audio tracks with similar controls.)

Except for the tracking adjustment, which can stabilize a shaky picture, and a "skew" control to adjust tape tension, you have no control over the video signal the machine reproduces from your cassette. If you have a problem tape and are using an editing system without a time base corrector, you might try moving to a system with a TBC. Other than that, there's nothing to do but make the most of the situation or let a supervisor decide whether to abandon the story.

Editing Machine

The editor records your edited product, your package. You can control the levels at which it records the audio and video signals being fed to it from a source machine, audio cassette or microphone.

One meter shows incoming video level. You want the needle to be in the green or "go" area. You can adjust this with the knob near the meter.

Another meter shows the levels of incoming audio on both channels (or four). Controls allow you to determine how much of that signal you will record, either with manual or automatic settings. (Don't use automatic if you are recording from a live microphone.)

Otherwise, you take the audio as it comes and make the most of it—not in the technical sense, but in terms of aesthetics and editorial adequacy.

Controller

The controller is the heart of the editing system. It can be a free-standing unit or built into the editing machine. Either way, this device lets you control what's happening. With two knobs called shuttles, and a lot of buttons, you can:

1. Select assemble edit mode or insert edit mode. Probably all the editing you'll ever do will be insert.

2. Choose video only edits, audio only edits, combined audio and video edits, and in audio, Channel One, Channel Two, or both (or four).

3. Pick editing points, with accuracy to within a single frame. You can choose points at which the source machine will start sending new material, and/or stop sending it, and the points at which the editing machine will start recording new material, and/or stop recording new material.

4. Instantaneously stop a tape playing on either machine as soon as you see the frame you want or hear the sound you want.

5. Play either tape backwards or forwards in slow motion or double speed, so you can refine your selection of edit points or look for scenes.

6. Preview your edit, so you can see what it will look like or sound like before you perform it.

7. Adjust a previewed edit by as little as a frame.

The magic of control track makes this possible, and on most professional editing systems accuracy is promised within a few frames—that is, within a fifth to a fifteenth of a second. Some equipment is accurate to a single frame, but in any case, all professional gear is remarkably precise.

You get single-frame accuracy from machines equipped for programmable SMPTE time code editing. Unfortunately for news staffers, these machines cost more and many stations, if they have them at all, reserve SMPTE editors for special production work and commercials.

A general rule to keep in mind is this: When building a package, you'll ordinarily end an edit manually rather than electronically. You edit manually by watching during the editing process until you get to the end of the picture or word that is your "out." When you hear or see it, *wait a beat* and push the button designated "end" or "stop edit" or something similar.

The editing process will stop. In some systems, the machines roll for another second or two, then stop and rewind, the source to the point where it began sending information for the edit and the editor to the point where you pushed "end." In other systems, both machines stop instantaneously and stay where they stopped.

When you set the next "in" on the package tape, you'll back up a little to make up for the beat you took before stopping the edit. The purpose of the beat is to provide picture pad in case the next edit is late by a few frames. If you have pad, you'll get continuation of picture rather than black or a "flash frame" from extraneous material that might already be on the tape from previous work.

Ending an edit electronically rather than manually is usually done when you are changing a scene or inserting a cutaway and need the greatest precision the machines can give you. To end an edit electronically, you set "out" points beyond which the source will send no signal and the editor will record no signal. That way you eliminate the risk of wiping out material you want to preserve. Generally, you set the "out" for only one tape, making the choice according to which is more critical—preserving what's already on the package tape or getting exactly what you want from the new scene.

Editing a Package

To edit a simple voice-over narration package with no sound bite or open sound, follow this basic procedure, using insert editing mode.

1. On your package tape, lay down the audio and video of a leader. (The leader audio is a "beep" called "tone" that is used for setting levels. The video is a numbered countdown, usually from ten seconds to zero.)

2. On the package tape, after the leader, lay down your narration, using audio only mode. The narration is usually on a video cassette, for ease of editing, but it may also be on an audio cassette or even recorded on the package tape live, through a microphone built into the editing system. Being on videotape is best because you can be much more accurate with it.

3. Cover the narration with pictures in video only editing mode. Try to make your scenes begin and end on phrases, on commas and periods.

If the package is more complicated than one piece of narration covered by picture, so is the editing procedure. But you still take the same logical approach. Suppose your package is a reporter narration and pictures, setting out a controversy, followed by an interview with a person on one side, followed by more reporter narration and pix as a bridge to a second interview, followed by an interview with a person on the other side, followed by reporter narration and pix explaining a bit more, followed by a reporter standup summarizing the story.

You'd build that package in segments, as follows, again in insert mode:

1. Lay down a leader, audio and video, on your package tape.

2. Lay down reporter narration on the package tape, audio only. Do just the first portion, up to the first sound bite.

3. Cover that narration with pictures, in video only mode.

4. Lay down the first interview, audio and video together.

5. Lay down the narration bridge, in audio only.

6. Cover the bridge, video only.

7. Lay down second interview, audio and video.

8. Lay down reporter narration, audio only.

9. Cover narration, video only.

10. Lay down reporter standup, audio and video.

11. If necessary, go back and add cutaways to the interviews, in video only.

Some tape editors might choose a slightly different approach. They might get the entire audio track down on the package tape before doing any picture, except for the picture that goes with the two sound bites and the standupper. That is, they would postpone steps 3, 6 and 9 until they had built the full narration track. Then they would go back and do those three steps, and step 11, the cutaways.

Editors make choices like this according to their own preferences. Many find that one or the other of the two approaches gives them a better feel for the picture in the package and lets them work faster.

Apart from individual preferences, each of the two approaches offers an advantage the other does not. The first approach allows you to build in transitions as you construct the package. If you want a little extra picture or a natural sound break between segments or in the middle of one, you can do it when you get there. This is better than having to make a decision in advance and guessing at the appropriate place and length of a natural sound break. Or, if you need to space out narration (that is, put in pauses) to take best advantage of picture, you can do it as you go along. You could space out narration using the other procedure, but you'd either have to re-dub and lose a generation of picture quality, or you'd have to start over from scratch.

The advantage of building the audio track first is that as soon as you've done it you'll know how long the edited package will run. At crunch time that information can be vital.

Some Fundamentals and Some Tricks

Along with knowing the right procedures, you must know and practice good fundamentals and take advantage of some tricks.

PACKING A CASSETTE: Run a tape from start to end in fast forward, then rewind it. This evens the tension between the two spools and ensures that the tape will move uniformly. Do this before you do anything else. By the way, in most shops this is also done with brand new tapes before they are taken to the field by photographers.

CONTROL TRACK: Your package tape must have control track on it before you start editing. Otherwise, you can't do insert edits. The practice in most shops is to maintain a supply of tapes with track by making them up every morning. Depending on your set-up, you can do many tapes at a time or just one. You need a recorder and a video source. Put the tape in the machine, check that the machine is receiving the video signal, and record. The popular term for this process is "blacking tape" because the video signal most commonly used is black from a switcher (rather than one of the colors the switcher can generate) or black from a capped camera (rather than color bars or a picture of the studio).

In an emergency, when no prepared tapes are available, you'll have to put track on a tape yourself just before editing. When this is necessary, be sure to lay down more than enough track because you can't add track without losing a few pulses. If that interruption coincides with an edit point, you won't be able to make the edit you want. If the package you're going to edit is supposed to run around two minutes, lay down at least four minutes of fresh track—some for leader, two minutes for the package, and the rest just in case. The extra minutes you spend doing this can pay big dividends, because running out of track just as you are finishing a package can be a disaster.

A tape that has track will make the numbers change on the machine's digital readout. If you run the tape at fast forward, the numbers will still change if there's track. And if you watch carefully, you can detect even in fast forward that a few pulses are missing and the numbers don't change for a split second. You don't want to use that tape. It may need fresh track or it may be physically damaged. In any case, don't use it until the problem is diagnosed.

STARTING: Put your tape with control track in the editing machine and run off at least 30 seconds of tape to help balance the tension between reels. Lay down a leader and you're ready to go.

LEADERS: They are quite standardized. Almost all leaders start at ten and count down towards zero, second by second, and have an audio beep or "tone" to help a program's audio director locate the tape and set levels.

The oldest kind of leader is an "academy" leader, a carryover from motion pictures to news film on television. An "academy" shows the numbers in a circle with a radius like a clock hand sweeping through each second until the number changes. Many modern leaders show seconds and fractions in numbers only, or combine numbers with postcard scenes of the station's city, or a station's logo.

Most leaders stop displaying numbers after two, and are blank until they show a dot or "X" or other symbol to indicate zero.

Different shops have different rules, but most agree that audio and video should not start at the same time and neither should start exactly at zero. That's to allow for human error in getting the tape on the air.

A common practice (not universal) is to start the picture one second *before* zero and the audio one second *after* zero. That way, if the technical director punches up the tape a split second early the viewer will see news story rather than black. And if the audio person is a split second slow the first couple of syllables of the report won't be lost, or upcut.

You can measure this "pad" with the machine's digital readout, which gives you seconds and frames. Fifteen frames make half a second; 30 frames make a full second.

Laying Down Narration

This can be done from a videotape or an audio cassette. It can even be done live if there's a microphone in your setup. Videotape is the most accurate and convenient, so most shops have reporters record their narrations on videotape.

The narration on videotape can come from the field, having been written and recorded on the scene by the reporter, or it can come from an audio booth at the station, where the reporter has written the story after returning and viewing the field tapes. The latter is generally better because the reporter will have had a chance to think about the story and will be able to write *knowing* what's on the field tape rather than *guessing* at scenes and at how sound bites begin and end.

Regardless of the source of the narration, you must set audio levels in two places before recording—on the audio mixer that is connected between your various audio sources and the videotape editor, and on the editor itself.

The mixer will be wired so that it has separate "pots" or controls for each of the audio channels coming from the source machine, and, if you have them, for an audio cassette deck and a microphone. In addition, a "master pot" on the mixer must be set for a general level that will accommodate the expected variations in your other audio sources. Ordinarily, a setting is found for this master pot and it is left there.

Many source machines send audio to the mixer at line level, meaning in effect that you have no control over what comes out of the source machine. You can't turn it up or down at the source machine. You can, however, boost it or back it off, as necessary, as it passes though the mixer on the way to the editing machine. Other source machines allow you to control their audio output level.

First, play a little source audio and set levels on the mixer. While it's still playing, push the record button on the editor and check the level on the editor's meter. You can then choose to have the editor operate on manual, meaning you, set the level with the knobs on the editor, or on automatic level control, meaning you leave the setting to the machine's electronics.

At this point, you've got to be paying strict attention to the channels you are using. You can record one audio source on two channels on your package, or you can mix two sources on one channel on the package, or you can turn Channel One from the source into Channel Two on the editor, and vice versa. You can do even more when using systems that have four rather than two audio channels. Whatever you do depends on the buttons you push on the controller, the mixer pots you are using, and the channels and pots you are using on the editing machine.

You've got to decide what you want to do. Fortunately, many shops make this easier by standardizing parts of the process. For example, narrations and sound bites may go only on Channel Two on the package tape, and effects (music or natural sound) may go only on Channel One. Or narration may go on Channel Two and bites and effects on Channel One (the advantage of this being that you can fade interviews up behind narration).

Once you have figured out what you're going to do, do it. Set the controller on audio edit only, pick your channel and level settings, and lay down your opening narration. Next, cover it with picture. Let's assume you began your audio a second *after* zero.

Keep in mind that when you are checking levels and actually editing, you can hear the audio from two television monitors, one hooked up to the source machine and one hooked up to the package machine. It makes sense to listen only to the package monitor when edits are in progress, so you'll know exactly what you're getting on your package. After you locate the source audio and edit points, turn the audio down on the source monitor and listen to the audio that comes out of the package monitor during the edit. That helps you catch distorted or "dirty" audio on your package.

Editing Picture Only

Now your task is to lay suitable picture over the opening narration. This time, you'll set the controller for "video only" edits.

First, you've got to find your opening scene. Unless you are right on top of deadline, you should inventory or log the field tapes so you'll know which scenes are good and where they are. This is especially important on features, where there can be so many field tapes you'll be lost if you don't log them. Log notes are far superior to memory, especially a day or two after viewing.

When you log, you take notes about scenes and sound bites according to the digital readout on the VCR. If you're short on time, you keep minimal notes—just the highlights. If you have lots of time you keep detailed notes. And if you're doing a documentary, you might log every scene and every sentence—which is one heck of a lot of work.

Now dub your opening scene, remembering to start it a second (30 frames) *before* the zero mark on your leader—or, at any rate, remembering to follow whatever is your station's practice.

Try to end the scene at the end of a phrase or sentence rather than in mid-thought, and do it on the tiny silence between words rather than in the middle of a word. This will give your tape a smooth, orderly flow. As an example, the script below is marked first with poor places to edit and then with good places.

Poor Edit Points:
> " The violence started in a courtyard outside the office of the university president, 36 hours [EDIT] after the protest began. Police officers ordered the demonstrators [EDIT] to leave.
> NAT SOT
> When they did not, the officers [EDIT] began arresting the protestors. One resisted and shoved an officer. Two officers [EDIT] reacted with nightsticks and bedlam erupted....."

Good Edit Points:
> " The violence started in a courtyard outside the office of the university president, 36 hours after the protest began. [EDIT] Police officers ordered the demonstrators to leave.
> NAT SOT
> [EDIT] When they did not, the officers began arresting the protestors. [EDIT] One resisted and shoved an officer. Two officers reacted with nightsticks [EDIT] and bedlam erupted....."

Assume you want your first scene to end after "protest began." Let the edit run until you hear "began." Take a beat and stop the edit.

When the tape re-racks, it will probably stop somewhere around "officers ordered." Using the shuttle, move back to between "began" and "Police" and set your next "in" or edit point. The system guards against getting black or a flash frame if the edit misses a bit. Find the next scene and repeat the process. Do this until you have worked up to the first sound bite.

Editing Audio and Video Together

This will be your first sound bite, perhaps one of the protestors complaining about the police. You'll locate your bite and set the controller for an audio and video edit. Try to set the "in" so you get a little picture pad (maybe 10 frames) before the student's words begin. Then you won't upcut the bite if the machine slightly misses the edit.

(Sometimes the pickup in the bite is so tight that you can't get it without showing a trace of "lip flap"—the lips move but there's no sound. One solution is to make the edit and re-lay the preceding scene, in video only, extending the scene so it covers the first word or two of the bite and masks the lip flap.)

Before editing, you'll have to check and set audio levels according to the procedures described under "Laying Down Narration" on page 144.

If you decide to use two bites, you'll have to butt them together and, unless you're lucky on the framing, you'll have to go back and put in a cutaway.

Be careful when you butt the bites that you don't wind up with a stray syllable, usually a leftover from the end of the first bite, or make the silence between the end of the first bite and beginning of the second abnormally long or short, noticeably long or short.

If you are interrupting the first bite rather than waiting for the interviewee to reach a natural pause, you may well pick up a spare syllable or two from the start of the word following your "out" word.

It's not fatal. Simply cue to a point a few frames before the start of the extra syllable and perform an audio erase edit to clean up your "out." You do this like an audio only edit, except that you go to your mixer and turn the master pot all the way down. That way, your new audio information will be silence and the silence will replace or erase the extra syllable on your package tape. (Alternatively, on some systems you can achieve an audio erase by going through an audio only edit using only the package tape. The machine receives no new signal, so it records nothing and therefore erases the spare syllable.)

Next, dub over your second sound bite, taking care to space the splice so the subject's speaking pace sounds normal. Put in a cutaway now, or wait and do all your cutaways later.

Editing Cutaways

You perform these bits of magic in "video only" mode. The question is, where will you start the cutaway and where will you end it? You have three choices.

1. You can cover just the end of the first bite.

2. You can cover just the start of the second bite.

3. You can cover the end of the first and the beginning of the second.

The decision will depend largely on what's being said. If there is something special about the ending words of bite one, or the beginning words of bite two, you might want to show the person's facial expression while saying those words. If that's the case, you put your cutaway over the picture you don't need to preserve, being sure it masks the edit.

The best way to do this is to set both the "in" and the "out" electronically on the package tape. On the source tape, the tape with the cutaway, simply pick an "in." When you perform the edit, the cutaway will be recorded from the point of the two "ins" to the "out" on the package tape, no more than that.

A cutaway, particularly if it's just a reporter's face, should be short—maybe one and a half or two seconds, three at the most. It can be longer if it is showing something, providing information about the size of the news conference or speech audience, or the barrenness of the locale, or opulence of the subject's living room, etc.

Cutaways should be as unobtrusive as possible. They should not seem to interrupt although, of course, they do. The way to minimize this is to lay them in on phrases or sentences, just as you try to do when covering narration. Where would you put your cutaway in this two-cut sound bite?

**"It was all I could take. No more. I saw the
paring knife and I couldn't stop myself. I took it**

and stabbed her right in the throat and watched
the blood gurgle out. [JUMP CUT, EDIT] Later,
when she was dead, I knew I had to clean up
good or I'd get caught........"

Forgive the rather gruesome example, but it helps make
the point. You want to insert the cutaway between phrases, not in
the middle of them. In this case, the choices are four.

1. You could lay the cutaway over just the end of the
   first cut, over: "...and watched the blood gurgle
   out" and come back on "Later."

2. You could overlap the cutaway, covering both sides
   of the edit, so it would start on "...and watched"
   and end after "Later" or on "... was dead."

3. You could lay the cutaway over just the word, "Later..."

4. You could lay the cutaway over all of "Later, after
   she was dead ..."

All of these would work technically, but the fourth
would probably be the best choice. Why? It's long enough, without
being too long, it starts and ends between phrases, and it doesn't
detract from the dramatic impact of "watched the blood gurgle out."
The third choice is just too short, one word. The second
is long enough but it suffers from the same flaw as the first: It
covers up what may be the most dramatic part of this tape, the individual's face as he or she says "... and watched the blood gurgle
out." Not a pretty picture, and probably not a preferred place for a
cutaway.

As for the cutaway itself, this is clearly a time for a neutral
expression on the reporter's face. A cutaway of a smiling reporter, or
one eagerly nodding his or her head, would be totally inappropriate.

Two additional points on cutaways:

1. When the cutaway is your reporter listening, look
   for one in which the reporter's head (the tightness
   of the shot) is the same size as the subject's or a

mite smaller. If one head must be larger than the other (and therefore visually more important), better the subject's than the reporter's.

2. Cutaways can be used even when there is no edit or jump cut to hide. In a long interview or speech, it can be a relief to get away from the speaker, even if all you get to see for a few seconds is the reporter or the audience. If you have the shots, you can go longer on the audience—three, four, five shots, before going back to the speaker. But you wouldn't want that much of your reporter listening.

Finishing the Package

Going back to the story you were editing, let's assume you've gone through all the steps that were listed—you've edited the voice-over bridge, the second sound bite, the voice-over narration and the standup at the end. There's one housekeeping detail you should be aware of and make a habit of doing—putting video pad at the very end.

If there's no pad, the picture will end just as the audio out cue is delivered—and the person running the video switcher will have virtually no chance of punching up the anchor before the tape feed goes to black. You do not want to put black on the air, so give the person at the switcher some video pad. Make it a continuation of the final scene rather than a new scene, to avoid a flash frame effect.

The story in the example ends on a standupper, so the final scene would be the reporter standing there, saying nothing, staring at the camera after having signed off. An experienced reporter will hang in there for at least five seconds, and an experienced photographer will keep rolling.

One second of video pad is an absolute minimum. Several seconds are better. Some editors run pad as long as 10 seconds, when they can do it without starting a new scene. It's best, too, to find a final scene without attention-grabbing movement that could catch the viewer's eye just as it is punched off the air.

A last-resort alternative is to "freeze" the final frame to make pad. This is done by stopping the source machine on the desired frame while allowing the editor to continue to dub the incoming, motionless signal. Unfortunately, viewers notice freeze frames—so this technique is regarded as undesirable but better than having no pad.

Timing and Cues

There's one more task before you are through: You must time the piece and write down outcues. For packages, you need the overall time plus the outcue (which is usually, but not always, the reporter's signature). It's also good practice to note the times for inserting supers, especially name identifications. For VOs, you need the running time. For VOBs you need the length of the VO to the bite, the length of the bite, the overall length, super times, and the outcue.

Sometimes the tape is edited to run beyond the final words, for applause, laughter, music or to finish a picture sequence. It's your responsibility to provide the person writing the story with information that will result in script notations like these:

> RUNS: 1-07
> ENDS: " .... AND A MERCEDES IN EVERY GARAGE." (HOLD 6 SECS UNTIL APPLAUSE FADES OUT)

> RUNS: 1-51

> ENDS ON VISUAL OUTCUE... BALLOON TOUCHING GROUND 4 SECS AFTER " ... RESTON, KJD NEWS." (PLENTY OF PAD)

Incidentally, some stations edit VOBs as two separate tapes, one with the voice-over and the other with the bite. The voice-over tape is called the "A" roll and the bite, the "B" roll (to which you tack on any additional voice-over after the bite. You must provide two sets of timings and cues, one for each tape.

When you edit this way, make sure that there's plenty of pad on the final scene of the "A" roll, plus a second of pad before the first audio of the "B" roll. This makes it easy to switch smoothly from one tape to the other during broadcast. Make sure the last scene on the "A" roll starts at least three or four seconds before the intended switch to the "B" roll. For example, if the air time of the "A" roll is 18 seconds, start the last scene no later than 14 or 15 and make it at least a 7-second scene, for pad.

Why do stations choose to edit VOBs this way? Because the "B" roll is rolled off the end of the script for the "A" roll, with the result that there's far less chance of dead air if the script is underwritten or the anchor reads too fast, or of upcuts if the script is overwritten or the anchor reads too slow or stumbles.

Editing Basics and Establishers

The goal in editing news tape (as well as shooting it) is to show the viewer what the viewer could have seen had the viewer been at the scene of the news event. To do that, you present your pictures the same way people look at things—that is, they take in the overall scene, orient themselves, and then check details.

This means you usually start out with what's called an "establisher"—a shot that locates the arena of the event. It may be a gas station, a battlefield, a river boat on the Mississippi, a used car lot, or a freeway pileup of half a dozen cars and a tractor-trailer. The next shot— a closer shot—may refine that location: a patron pumping gas, two soldiers in a fox hole, a gambling salon inside the river boat, a customer kicking a tire on a 1978 Pinto, a knot of men working where the tractor-trailer is lying on top of a car. After that, something even more specific: the gas pump's numbers moving, one of the two soldiers talking, a roulette wheel spinning, the price sticker on the Pinto, a man with a blow torch trying to cut into the squashed car to rescue the driver.

As a general proposition, you follow this pattern throughout the story—establisher followed by details going from medium close-up to close-up. You do it every time you change location in a story, or every time you change the emphasis from one part of the activity to another. That's a general proposition, a guiding principle, but far from inviolate law. You depart from it all the time for any number of reasons: it's too predictable for the viewer, it takes too much time, you don't have the shots, the script won't permit it, you have a moving shot that does it for you faster, or the next thing you want to show doesn't need an establisher.

Scene Length

In very rough terms, you should edit static scenes no shorter than three seconds nor longer than eight. And as a rule, you should vary the length of scenes in a sequence. Only rarely would you start a story with three straight three-second shots, or three straight eight-second shots. In real life, you might actually edit any of the 3-scene sequences described a moment ago at anything from 11 or 12 seconds up to around 18, although based on the 3-second minimum, 8-second maximum guide, the sequences could be as short as 9 seconds and as long as 24.

How might it work out with the gas station/customer pumping/ moving numbers sequence? This is easily digested visual information. Viewers can take in a gas station in three seconds, and a person pumping gas in three seconds. But it takes longer to get information from the face of the pump, unless all you want to do is indicate the pump is working. If you want the viewer to note the price per gallon you might have to allow 5 or 6 seconds, so this very simple sequence might take 11 or 12 seconds—3 plus 3 plus 5 or 6.

On the other hand, if you were to run the same three scenes for eight seconds each, the sequence would limp along. "Gas station" will register with the viewer long before eight seconds is up. So will a customer pumping gas (unless there were something unusual about the person that you wanted the viewer to note, in which case you really should have an additional close-up scene), and eight seconds is too long for the face of the pump, unless you are scripting the viewer through everything there is to see on that pump.

In the example of the freeway accident, three-second scenes are just too short. You want the viewer to see what a mess that accident is: six cars and a truck! That takes more than three seconds. It could take eight, or even more. You want the viewer to see the men working and see clearly that there's a car under the truck. That takes more than three seconds. The individual working with the torch is easier to comprehend; you might do that in three or four seconds. This sequence could come in at 18 to 20 seconds, and anything significantly shorter—down around 11 or 12—might be too short to tell the story of this terrible accident and the dramatic rescue that was made.

Or you might actually edit the sequence to 10 or 11 seconds if you were using the footage to illustrate a different story—not this particular accident and rescue, but a story about freeway accidents in general, or about the value of blow torches as standard equipment on rescue vehicles.

The nature of the story can play as important a role in determining appropriate scene length as the contents of the scenes themselves. An aerial shot of undulating farm country, a wide shot of a green pasture with many cows, and a closer shot of three or four cows could be cut quite short in a story about milk prices, where all you are doing is showing that milk comes from the country, but they'd be much longer in a mood piece about the pastoral beauty of the rolling farmland of Middle Tennessee.

The script, as mentioned earlier, is another factor in scene length. You try to edit on phrases, without running individual scenes longer or shorter than they deserve. In this respect, you sometimes can't have it both ways. No matter how careful and professional the writer was, at times you've got to stay with a scene even if it means ending in mid-phrase.

Scenes with Movement

When you switch from editing static scenes to scenes with movement, the guidelines change. Scenes with movement generally hold a viewer's attention longer than static scenes, so you can let them run if the movement helps tell the story.

A scene of moving traffic on a highway is too ordinary to hold very long, unless there is something exceptional about the traffic load or the vehicles that you want the viewer to notice. A scene of a kickoff being run back for a touchdown will take as long as it did in the game, or at least from the time the player catches the ball until he reaches the end zone. If you condensed this you'd ruin it. If all you show is the runner catching the ball and starting out, then some wildly cheering fans, and then the last five yards of the run, you would not have shown the run.

The same principle applies when using movement created by the camera or the camera lens—that is, with pans and tilts, and zooms and pullbacks, use the whole thing or don't use it at all. However, there is an escape clause—how much constitutes "the whole thing"?

A competent photographer will give you plenty of the beginning scene and plenty of the ending scene—at least 10 usable seconds of each, plus the pan itself. In the case of a pan that takes 8 seconds to go from opening shot to closing, you might be able to edit the scene from 10 seconds up to 28 seconds, although it's unlikely that either extreme would produce a good result.

The rule for photographers is that they don't even shoot a pan or tilt (or pullback or zoom) unless the beginning and ending shots help tell the story. With the pan shot edited at ten seconds, you'll be giving viewers eight seconds of movement and only one second each from the starting and ending scenes, hardly enough time for viewers to absorb them.

The other extreme—ten seconds of the opening, eight of the pan, and ten of the ending—quite likely will be too much. Chances are there's not enough in the beginning and ending shots to warrant holding them that long.

In fact, if you have 8 seconds of movement in a pan shot you'll probably edit it at 12 to 18 seconds, total. At 12, the beginning and ending shots would be about 2 seconds long, breaking the rule of 3 seconds minimum. But with pans, tilts, zooms and pullbacks you can go below three seconds because a bit of the beginning scene remains recognizable as the camera moves away from it and a bit of the ending scene becomes recognizable before the camera settles on it.

Pans, zooms and other shots with movement can be difficult to work with. It's a good idea, therefore, to determine the time you are trying to fill with the shot and then examine the shot to check how it will work in that time. Pick what looks like a good spot to start or end the movement shot (the ending sometimes can be more important), measure forward or backward for the number of seconds you need to fill, and play the tape. Is that a good spot, or do you need to adjust a second or two one way or the other? If you think an adjustment would help, try it. When you have made up your mind, and if you have time, do a preview edit. If you like it, make the edit. If you don't, adjust as necessary.

Sequence Building and Transitions

The general rule is that each voice-over portion of a story, whether in a package or an anchor's live script, requires a new sequence—a new establisher followed by closer, detailed shots until the voice-over is completed. In a typical example, you might have a 20-second voice-over into a sound bite, the bite and a 15-second VO bridge to another sound bite, the second bite and another 20 seconds to the signature. That's three voice-overs. You have three little sequences to build.

In stories with longer VOs or stories that are all VO, the likelihood is that you'll have to build a number of separate sequences (establisher, etc.) within the same VO, one after the other. This is largely determined by the script or scripting plans. Sometimes the script will take you from a generalization to specific examples. Sometimes it'll guide you through a number of locations. In the first instance, it won't hurt if your pictures all look like one thing or one place, because that will probably be the truth. In the second instance, you want it to be very clear that you are showing different things—different locations or different subjects.

Either way, you will need transition shots to indicate the start of each new sequence. They might be routine wide-shot establishers. They might be tight shots. You might find—in fact, you will find—that you can employ both transition techniques to bring variety to your package.

Let's make a tour of your local arts and crafts fair.

Unless you make a point of departing from tradition, you'll open with a wide shot establishing that something is going on at a park or the football field or the county fairgrounds, wherever your arts and crafts fair is held. If the scene doesn't include a sign indicating it's the arts and crafts show, your second scene probably will. If you have a shot showing people as well as the sign, so much the better, far better.

Now you are inside. The next shot may be a wide shot indicating the scope of the event. After that, a medium-wide shot of a row of display booths. That might be the end of the opening sequence. You might start another sequence by isolating one booth, then indicating the exhibitor is a painter by showing a group of three or four pictures hanging from a partition. Then you might show close-ups of some of the paintings before going to another booth with a transition shot.

Here the field is wide open. A wide shot showing several booths before you isolate one of them would do the trick, except that you've already used that kind of shot and in tape editing, repetition is anathema.

Better possibilities are a medium shot of a display of the work you next want to show, so long as it's not more paintings; the difference must be great enough that the transition announces itself visually. While paintings might not work, a medium shot of pottery on a shelf would. You would follow that with close-ups until you are through with the pottery.

The next transition might be a front view of people looking at something unseen. Then show what it is they are looking at (or could have been looking at, if you take a little license). Make it handmade jewelry—perhaps a display tray of pieces, followed by a series of close-ups. After the jewelry, you could make a transition with a close-up of something very clearly different from the jewelry, let's say a ship in a bottle. After some close-ups of more of the same, you might show an exhibitor, from the waist up, reaching for a sample of the leather work she does.

After several shots of leather goods, you might show an exterior shot of the pavilion where winning entries in the fair are displayed. This would provide a piece of information for your viewers (where to see the winners), as well as a transition. Next you might show a wide shot of the interior and then close-ups of various winners until, perhaps, you sneak outside with a transition that is both aural and visual, a close-up of fingers strumming a guitar with natural sound of the music for several seconds, and then a pullback revealing a guitar-maker playing one of his instruments in his display booth. Audio transitions are very useful and effective, if not overused. After that, show a few more instruments.

You could keep the guitar music going through the rest of the guitar sequence. You could even keep it going for the rest of the story. Or, you might have used the guitar sequence earlier in order to run the music through most of the piece. Please note that this music is natural sound, sound occurring and recorded at the event. Few editors or producers, if any, would complain if you used this music throughout. They might complain, however, if you used music from a record or compact disk, music that was not a part of the arts and crafts fair and not recorded by your crew while covering the scene. They would tell you that in news—and the key is news work, not industrials or theatrical productions, but news—use of canned music could be construed as misrepresentation, which it is.

Most of the transitions mentioned in our let's pretend tour of the arts and crafts show have depended on the principle that the new subject must be instantaneously discernible as different from what preceded it. Strictly speaking—at least according to some definitions—most of these shots haven't really been "transitions."

The scene of pottery on shelves works because pottery is so different from paintings. Likewise the shot of a ship in a bottle after scenes of jewelry. The shot of people looking at something (we can't see what) is as much a cutaway as anything else, except that it serves as a transition, allowing you to go to virtually anything else at the arts and crafts fair. The pure transition shots are the establisher of the pavilion and the pullback from the guitar-strumming close-up.

Oftentimes, the best transitions are shots with camera or lens movement, or with movement within the scene. They work especially well if the preceding shot is static. The worst transitions tend to be signs and exteriors of buildings; they are boring clichés which seldom offer useful visual information.

Assume you are editing a medical feature about progress in treating a disease. Patients and doctors are interviewed in a number of different hospitals, and you need to get from one to the next. Building exteriors and/or name signs will do the job for you—but is a viewer's understanding of the disease enhanced by knowing that one hospital is red brick and another yellow brick? Not likely.

Avoid using buildings and signs when you can. Look for something better to get from place to place. Let's say the first sequence ends on a sound bite of a doctor at the first hospital. Maybe in the footage from the second hospital there's a shot that can be used for transition even though it is inside the second hospital. Maybe the photographer has given you a close-up of the feet and ankles of a patient pedalling an exercise bike, with a pullback revealing a clearly new locale. Open up the narration for a couple of beats of natural sound of pedalling before the pullback and you're in business. Another good transition might be a close-up of a medical device with flashing numbers or wave forms, with a pan to the face of a new patient hooked up to the machine, or a new doctor watching it. Script and supers can take care of the rest of the transition.

On the other hand, routine establishers would be desirable if you were editing a story about war in the Balkans and jumping from battleground to battleground. The look of a village in the countryside, the walls of an ancient city, the rugged mountains, these would give viewers some sense of the region's terrain and history, and with that a sense of the difficulty and tragedy of the fighting. You would use these establishers because they are part of the story and will help viewers understand.

Layover and Cover Footage

The terms "layover" and "cover," like a good many other television terms, are vaguely defined and loosely used so they verge on being synonymous even though they are not. Strictly speaking, "layover" is footage shot specifically to illustrate what someone says in a sound bite. "Cover" is footage that covers narration. It can be generic or specifically shot for the story at hand. To purists, the use of generic cover in spot news, even when adorned with "file" or date supers, is a misrepresentation that borders on fraud but tape editors who make a fuss about it probably will be seen as editors who make a fuss.

With layover, it's best to show the person who is talking before starting the cover footage. (See how easily the terms merge?) Wait through one or two phrases, then begin. Layover works best when the first scene matches the person's words. With layover, wholesale editing of the interview is possible because you won't be showing the person and won't have to worry if the editing produces choppy video of the interviewee and reporter. Once the layover starts, they won't be seen. So long as you take care not to distort the content of the interview or the person's manner of speech, you can do a lot to make words and layover pictures work together.

Interview Setups

It's worth paying attention to how you get into interviews. Your options often are controlled by the photographer and the script. Both can hamstring you. Both can help you.

The tried and true and most boring way to get into an interview is to use a shot of the interviewee and your reporter together, at a desk, on a park bench, etc. The typical sequence is the two-shot followed by a cutaway of the reporter followed by the sound bite. When the framing is right and the script is short, the cutaway can be skipped and you can go direct from the two-shot into the bite. When there's a lot of script—maybe 12 to 30 seconds giving the interviewee's credentials and setting up the bite—you might have to use two two-shots, and maybe a cutaway of the reporter and a shot of the interviewee and yet another cutaway of the reporter before starting the bite. It will look awful, but sometimes the script and available scenes offer no choice.

It's much better, if you have the footage and a properly written script, to show the interviewee going about some activity before starting the bite. When it's shot right, you'll have the person moving in and out of frame, or shots that show the person's face and then allow you to cut away to related scenes before coming back to the interviewee. In the case of a tattoo artist, for example, you could show the tattooist at work on a customer, then go to close-ups of hands at work tattooing, then go around the tattoo parlor looking at sample designs, and finally come back to the interview. This easily sustains for 30 seconds or more and adds visual information.

Sometimes the script provides little or no time for setting up the interviewee. In such cases, you have a choice of approaches. Let's say the story is about an environmental problem with salmon, and the lead-in goes like this: "... and a growing number of ichthyologists believe the loss of spawning grounds may be irreversible. Katherine Pescadora is one." There are at least four ways you might handle this.

1. Come to Pescadora cold. See her and hear her right after "Katherine Pescadora is one." Bang! Sound bite begins. This lacks style, but it works and it's easy, which is why it's done all the time.

2. Introduce her sitting at her desk or working in a laboratory, over the line, "Katherine Pescadora is one." Then, so long as you don't do it with a jump cut, start the bite after "one." This can work, but in this case it would be a bit choppy because the set-

up scene would only run about two seconds, the time it takes to say "Katherine Pescadora is one." If the set-up line were longer—"Katherine Pescadora is one of those scientists"—you'd have around three seconds and it would look better. If you had two scenes of Pescadora, or one with some movement, you could go back farther and show her first on "... and a growing number... ." Bringing her in on that phrase would make it clear that this new person, whoever she is, is one of "a growing number of...."

3. Backtime her bite so you show her at "Katherine" but don't have her talk until "one." You do this by timing the line "Katherine Pescadora is one" on your digital readout. Let's say it takes two seconds and two frames. Find the pickup point for your bite and measure backwards two seconds and two frames plus another two or three frames for safety's sake if the edit misses. Make that your editing "in."

Then make an insert edit that will give you her picture with no sound until the pickup, to preserve the identifying narration line "Katherine Pescadora is one." After that, she would start talking and you would make an audio and video insert edit. How you do this will depend on your equipment and whether your station's practice is to put narration and sync sound on separate tracks or the same track.

If it's separate tracks, you do a video and audio edit, with the audio going to only one channel, the sync sound track. That preserves the narration while giving you the picture of Pescadora and her voice. You even have two options on how you bring in her voice. You can fade it up from nothing to audible under the narration "Katherine Pescadora is one" or you can simply start it full after "one." First, you predetermine the appropriate level setting for her voice and make note of it. Then, to fade it in, you turn the level down to zero and make the edit. Once the edit starts, you gradually turn the level up to the predetermined setting, listening to the narration as you go so you don't drown it out. Or you can turn the bite level up abruptly, just as the narration says "one." (With some equipment, you can accomplish the same effect by starting out with a video only edit and pushing the appropriate audio edit button right after you hear "one.")

If you are using the same channel for narration and synch sound, you can accomplish the edit in two ways. Easiest, if your equipment will do it, is the method just mentioned, where you switch from a video only editing to video and audio editing when you hear the word "one." Another way is to erase whatever Pescadora says immediately before the sound bite pickup, then erase a line or long phrase of narration up until "one," and make the desired audio and video edit. Then go back and re-insert the erased bit of narration with an audio only edit. What you don't want to do is lay in her picture with a video only edit and go back and add her voice after "one." If the edit is precise, you'll be OK. But if it misses by more than a few frames you'll have an out-of-synch ichthyologist, heaven forbid.

4. Start her audio *before* you show her in sync sound. This works nicely if you have pictures worth looking at to cover "Katherine Pescadora is one" plus one or two phrases of her bite. Do an audio and video edit of her bite, starting right after "one." Then go back and do video only edits over the first couple of phrases or sentence of her bite. This delays her appearance in sync sound and produces a nice effect.

When to "Hit" and When Not to Worry

When picture and script coincide they "hit." Most hits are deliberate, the result of cooperation between the writer (who often is also the reporter) and the tape editor for the benefit of the viewer. The hits keep the script and pictures working together rather than fighting each other. For example, if the narration prepares viewers to see the Queen of England and the videotape shows Smokey the Bear, viewers will be confused (and maybe amused) and the story, certainly at that point, will be a failure.

In the sense of who can blame whom for missing hits, the onus is on the person who goes last. If the tape editor is given the narration and has to make the pictures work with it, the responsibility is the editor's. If the editor gets that rare chance to edit picture to tell the story, without being limited by a script, the responsibility for making the words and pictures work together falls to the writer (reporter), who goes last. True professionals, of course, cooperate for the benefit of the viewer rather than create problems. Pragmatically, unless the editing or the writing is outrageous, it's easier for editors to hit narration than for writers to match edited hits.

The important thing, however, is to know when you need hits and when you don't. Television that literally tells and shows— television that hits everything—tends to be sophomoric and dull. There are exceptions, of course. Coverage of a basketball game, for example, demands that players be seen when they're named. You don't want to show Scottie Pippen popping a three-pointer when the script says Shaquille O'Neal blocked Pippen's reverse layup.

This is obvious. So are most instances when picture and script must coincide or hit. They must do so when the script or story line is specific—when people, places and things are pointedly mentioned and play leading roles in the story.

Sometimes the length of scenes or the nature of the script are such that you if you are to hit something exactly as it is mentioned you will have to sacrifice editing smoothness. If you don't want to do that, show the scene that has to hit a couple of seconds late rather than early. If the scene precedes the script mention, the viewer may never put the two together. But if script comes first it may put the viewer on the alert for the upcoming scene.

Watch out for accidental false hits. Suppose you are editing a backgrounder on American foreign policy in Somalia. If the name of Secretary of State Warren Christopher comes up just as you show scenes of (the late) actress Audrey Hepburn working with starving children in that country, viewers will notice and a question will occur to many of them: does this news program know what it's doing? You don't want that, so watch it! Make sure you are not showing oranges while the narration is talking about apples. It's the kind of thing that sounds like it can never happen, but it does.

Wipes and Dissolves

Wipes and dissolves are electronic editing techniques. In a wipe, a line moves across the screen and apparently pushes one picture out of the way while pulling a new picture behind it. The new wipes out the old. The wiping line can move horizontally, vertically or diagonally. In a dissolve, one scene evaporates while a second materializes and replaces it.

Most news editing systems don't have the capacity to wipe or dissolve or do any electronic tricks, which many editors feel is just as well. Wipes and dissolves have their places, especially dissolves in features, but they really are not "editing" in the traditional sense. Rather, they offer a quick way to cover up deficiencies in shooting and writing, or mistakes in editing sequence. Wipe, and the problem's solved! Dissolve, and the problem's solved!

A presidential address from the Oval Office offers an exception few would argue about. That's because the broadcasts seldom provide usable cutaways. All anyone sees is the president. You might get lucky and be able to edit with a frame change. Otherwise, an electronic trick—a wipe or dissolve—is the only way to edit. One thing about wipes and dissolves is that there's no deception:

they are uncompromisingly honest about the fact that an edit has been made, which may account for their increasing use in editing news conferences and speeches.

Time Code and SMPTE Time Code Editing

Time code editing means using time code as a reference in ordinary editing. SMPTE time code editing is automatic computerized editing, according to SMPTE time code.

Ordinary time code gives you the hour, minute and second that the original footage was shot. Reporters (and shooters) can synchronize their watches to the camera's time code and keep excellent track of when scenes were shot and things said at news conferences, or when key plays were made in a basketball or football game. They can include these times as notations to field narrations, telling the editor where to find the correct footage. Or even better, they can return to the station, log tapes according to time code, and then give you notes of what they want by time code—including the ins and outs of sound bites.

SMPTE time code is another matter. SMPTE (Society of Motion Picture and Television Engineers) time code employs eight digits to put the hour, minute, second and frame on every picture—not just the hour, minute and second, but down to the frame, to the thirtieth of a second! Editors, reporters and producers can screen footage, make precise notes with SMPTE time code and prepare a shot list that gives the exact time, to the individual frame, of the in and out of every scene they want. The editor then enters the numbers in a computer, and when ready pushes a button. The computer takes over and directs the machines to perform the programmed edits. When the machines are right, their accuracy is to the frame, to the exact numbered frame. Their performance and speed are remarkable. But few stations have SMPTE editing capacity for day-to-day news work. If they have it at all, it's often reserved for commercials and special production work.

Music Editing

Music gets into news stories and news features in one of two ways. Either it was recorded as part of the events that make up the story, or it was added. If it was part of the event, there's no question it can be used legitimately in the edited story. If it wasn't, when the music comes from a record, CD or tape, professionals will disagree as to the ethics of adding it. Strictly speaking, that music is no different from canned sound effects, and very few professionals would mate their own silent footage of a lion with a lion's roar from a sound effects record, or the crackling of pistol fire from an effects record with the tape of a police shootout that the news department bought from an amateur whose sound recording was unusable.

Except for purists who contend the only sound you can use is sound that was taped as part of your coverage (and there are a lot of them), the legitimacy of using recorded music comes down to two questions—is this straight news or a feature, and will viewers think the music was part of the event they are seeing?

In the case of straight news, most people are pretty strict: they won't add music or effects. In features, the question of whether or not viewers will be deceived comes into play. If they will, don't deceive them (and thereby cheapen the news) but if they won't, if it's too obvious, go ahead and use the canned music. This reasoning permits the use of recorded music as an enhancement to the video, as a means of trying to arrest the attention of viewers whose interest might otherwise be expected to wane. Some professionals, the real purists, will argue that the moment you add anything artificial to news it stops being news and becomes a video production. Who, they say, would care to call their news program "Eyewitness Video Production at 6"?

Ethical considerations aside, if you are going to use music, take care to do it right.

1. When you are editing picture over open music, change scenes on the beat of the music. It's disconcerting to viewers when you do otherwise, although it takes a while for them to notice. If you run only 10 or 15 seconds of open music it might not make a difference, but if you run it for 30 seconds or a minute you're much better off editing on the beat. If you're using a subtle music mix with narration, however, don't worry about the beat.

2. Don't use vocal music behind narration or a sound bite. It will compete with what you really want viewers to hear—unless it is very quiet, undemanding music, and your mix is very soft.

3. In a mix, keep the music low. If you allow it to fight for the viewer's attention (which strident music and vocal music almost always do) the viewer will miss some of the reporter's narration.

4. Fade music up at the start and down at the end in a mix, unless you start it as an audio transition. In that case, start it full sound at the end of a beat and then fade. If the narration is spaced out in a mix, bring the music up a little if the pauses are more than a second or two.

Editing Trends, Admonitions, Ethics

In the days of 16 mm film, effects like slow motion and dissolves seldom found their way into news programs. They were expensive and very difficult to accomplish in the rush of daily deadlines. When they got into news, it was in special features or documentaries.

But electronic news gathering has profoundly changed that. Newstape editors have access to all the tricks and gimmicks that electronic equipment delivers. The gear may be in the production department rather than the news department, or it may be down the street in a commercial house rather than at the station, but one way or another it is available—increasingly so as costs fall and sophistication increases.

If it's available, is it any wonder it's used? Especially when it can be done in minutes rather than a day? Is it any wonder that techniques used in commercials and in entertainment and sports programming are emulated by news producers and tape editors who may, for example, want their work to look as up-to-the-minute and exciting as non-news programming, or who simply want to experiment, to get in on the fun of electronic editing?

Once started, trends can be hard to stop. That's why on some programs some news stories look as much like music videos or commercials as they do news; quick cuts, one- and two-second scenes, dissolves, attention-grabbing music beds, wipes and squeezes and other video pyrotechnics. This can be called "using the medium" to best advantage, or it can be seen as putting appearance ahead of contents, as relegating news content to a kind of second-class status even on news programs.

These techniques aren't yet widespread in news programming, but lesser transgressions are. Slow motion is an example. It's easy to do, so easy that it's almost irresistible when, for example, the footage of a suspect being placed in a paddy wagon isn't long enough to cover the narration; just run it slo-mo and you'll have enough. Or run it slo-mo and freeze it as soon as you get a good view at the suspect's face; freeze it and hold it. Producers and editors may see this as merely solving a problem. But viewers can't avoid noticing this special treatment. If they infer the reporter or program is telling them there's something especially sinister about the suspect—who's to blame?

Videotape also makes it possible to recut footage and use the same scenes over and over, and over and over, day after day in running stories. With film, you nibbled away at scenes with each recut and left the scraps on the editing room floor. Unless you spent money and waited for prints of the original film, you slowly destroyed it. Because you didn't want to do that, you didn't recut and use the film again and again. As a result, your regular viewers might see the body of a DWI accident victim or a stabbing victim only one or two times, and the handcuffed suspect at the scene in police custody only one or two times. Today, thanks to reusable videotape and the insistence of news consultants on pictures, pictures, pictures, regular viewers may be treated to those emotional and potentially prejudicial scenes a dozen times before a trial, and sometimes during it. It's worth pondering if that's healthy.

Sound

Vocal music and narration don't mix.

Keep background music in the background.

Put the viewer on the scene with natural sound.

Keep that microphone down.

Remember, fluorescents make noise.

Good sound is essential to professionally-produced television news stories. Obviously, the voices of reporters, interviewees and speakers must be recorded and broadcast so they can be understood. More than understood, they must also be easy to listen to, recorded in natural tones free from distracting background noise, static or echoes. It's also important to give viewers the "natural sound" from the news event being reported. Be it airport bustle, factory clatter, surf, sirens, rifle fire, or babies crying, the realism of "nat sot" puts viewers on the scene.

Sound waves are vibrations of the air that our ears "hear." Sound is high or low, thin or strong, according to the frequency and size of the vibrations.

The greater the number of sound waves (or cycles) per second, the higher the frequency and the higher the pitch of the sound. The larger the sound waves (amplitude), the louder the sound is.

A soprano sings, creating sound waves. A cannon booms, creating sound waves. A pin drops. A rooster crows. The sound waves hit the eardrum and cause it to vibrate. These vibrations are converted into nerve impulses which go to the brain and are translated into the various sounds we have learned to recognize.

Microphones and loudspeakers work like the ear, except, of course, that they have no memory system enabling them to recognize the sounds they are reproducing.

All microphones have diaphragms which, like the eardrum, vibrate when sound waves strike them. The vibrations are converted into electrical currents which, in electronic news gathering, are transmitted through wires to storage on video or audio cassettes.

When a cassette is played back, the signals stored on the tape reproduce the electrical currents that brought them to the tape. These currents eventually reach a loudspeaker, which has a diaphragm that vibrates according to the electrical impulses it receives. This replicates the original sound waves, which we hear when they strike our eardrums.

Microphones commonly used in news work are either dynamic, usually the big mics, or electret condenser, usually the little mics. Most dynamic mics are hand-held or stand-mounted. Most electret condenser mics are clip-ons.

Dynamic microphones are the workhorses of the business. They are ruggedly built to take a lot of abuse, which is essential in news work. They are large, compared to electret condenser mics, because they house permanent magnets and wire coils to create electrical impulses from the vibrations picked up by their diaphragms.

Most electret condenser mics, on the other hand, are small and much less rugged. Their electrical impulses are created by the movement of two tiny metal plates, in a signal so weak it must be amplified by a battery. But the battery can be very small, like those in a calculator or hearing aid, so the mic can be small.

In the field, whether a mic is dynamic or electret condenser is seldom important to you. Your concerns are the microphone's size and convenience, and its pickup pattern.

Some microphones are omnidirectional, meaning they are sensitive to sound all around them and have spherical (like a ball) pickup patterns. Others are unidirectional, meaning they are sensitive to sound in a limited area and have what are called cardioid (heart-shaped) pickup patterns.

As a rule, hand-held mics are omnidirectional, all-purpose mics. Their spherical pickup pattern enables them to pick up all the sound around them, from any direction. You can use them for interviews. You can use them for the sounds that abound at a five-alarm fire. You can use them for a speech, and pick up the speaker and the audience's applause or laughter. You can use them to get a kindergarten class singing carols.

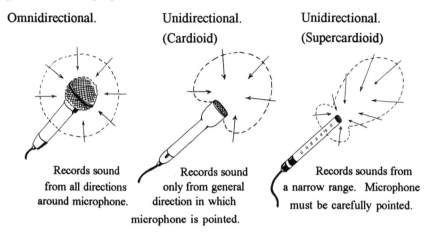

Omnidirectional.	Unidirectional. (Cardioid)	Unidirectional. (Supercardioid)
Records sound from all directions around microphone.	Records sound only from general direction in which microphone is pointed.	Records sounds from a narrow range. Microphone must be carefully pointed.

But sometimes the very thing that makes them all-purpose limits their usefulness to you. Because they are omnidirectional, they will indiscriminately pick up whatever is within range. As a result, they are hard to use for interviews when there is a lot of background noise—as at a five-alarm fire, in a noisy factory, or standing by the side of a freeway during rush hour.

In such instances, the voice is apt to be overwhelmed by background sounds unless the mic is right in the subject's face. Putting the mic that close can make for a bad picture, and sometimes having it there still won't solve the audio problem.

If that's the case, bring out a unidirectional or cardioid mic, one you must point directly at the sound you're trying to get.

When you go to the unidirectional mic, you have two choices —cardioid and supercardioid. Just as the name implies, the supercardioid is more directional, more limited in its pickup pattern, than a cardioid mic. This makes it better for isolating the sound you are aiming for, but it also makes it unforgiving if your aim isn't on target.

This brings us to the three styles of microphone used in news work: the hand-held, the shotgun and the lavaliere. All three are made in omnidirectional and unidirectional models, but as a general rule hand-helds and inexpensive lavs are omnidirectional, and expensive lavs and shotguns are unidirectional—with lavs being cardioid and shotguns supercardioid. Hand-helds for singers and solo instruments are cardioid rather than omnidirectional. Most lavs for anchors are unidirectional and, except when a special situation demands cardioid, most lavs in field use are omnidirectional.

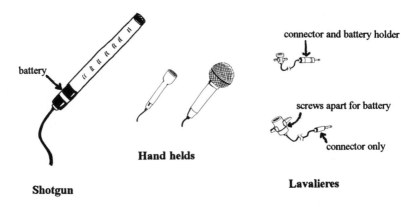

battery

Shotgun

Hand helds

connector and battery holder

screws apart for battery

connector only

Lavalieres

Any of these microphones can be plugged directly into the photographer's camera and/or video cassette recorder, and the photographer can monitor the sound that's being recorded with a headset or earpiece. The headset gives a good idea of the quality of the sound; the earpiece does little more than tell the photographer he's getting sound. (Some cameras avoid the potential nuisance value of a headset or ear piece by building a small loudspeaker into the camera body, right where a photographer's ear will be during portable operation.)

It's much better, and obviously more expensive, for the photographer to have an assistant working as a sound technician, operating a field audio mixer. In many setups, such a person is necessary because there's more work than one person can handle. As a rule, field mixers have four inputs, allowing the use of four microphones, with a master pot plus a pot for each input.

A sound technician will wear a headset allowing him or her to monitor the sound that is passing through the mixer to the camera's recorder. A good headset provides the sound recordist with all the nuances of the signal. What the technician hears is what will be recorded.

Situations calling for a sound technician with a mixer include:

1. Multiple microphone setups for musical performances, round-table and panel discussions, walking interviews with wireless mics, two-lavaliere
interviews in cars, formal, controlled news conferences, question and answer sessions, etc. Multiple
mic setups a photographer can handle easily without a soundperson are two-lavaliere interviews or
occasions when one mic is for ambient sound only.

2. Specialized single microphone setups—surreptitious recording with a wireless, long, meandering
standups with a wireless, most uses of a shotgun
when it's not mounted on the camera (including
news conference questions, walking interviews
with the photographer walking backwards, chase
and ambush interviews, etc.), and instances in
which ambient sound is regarded as very important
and the mic should not be close to the camera.

One of the biggest mistakes a photographer or reporter can
make is to undervalue the importance of sound to the finished
product. Nothing is appreciated less when it's present or missed so
much when it's not, than high quality sync sound and natural sound.
Never take sound for granted. You must work to get good sound.

Placement of Microphones

Here are some helpful hints covering a variety of situations that are
sure to come up as you work in the business.

1. Hand-held microphones usually are better kept out
of camera view in interviews. If you're the reporter,

stand about two feet from the interviewee and hold the mic chest-high and out of frame. Tilt it toward the subject, then toward yourself, as the interview proceeds.

Whenever possible, avoid holding a microphone right in the face of the subject. Some people take this in stride and behave naturally. But others take it as a sign you want them to talk and talk and talk—or you wouldn't thrust the mic in their face. Still others are determined to finish what they're saying even when you withdraw the mic, and they look pretty silly chasing after it with their mouths. Either way, a visible, moving mic is apt to cause problems in the editing room.

For a speech or news conference, clamp or tape a hand-held mic to the podium so it'll be around eight to ten inches from the speaker's mouth.

2. Lavalieres should be placed six to eight inches below the Adam's apple, clipped to a necktie, shirt front, blouse, etc., or hung from a string around the neck. Lavs are designed to be close to the body; if they're not they lose lows and resonance.

If you want to hide a lav, be careful not to cover it so much that the sound is muffled, flat and devoid of highs. You can use double-faced gaffer's tape to secure a lavaliere under a lapel while keeping it close enough to the lapel's edge that it isn't smothered. When hiding a lav, remember also to run its cord under clothing.

Dealing With Noise Problems

1. When there's a lot of ambient noise, put the microphone closer to the mouth of the person being interviewed, even though you risk picture and editing problems.

2. If that doesn't help, switch to a cardioid mic. Most companies now make hand-helds in cardioid as

well as spherical pickup patterns. Try to hold the mic so that the handle points toward the source of the background noise you are trying to avoid. The handle, of course, is in the center of the dead part of the cardioid pickup pattern.

3. As the reporter, sometimes you can reduce the undesired noise by placing your body between the interview subject and the source of the noise.

4. If there's annoying but not overwhelming traffic noise, it helps if the shot is framed so that traffic is visible, if only in a corner.

5. If you are running sound with a mixer and you get a reading at normal settings even when the reporter or interviewee is not talking, you've got so much background noise you should move.

6. Never hesitate to move in order to get legible sound. It's a mistake to think a particular shot or background is more important than legibility. It's not. And often you don't have to move very far.

7. If an interview is going well when a plane flies over or a bus roars by, make a mental note of the question or answer at the time and return to it later. This is usually better than interrupting the flow of the interview by stopping then and there to redo the question and answer. Stopping can unnerve the interview subject.

   On the other hand, if the occasion is a group shoot (in the business, it's often called a "gang bang") and you aren't quite ready or have run into an equipment problem, don't be afraid to ask the news maker to give you a minute or two. That's better than being the only crew to miss the story. The request for a moment's time has been granted even when the first words were, "Mr. President, please..."

Wireless Microphones

They are marvelous. They make simple work of taping or filming sequences that used to require elaborate editing room sound mixing, or hundreds of feet of painstakingly hidden mic cable, or that couldn't be accomplished at all.

Wireless mics (omnidirectional) are used for standuppers, for walking interviews, for miking the principal figure in uncontrolled action (for example, an antique collector taking you on a tour of his house, a coach giving a Rockne-like speech at half time, a classroom teacher interacting with pupils), and for surreptitious filming and recording.

Wireless mics consist of a small transmitter about the size of a cigarette package, and a slightly larger receiver. They operate on pre-set radio frequencies. To do an interview, you need two wireless mic systems, preset on frequencies sufficiently far apart that one won't interfere with the other.

The transmitter is hidden from the camera, often stuck in a back pocket or clipped to a belt. From the transmitter come two wires. One is about three feet long and has a lavaliere mic on the end. The other is about a foot long and dangles from the transmitter to serve as an antenna.

The receiver has an antenna and an output wire that can be plugged directly into a video recorder or a sound mixer. You can usually get adequate results with an interview just by plugging one wireless into Channel One audio and the other into Channel Two. If genuinely high quality sound is an absolute requirement, you should have a sound recordist and mixer.

Leaving the lav microphones visible or hiding them depends on the situation and individual preference. They can be hidden under clothing, in which case it really helps to have a sound mixer for careful monitoring. Take care that the mic is firmly fixed so it won't move around under a shirt or sweater, and place it so clothing doesn't rub against it or rustle around it.

If the wireless is being used for surreptitious recording, it's best for the reporter to wear the mic to the left side or the right and then make a point of getting the subject on that side, the closer the better. It helps enormously to have a soundperson on the job to "ride the pot" and make sure you get the person who isn't miked. Riding the pot usually produces an annoying inconsistency in background noise—it's way up, then it's down, then it's way up again. But in this case, getting the voice you are recording surreptitiously is more important, and a soundperson really improves the chances of being able to hear and use both sides of the conversation.

Walking interviews are done with wireless mics. You should determine before shooting who's is going to be on the left and who on the right. Put the mic toward the left of center on the person who'll be on the right, and toward the right of center on the person who'll be on the left. As the reporter and subject walk along, they'll tend to turn toward each other; if properly miked, they'll be turning toward their mics rather than away.

Wireless microphones need batteries to run their transmitters and receivers, so carry extra batteries. Don't get caught dead.

Recording Music and Performances

What you do depends on whether the music or performance is central or incidental to your story.

If it's incidental, like the band at a political picnic, make sure you record one complete song in one take. Because the music is incidental, the camera can be on the band for a while and then roam around getting cutaways, inserts, etc., until the song is over. This will give the editor enough music for a mix and make it easy to do.

If the musical performance or, say, a poetry reading, *is* the story, and the situation is controllable, get the performers to run through it at least twice. Use the first rendition to get the basic sound while the group or orchestra is taped in wide and medium-wide shots to use as establishers or masters. The second time, the sound can be recorded for reference only while the camera gets closeups of soloists, instrument sections, inserts, side shots, etc. When doing this for music, try to power your equipment with a transformer and AC current rather than batteries. This eliminates the risk of recording at an inconsistent speed because batteries are running low.

To successfully record an orchestra, you'll need at least two or three omnidirectional microphones on mic stands, and a mixer. To get a three-piece combo, one mic feeding directly into the video recorder should do it. Watch out for over-modulation during your music take. If it happens, get the orchestra to run through it again, from start to finish, after you reposition your microphones and adjust your levels.

For a poetry reading, use a lavaliere. Get a complete take in a master shot. Inserts can be shot during a full repeat reading of the poem.

For a scene from a play, try two wireless lavs and shoot a full take and then inserts. If you need more than two microphones, a mixer and soundperson are necessary—and, if you can get it, a script, so the soundperson will have outcues for raising and lowering the pots.

Windscreens

Windscreens are microphone covers made of foam; they're the things that make a hand-held mic resemble an ice cream cone. Their primary purpose is to prevent wind from making noise by moving across the grill of a microphone head, but they can also help to reduce other undesirable noises. You can get them for every style of microphone. One rule is: When in doubt, use the windscreen. A better rule is: Always use a windscreen.

Mults, Mult-Boxes, Repeaters

These are terms for multiple outlet sound systems—that is, one or several microphones feeding a distribution system—a box—that many news people plug into simultaneously. They are commonly found in hotel and auditorium sound systems and in meeting and conference rooms operated by government and business. Some are portable and some built-in. Where they're built in, the installation often includes built-in lighting systems.

Mults eliminate the forest of microphones (often replete with station call letters or network logos) that can obscure a speaker's face. They eliminate mic cables spreading all over a conference table or a banquet dais in multiple mic setups. Altogether, mults are a blessing—so long as the people running them do it right. If they don't, the only advantage, if you can call it that, is that even if your sound is poor your competition's won't be any better.

Speeches

Usually an omnidirectional hand-held microphone, clamped to the podium, gives best results. It can pick up applause or laughter adequately, unless the audience is very quiet or a long distance from the speaker. Avoid the temptation to raise the pot to bring in applause: You might make 200 people sound like 2000. Worse, if you ride the pot it will be noticeable because it makes the background noise fluctuate. If a speaker gets excited and over-modulates, you should back off on the pot. Otherwise, find a good mid-range level setting and leave it there, come whisper or bellow.

If you were involved in high quality production work you might record the speaker on one channel of audio and audience reaction on the other channel, using a hand-held shotgun mic.

Round-table Discussions

If the people are close and the room is dead, a single omnidirectional mic on a desk stand can do the job marginally. Two mics will do it better. More often than not, you need three or four mics, a mixer and deft riding of the pot. Keep all mics in a low, waiting position—up just enough that you can pick up a person who jumps into the talk; when it happens, fade that person up while fading the previous speaker down to the waiting position, and so on. If you have all mics up all the time you'll get too much background noise, stray reactions, comments and throat clearings (which are disconcerting to the viewer when the camera doesn't show the source), and possibly feedback.

You can also do round-tables with a shotgun, but you can count on losing a degree of naturalness and spontaneity because it is very difficult to get both the end of one person's comment and the start of another's, unless the two people are sitting next to each other.

Question and Answer Sessions

You can get remarkably good results picking up questions with a shotgun or shotgun on a boom, in part because people asking questions are apt to be pitching their voices anyway. If you're anywhere but behind the person and if your aim is good, you can get a question from 20 or 25 feet away. This means you're set for a news conference, but in trouble after a speech in a large auditorium. At the latter, it's best to have the questioners stand at microphones you've set up in the aisles. If that can't be done, try to arrange to have the moderator or speaker repeat the questions. Even if the repeated question isn't used on the air, reporters and writers will have no doubt what question was being answered.

Recording Off Loudspeakers

This is a last resort, the very thing you never want to do—but wind up doing anyway because it's inevitable. It's inevitable because the assignment desk is always sending you late to luncheon addresses, awards banquets, public policy forums and the like. So when you must, use a supercardioid microphone, a shotgun, and hold it as close as possible to the loudspeaker. This minimizes distortion and mugginess caused by the feedback and room noise you're sure to pick up with an omnidirectional mic held far from the loudspeaker.

Interviews in Moving Cars

This is an increasingly popular way to get more from an interview than just two people talking in an office or living room. You get a transition and often you get street scenes that are part of the story—a plush residential area, a rundown factory district, a ghetto.

Use lavalieres. If the subject is driving and the reporter sitting in the passenger seat, put the driver's mic a little off center to the right and the reporter's more off center to the left, keeping them nicely on mic as they exercise the tendency to turn toward each other during conversation. If you're shooting only the subject driving alone in the front seat, keep the mic centered.

Standing on the Mic Cable

Some reporters can't resist raising a microphone from diaphragm level into camera view during an interview or standupper. You can prevent it by having the reporter bring the mic to the right height and then putting his or her foot on the cable with no slack.

"Memorizing" a Standupper

More reporters than might like to admit it have a very tough time memorizing standuppers, especially those that are long or in which wording must be precise. Many overcome this problem by recording the material on a pocket tape recorder and playing it back to themselves through an ear piece while videotaping the standupper. The key to making this work is recording the cue tape at the pace desired for the standup. If it's too slow, the standup will drag. If it's too fast, the reporter will fall hopelessly behind.

Interviews

When you record an interview with a pair of lavalieres rather than a single hand-held microphone, you can record the audio mixed, with both mics on one channel, or both mics on both channels, or you can record each mic on its own channel. Separating the mics provides an editing advantage, because overlap—when the subject and the reporter are talking simultaneously—can be eliminated. When you do this, put the interviewee on the audio track farthest from the edge of the tape (usually Channel Two), because if you are to lose either track due to tape damage, it's better to lose the reporter.

Feedback

Feedback occurs when microphones pick up a signal, send it through the recording system and pick it up again from a loudspeaker that is part of the same system, so that the signal is feeding into itself. When this happens you get strange noises—squeals, whistles and whines—that ruin the audio you are trying to record. To combat feedback, you must change the relationship between the microphone and the loudspeaker. Move the mic away or turn down its pot, or turn the loudspeaker off or down.

You are most apt to encounter feedback in a poorly balanced public address system, and pick it up as you record. You could also get it in situations where you use two microphones and loudspeakers are present. Another way, surprisingly, is when you are using a camera-mounted shotgun mic and monitoring sound with the loudspeaker built into the camera body (next to the photographer's ear) rather than monitoring with a headset plugged into the camera. If you crank the loudspeaker output too high, the shotgun can pick it up and create a feedback loop.

Interviewing

Good interviewers want to know everything.

Successful interviewers listen.

When you get a one-word answer, try one more word: "Why?"

Don't intimidate; put your subject at ease.

Clarify. If you don't get it, who will?

Television journalists conduct interviews in three distinctly different ways. The differences arise from the purpose of the interviews.

One kind doesn't require a camera. That's the interview for gathering information to be used in reporting and tracking down additional information from other sources. It can be done face-to-face or on the phone.

A second kind requires a camera and is usually done in the field. That's the interview for sound bites to be incorporated in news stories and documentaries.

The third ordinarily requires two cameras and is conducted in a studio, in a carefully chosen location outside the studio, or sometimes with the interviewer and interviewee in different places. A long interview in this category may constitute a program in itself, while a shorter interview may be used as a segment of a program, often a live interview in a news program.

Regardless of the type of interview you are conducting, to succeed you must focus on what you are trying to get from the interview and how it is going to be used.

In the information interview, where you will probably take notes but might use a cassette recorder for convenience, you are usually after 5-W information and leads to other sources. Where did this happen? When? Who did it? How do you spell that? Did anyone else see it? Why were you there? How many are there in the city? How many in the state? Is that a lot? Who pays for these things—the city? The state? What do they cost? How many vendors bid on it? If you can't tell me the price, who can?

Your questions will be spontaneous and unrehearsed, although your may have jotted down some topics to cover. They'll flow from your experience as a reporter, your background in the subject, if you have any, and your curiosity, your desire to learn as much as you can about the subject. You can never be a reporter if you aren't curious. You might make it as an anchor, but not as a reporter and not as a writer.

Field interviews for sound bites require curiosity, news sense and a feel for the story you are covering. The more you know about the story the easier it is to focus on what the interviewee may be able to say that you can use in the story.

As a rule, you don't just roll tape and reel off questions. Tape is cheap, yes. Tape is reusable, yes. But time is always limited and it's not recoverable. The videotape editor who is going to put your story together won't have time to view and log an hour's worth of interviews. It takes more than an hour to do that. And in most instances, you won't have time to conduct an hour's worth of interviews, anyway. That also takes more than an hour.

So you need to know where you are going before you start. You might begin this process on the telephone, when you call to try to find out whether the individual knows anything useful and is willing to be interviewed, or you'll do it at the scene when you first approach the person. You try to determine in advance what the interviewee knows, so you can economize on time when you do the interview. This is not to say that you rehearse the interview, or tell the subject what you want him or her to say or not to say. That could amount to staging. Nor do you get into so much detail in your chat that the subject is apt to lose spontaneity and say during the real interview, "Like I told you a minute ago ..."

But very often with a few questions you can get a good idea of what the interviewee can add to your story. This little conversation also allows you to try to put the subject at ease—to make him or her comfortable with your personality and with the circumstances, the microphone, the camera, and, when they are used, the lights. Of all the trappings of a television interview, nothing reminds the average interviewee more than lights that something unusual is going on.

You can say, "Wow, those lights are bright. As long as I do this, I'll never get used to them" to let your interviewee know he's not alone in discomfort. You can say, "Mr. Morrison, I'm going to hold the microphone down here, where the camera won't see it. But don't worry. Even though it's not close it will work fine. Just talk about as loud as I do."

When the interview starts, it's imperative that you listen to what the subject says. If you commit a dozen questions to memory and rattle them off without listening to the answers—really listening—you will be opening the door to disappointment. You could, of course, obtain a successful interview without listening. But you could also have long, rambling convoluted answers that defy editing. And you could also fail to pick up on a comment that would have led to special, unexpected information had you heard the clues and followed up.

So you must listen carefully for two reasons: to coax the interviewee into talking in simple, declarative sentences, if he or she isn't, and to keep yourself alert to new avenues of inquiry that the answers might suggest.

There is absolutely nothing wrong with going over the key points of an interview a second time—doing them over. In fact, interview subjects often welcome a second chance because they feel uneasy about the wording or content of their first responses. You can say, "Well, Mr. Morrison, just to review…let me ask you again …." and ask the questions you now know—from having already asked—will produce sound bites you can use. Just as you are giving Mr. Morrison a second chance, you are also giving yourself one because you can rephrase and sharpen your questions.

Be very careful during the interview to avoid saying "uh-huh" and "okay" and "yes." You may intend these interjections as encouragement to the interviewee, but they can appear to a viewer as agreement, as if you are taking the interviewee's side. And even if they don't, you're going to look a little unprofessional saying "okay" six times. Moreover, these little words can be so difficult to edit out that it's best not to utter them at all.

In most cases, when the interview is over you will do cutaways, the shots that tape editors use for condensing interviews. There are two types: silent cutaways of you listening to the interviewee, and sound reverses, in which the camera is on you while you repeat questions you asked in the interview.

It goes without saying that your sound reverses must be the same as the original questions. You can clean up the language or make them a little sharper, but don't change their content in any substantive way so that you abuse your interviewee. Guard against this by doing the sound reverses in the presence of the interviewee, and ask to be told if you accidentally misstate a question or give it a different nuance. If the interviewee tells you that happened, do the question over. Fair is fair—and if necessary you can always compare original and revised reverses with the original interview question when you're in the editing bay.

In the silent cutaways, make sure you always do at least one absolutely blank and reactionless, dumb listening shot. Anything else—smiling, frowning, nodding "uh-huh"—carries editorial overtones. You're better off looking stupidly uncomprehending than appearing to agree or disapprove, or smiling radiantly while the subject tells you how he attempted suicide.

In extensive field interviews, when you expect to use a lot of material, it's helpful if a field producer or writer comes along to keep track of questions for reverses. Or if you're lucky you'll have a photographer who is interested enough to remember questions. But the responsibility is yours, and the more interviews you do the easier remembering becomes.

In production interviews—such as the long sessions that make up a personality profile—you'll probably have the luxury of two cameras, one on you and one on the subject. You won't need separate cutaways because you'll be getting them all along.

Live interviews (or pretaped interviews that aren't going to be edited) are decidedly different from interviews for edited sound bites. They are little productions or programs in themselves. You want them to flow smoothly and naturally, to have a beginning and end and to disguise the fact that most of the time you, the interviewer, know the answers before you ask the questions. You also want to bring them in on time—to do the whole business in three and a half minutes, if that's what your producers have planned, and not five or six, just because you are happy with the way it's going, or because the guest is uncommonly loquacious.

You know the answers before asking because a live guest is never a face from the crowd. The guest is a celebrity actor or athlete or author, or an expert in the subject at hand, or the proponent of one side or the other in a controversy, or a person who has been invited on the program after rescuing a baby from a flaming building or surviving three weeks lost in the wilderness, or winning the state lottery, or asking the news director for a little publicity for an upcoming theatrical production or a charity street fair.

These people are there for a reason; otherwise they wouldn't be chosen. You will be familiar with the subject or the individuals because to greater or lesser extent; they are in the news and you have read or heard about them. In large markets or at the network level, the interviewees usually are "pre-interviewed" by a writer or producer who provides you with biographical and background information, a rundown on what the subject has to say, and a list of proposed questions (with a summary of the answers you can expect, based on the pre-interview).

You are armed and ready, or should be. Your job is to get the right information out of the guest. Take advantage of any opportunity to put the guest at ease. It helps.

Most of these interviews are done on your studio interview set, where the rigmarole of setting up is minimal because everything is there—a clip-on mic is ready at each chair, the chairs are comfortable, the lights are permanent and out of the way, and the cameras are in place—one for you and one for the guest.

You and the guest usually are sitting in your chairs well before the interview starts. During a commercial break or while another program segment is being aired, you'll have a chance to visit with the guest and establish yourself as a pleasant, non-threatening person who is sincerely interested in the guest. You can review the topic, remind the guest how long the interview is scheduled to run, tell her you'll be getting the cues and all she has to do is relax and chat with you.

Live remote interviews, where you are in the studio and the guest is at another location, tend to be more difficult than in-studio interviews. The primary reason is that the set-up for the guest is one hundred percent abnormal, unless the guest is experienced at being interviewed.

The guest may be in comfortable surroundings, in her own living room, or office, or at a school board meeting, and feel relaxed, or she may be seated on a stool in your noisy and intimidating newsroom, and feel uneasy. Either way, there's a good chance that except for a telephone call, she has never conversed with you or seen you, she's never had to listen to an interviewer through a tiny earpiece that feels like it's going to fall out, and she's never had to talk to a camera just as if it were a person.

In these cases, you must rely on your colleague who is with the interviewee (the cameraman or a field producer) to put the subject at ease and explain that all of a sudden, she's going to hear your voice asking her a question and she's going to have to look into the camera and reply. You can help by making your voice as friendly as possible, perhaps by thanking the person for being there and giving her a chance to test her voice and wits by saying "You're welcome" or "It's a pleasure," and by making the first question as easy as possible.

Still another type of live interview is the remote in which you and the interviewee are in the field—when you interview a fire captain at a four-alarmer, a city councilman who's about to step into a hearing room to undergo an ethics inquiry, or the basketball player whose buzzer shot won the big game.

You need to explain to the interviewee just what's going to happen. The two of you will stand side by side and the segment will begin with both of you in the shot, or it will begin tight on you and widen to both of you after you tell the anchor, "Jim, So-and-So is with me right now ..."

With the fire captain and the basketball player, the subject matter is obvious and you don't really need to discuss what you're going to ask. But you'll improve your chances for a good interview with the beleaguered councilman if you tell him in advance just what the questions will be. It's likely he's busy phrasing in his mind the denial he's going to make to you, and he doesn't know that you don't want a denial because it has already been in the papers and on the air. What you want to know is how he plans to persuade the panel of his claim that the facts have been misstated and his actions misrepresented—what exactly is he going to say? You'll both be helped if the councilman has been able to think about the answer.

You can also help yourself by rehearsing your questions, out loud if you have the privacy or in your mind if you don't. Practice getting the words out, especially if the question is at all sensitive. And when the words do come out, when you hear them with your ears or in your mind, try to judge how the interviewee might react to them. Maybe you'll need to rephrase the question before you ask it. If so, now's the time to work on it.

Now, how do you know what to ask? Your questions will stem from your sense of curiosity and your background in the subject. You should want to know what's going on here, why is this happening? You should want to understand the issues. You should want to understand the interviewee's point of view, and you should want to help him or her get it across (because that is useful to your audience, not because you are taking sides). Then, you need to know something about the subject before asking questions. In the case of issues in your community, you should know at least something about everything (you are, after all, a reporter) and, in fact, you should be an expert about some of them. This just happens, if you are a serious journalist. It may never happen if you are a preening prima donna aiming for a glamorous seven-figure network job on the strength of your good looks and charm.

Even serious journalists can't know everything. So if you are in the dark on the topic, ask the assignment desk for a fill-in. If the desk assigns the story, the desk is duty-bound to know something about it. The desk should have newspaper clips and useful press releases. You can even ask other reporters; most will cooperate with you if you do the same for them. As a last resort, you can ask the person you are going to interview. A confession beforehand often serves you better than having your abject ignorance manifest itself during the interview; that can make the interviewee think of you as a jerk during the interview and that opinion can be reflected in the interviewee's answers. Still, the more you know the better your questions will be. Better questions tend to get better answers because the interviewee will have greater respect for you and feel more cooperative.

Another factor in knowing what to ask is knowing the purpose of the interview. If the story is brand new, you more or less start from who, what, where, why and when and work from there. If it's a running story, you won't want to rehash it if you are covering it as spot news. You'll want to deal with the latest development, or try to push the story ahead by asking questions that look to the future. If you are putting together an expository feature or documentary segment, background questions will be appropriate and necessary. It's important to conduct the interview within the context of its purpose.

A lot of the stories you will cover will have nothing to do with important issues facing a democratic society. Instead, they'll be police and fire stories, personal tragedies or triumphs, stories about children or animals or lottery winners—in sum, stories that depend on emotions, stories television news sometimes seems to be obsessed with. One of New York City's early television reporters was famous, or infamous, for getting the emotional responses his bosses wanted by asking the "How does it feel..." question, as in:

- "How does it feel to watch your three-year old boy get run over by a garbage truck?"

- "How does it feel to be the only survivor of an automobile accident you admit you caused because you were drunk?"

- "How does it feel to burn down an orphanage because you carelessly tossed a cigarette?"

The questions this reporter asked could not have been coarser or more unfeeling, but he often walked away with terrific answers that went right to the heart of the story and were, in fact, what everyone wanted to know.

The trick is to elicit the same answers without asking how it feels. Sometimes you can do it by carefully leading the interviewee to the point—more or less like this, in the case of the father who saw a garbage truck run over his son:

Q. Where were you when it happened?
A. I was right there, right across the street.
Q. And...and...did you...?
A. I did. Oh, God I did...
Q. And...? (Then wait— you'll usually get an answer.)

That's rough but gentler than "How does it feel to watch your three-year-old son get run over by a garbage truck?" The grieving parent has the choice of talking about it or not, without being directly confronted with the question and feeling obligated to respond.

You can, of course, charge right in with the offensive question, get the answer and use it without airing the question. The public will never know how crude or cruel you were. This is a question of individual conscience, but you should know the best people don't do such things.

In stories involving issues and controversies, you often need to challenge the answers you get. If you can, phrase it so the challenge comes from someone other than you. For example: "Senator, your critics say..." or "Your political opponents claim.... etc." When you do this, you'd better have on the tip of your tongue the name of a critic or political foe, in case the senator challenges you. If you don't, you'll look biased and silly.

Frequently, you can clear up fogginess by making a question out of what you think the subject said or meant to say: "Senator, are you saying ...." This can clarify, which is very important, and it can produce a restatement of the subject's position in shorter and more precise and useable terms. Of course, the subject could just say "Yes" or "No." Then your response would be "Why" or "Please explain why."

On occasion, you will know that not only do one or two key points require clarification, but the entire interview needs to be done over because the interviewee's answers are terrible. He rambles. He contradicts himself. He's nervous and it shows, and that doesn't suit your purposes. What should you do? You can allow a look of puzzlement to come over your face and say to your photographer, "What's that, Bill? A sound problem? Intermittent? You say we have to do it all over—from the beginning? Mr. Morrison, I'm terribly sorry, but did you hear that? Do you have the time...?" While the photographer is "fixing" the problem, you can go over with Mr. Morrison the ways you and he can do the interview so the second one will take less of his time. Depending on the nature of the material, there's nothing at all wrong with asking him to summarize his views in 30 seconds.

When it comes to questions you know the interviewee is sensitive about, do not be afraid to ask but do try to time them carefully. If there is information you want from the interviewee in addition to his answer to the sensitive question, get the information first and save the sensitive part for last. If the sensitive question is all you care about, it may still make sense to build up to it by asking questions you don't care about. That will give the interviewee a chance to get used to you and to being on the hot seat.

On rare occasions, you may accept pre-interview conditions from the interviewee. You may agree to ask no questions about a lawsuit, for example. Or no questions about his or her divorce. Or no questions on a hot issue he or she's been ducking from for two weeks. Some news organizations will agree to conditions and others won't. You should clear it with your assignment desk or news director first, but you should not automatically tell the interviewee that the request is out of the question. If the person's knowledge or views are necessary to the story you are doing, some give and take may be necessary. If staying away from the verboten subject is going to be obvious to viewers, you may wish to work into your script mention of the agreement; that keeps everyone honest. One way to script it is to say the interviewee declined comment on the hot topic.

When you are interviewing a person just for information, the form of your questions is much less important than it is in on-camera interviews. No particular harm is done if a person tells you on the telephone, "I don't understand that question" or, "That's really two questions. Which do you want me to answer?" When this happens on camera, especially during a live interview, you might be embarrassed, you will probably waste time, and you can lose control of the interview.

Try, therefore, to make your questions clear. Ordinarily, the simpler and more direct, the better, and the longer and more convoluted, the greater the risk.

Avoid two-pronged questions. Ask one and after it has been answered, ask the other. Don't ask two at the same time.

Avoid closed questions, except when you really want a "Yes" or a "No" to pinpoint a person's position or try to overcome evasiveness. After "Yes" or "No" you can always ask "Why?" or "Will you explain that, please?"

Most of the time, keep your questions open-ended. They elicit answers in the interviewee's own terms, and allow the interviewee, sometimes at least, to provide good information and answers you might not have gotten otherwise.

Listen for jargon in answers. If you don't understand it, viewers won't either and the question and answer are wasted. Sometimes you have be very frank, tell the subject you don't understand, and ask the subject to try to answer in layman's language.

Finally, some points to keep in mind on how to treat the person you are interviewing on camera:

You should look at the interviewee during the interview. In a friendly way, frequently look that person straight in the eye. If you don't, you are telling the interviewee you aren't really interested in what he or she is saying. That will harm the interview.

You should remember the interviewee is the star, not you. The purpose of the interview is to get information and opinions from the interviewee, not to show how smart you are. If viewers wind up noticing you more than the interviewee, the interview may be a failure.

You should talk with the interviewee, chat with him or her. Don't project your voice in any unnatural manner. Television is an intimate medium, one on one. In most cases (there are always exceptions) you don't want to intimidate the interviewee with your voice and manner, nor do you want to appear intimidating to viewers.

Producing

It's live, but is it news?

Stay ahead or you'll fall behind.

Make it work now, fight it later.

The golden words of producing: please and thank you.

Start strong, end strong.

Producing television news programs is hectic and stressful. You live by Murphy's Law—if anything can go wrong, it will—and you live with it all day long, without relief. At the very second your program is scheduled to start, you start. Not a minute later, or 12 seconds later, as might happen in ordinary endeavors, but at the very second. No matter that it has been a horrible day. Two editing systems broke down—two! Your male anchor was carted off to the emergency room with appendicitis 45 minutes before air time. The live shot with the governor is up and ready to lead the program, except the governor's not there and his press secretary can't find him. No matter. You broadcast live, without rehearsal. Ready or not, you grab the script and hit the air, on time, to the second.

With luck, you'll never have all those problems at once, but they do happen. As producer, it's your job, your responsibility, to persevere. You are the leader of a team of writers, reporters, news and sports anchors, meteorologists, photographers, tape editors, directors, technical directors, board operators, teleprompter operators, graphic artists, engineers, camerapersons, floor managers, electricians, couriers and helicopter pilots—many of them as wildly individualistic as any person in your city. Collectively, you and they and the other producers put the news out three, four, five times a day—sometimes more—starting with thin air as your basic raw material.

You pull off this "daily, small miracle" because you care about your work far more than the average person. You do it not by barking commands like a general, but by earning the team's respect, leading by example, persuading, cajoling, cheerleading, and being professional. One of the hallmarks of of professionalism is maintaining grace under pressure. An essential ingredient of that is politeness—saying "please" and "thank you." Treat your co-workers as you prefer to be treated (however out of the ordinary *they* may be). Say "please." Say "thank you."

When a production looks like it's about to fall apart, those respectful words can save it. They can prevent the screaming and cursing and personal attacks that make bad situations worse at exactly the moment everyone should be pulling together. They can also make your reputation as the kind of producer people like to work for and with. Say "please." Say "thank you."

In small to medium market newsrooms, producing jobs are often given to relative beginners, to people who have demonstrated they are reliable and organized, and can write fast and accurately. Writing ability is the key ingredient.

You may have wanted to be a reporter and, eventually, an anchor, or you may have wanted to be a photographer. But you find out you don't quite have the performing skills for anchoring, or the ego that is often required. You find out you don't quite have a photog's eye for pictures; you recognize the good shots and appreciate them, but out there in the field you don't see them, or don't realize they were there until it's too late.

But you can write. In fact, you love to write. You see producers writing, and doing many other things which altogether add up to having enormous influence on the news the public sees on television. You may start out as a writer or assistant producer. After a time, a weekend or early morning producing slot opens up and you get it. You prove yourself and move up to a better shift with a more important program.

In the best of situations, as the producer, the major decisions of the day are yours to make. It's like being a newspaper editor, only better, because you're more intimately involved with the people and decisions than most newspaper editors.

Few situations are ideal, however, and as a hired producer, you must operate within a system established by others and sometimes you must do things you might not agree with. Fortunately, few if any of them will involve dishonesty or unethical journalism. With a modicum of luck, nothing that big will ever come up.

Instead, the only compromises you'll have to make will involve degrees of quality and your efforts to conscientiously husband the precious few minutes that today's news programs devote to real news. You'll make the best of it, you'll have fun, and you'll look to the possibility of introducing improvements over the long haul rather than tomorrow.

The kind of program you produce is going to depend primarily on factors you don't control. What sort of news is supposed to be in your program—local only, all national and international, some of all? What is the format—one anchor or two? How long is the program? How many commercials? How much time is devoted to special features? To sports? To weather?

Basic Content

Is your program entirely local news or mixed news? This usually depends on the hour your program is broadcast. If it airs directly before or after your network's news, your program is likely to be local news only, plus, of course, sports and weather. If it's not all local, the current style is to run two or three or even four or five major national and international stories, either in a short package, or in a full segment of their own (or in some rare unfortunate instances, sprinkled randomly into the program to the confusion of viewers). If you are producing the late news, at 10 or 11 p.m., it always will be a program of mixed news—a wrap-up, as the cliché has it, "of the major events in the city, the state, the nation and around the world" plus, of course, the sports and weather.

Your program, regardless of when it's broadcast, will likely also devote a significant portion of its allotted time to non-news features chosen by someone above you in the chain of command—usually the news director who, in turn, has consulted with or received orders, or strong suggestions, from someone still higher up.

You can gripe, and a lot of producers do, but you still must make time for these non-news features: medical and health segments; catch-a-crook segments; pet of the week in need of a home; unfortunate children in need of a home; movie, arts and restaurant reviews; consumer segments; best buys at the greengrocer's and what to do if you happen to have a rutabaga in your refrigerator; personal finance and money management; appeals for employment by out-of-work citizens; gardening advice; and on and on.

Some of these segments are proven audience builders. Others provide genuinely needed service to the community. Some exist only to promote the station as a concerned and important citizen. Almost all of them replicate material found in every newspaper in the country, where increasing emphasis is being put on the fabricated category of "news you can use." For competitive reasons, for better or for worse, television is doing it too.

The problem for television news producers is that these segments shrink the news hole. A newspaper, on the other hand, varies in size from day to day according to how much advertising it has, and "news you can use" doesn't necessarily mean fewer column inches of straight news. But television is different. Programs aren't expanded by three or five minutes to accommodate non-news features; instead, the features run where news would have run and the programs start and end on television's regular on-the-hour and half-past-the-hour schedule.

Basic Format

Does your program use a single or dual anchor? Are anchors allowed to read an entire story or lead-in by themselves, or have higher-ups (the news director, the general manager, the group owner, the news consultant) decreed that your station's anchors will split stories—alternating as each does one or two or three sentences of the same story? This may seem dumb as heck—after all, if the anchor is being paid $75,000 (or $1,000,000) shouldn't he or she be good enough to deliver a 20-second story without assistance?

Of course the anchors are good enough. Of course they can do it. But you and they are stuck with whatever management has decided on the subject. The positive spin is that splitting stories steps up a program's pace and keeps viewers tuned in. What's the point of doing the news, bosses ask, if viewers are tuned to another station? The negative view is that splitting stories is a patently silly practice that encourages anchors to be more concerned about performance than journalism, which in turn attracts a different type of person into the business, changing the business for the worse.

In any event, you do it the way the bosses want it done until, if ever, you have the clout to change it.

Another factor is story length. Are any limits put on how long a story without videotape pictures can run? Or on how long a reporter's package can run? When these limits exist, the theory again is that brevity and variety speed up the program and hold the audience by reducing the possibility of boredom. Naturally, the quality of journalism suffers. This is inevitable and incontrovertible. But if higher-ups order it, you do it—most of the time, anyway.

Do higher-ups care about journalism? Do they share your commitment to informing the public? Even if they do, and many say they do, their top priority—and, to be fair, their major responsibility—is to build audiences and advertising revenues. Again, you live with it, and hope to make changes if your position grows stronger.

As you establish yourself as a producer and news professional, you'll frequently come up against the insidious argument that wins over a lot of well-intentioned journalists, that often makes them the managers of the future. Already alluded to, it is this: You can't do a good job with the news if you don't have the tools (the best personnel and latest equipment) and if you don't win the audience you won't have the money to buy the tools. Unfortunately, the logic of this position often is distorted into a rationale for emphasizing gory violence and gratuitous sex in local television news.

Remotes

Is it standing orders that you always have at least one live remote in your show? Does your station count a remote to the news room (which might be only a few steps removed from the anchor desk) as a real remote, or must it be out of the building somewhere? Must you have two remotes? Three? The vogue today is to do as many remotes as can be excused, so long as they don't cause too much overtime.

How many times does being live on the scene really add to the content of the reporter's story or the freshness of the information? The answer, as anyone with any critical sense knows, is very seldom. For the most part, what the news audience too often gets is a picture of the scene of a news event, from which everyone has either gone home or at which no one has yet arrived, followed by a pretaped package of what happened earlier in the day, or what happened over the past several weeks to set up the story of what might happen at this live remote location when the people get here tonight, followed by a brief live interlude in which the anchor may ask the reporter an inane question or two before thanking the reporter for being out there and doing such a good job, LIVE!

This is show biz unadulterated. As the producer, you can mitigate it by assuring that the remote moves smoothly, that the pretaped packages are meaningful, that the cross-talk between the anchor and the reporter actually adds useful information, and that time-wasting and silliness are held to a minimum.

Fact is, "live" can be regarded as the very essence of television news—what's happening, right now, this minute. See it with your own eyes, right now! When used judiciously and carefully planned, live remotes can be effective. They work very well for anchor interviews of people who might be unable or unwilling to go to go to your studio, but they succeed only insofar as the person being interviewed has something newsworthy to say and will say it on the program. They work very well to show a fire in progress, a demonstration continuing, flooding on the south side of town, the raucous nature of a school board meeting—but again, they work only insofar as what is being shown live is newsworthy.

When it's not, all you are giving the viewer is unedited pap and there's no journalism involved in doing that. Getting a station manager who has spent tens of thousands of dollars on live equipment to agree with you is another issue entirely.

LIVE! "This is Sidney Stunning with a live update of the news at eight." Or, "For more on the story we bring in Marcia Marvelous reporting live." Well of course Sidney and Marcia are alive. Would the quality of what they have to say suffer if they were on tape? Nine times out of ten, no.

Weather and Sports

Are there required formats for your sports and weather segments? These can be dictated by management (and indirectly by sponsors because sports and weather commercial time is sometimes sold separately from the rest of the news program) and by the contracts of sports anchors and weatherpersons, which sometimes commit or guarantee them a specific number of appearances and amount of air time.

The result is that the format for the weather segment could be simple or complicated, possibly a little longer than the producer might prefer but shorter than the talent would like.

The simplest format might be an introduction from the anchor, who says now here's Joe with the weather, followed by Joe doing three and a half or four minutes of weather and saying he'll see everybody again at ten.

Another format might require a tease to the weather—that is, right before a commercial the anchor comments on the day's weather and says Joe's forecast will be coming up next. That's followed by a weather-related tape or graphic, followed by a commercial which was sold with the guarantee it would be used right before Joe's weather, when audience attention and anticipation are thought to be high. After the commercial, you go to Joe with no further ado. Joe might then do his weather and say goodbye. Or he might do the national weather, break to a pair of commercials sold at a premium to be in middle of the weather forecast, and come back for the local forecast.

A slightly more complicated format might require Joe to slip onto the set before the commercial break preceding the weather. The director includes him in the shot while an anchor says Joe will be giving his forecast in a moment. Joe will probably banter with the anchors before the commercial break, possibly giving a preview of his forecast or weather report. Or he might do a 15-second voice-over on a tornado in Kansas or ice-covered highways in Pennsylvania before promising to be right back with our local weather. Or in a slightly different format, he might launch right into the national weather before breaking to commercial.

The variations are endless. Many sponsors want to be associated with the weather and will pay extra for it. Many stations, therefore, devise weather formats to allow maximum participation by such eager sponsors.

The weather forecast is a genuinely popular part of television news programs; many viewers say they tune in for the weather more than anything else and choose one channel over because of the weather forecaster. As a result, stations and producers are constantly experimenting with the weather segments, and today it's not uncommon to have the forecaster appear three times in a half-hour newscast—once with a brief weather preview early in the show, then with the full report and forecast near the middle of the program, and finally with a brief summary in the last couple of minutes.

For the most part, as the producer you'll have little or no control over this. Management will decide the emphasis the weather gets, and your job will be to make it work. This can turn the weather report and forecast into an interminable and repetitive project (imagine presenting a news story two or three times to make sure people get it), and it may guarantee losing some viewers to glassy-eyed boredom, but research and revenue records show many viewers lap it up and many sponsors will pay what they must to reach them.

The sports segment is somewhat different. Some sponsors will insist on being part of the sports segment, and even pay extra for a guaranteed location, but the sports audience is smaller than the weather audience and it's primarily a male audience. Your job as producer will be to see that the sports is smoothly integrated into the program, is presented without technical flaws, and doesn't run over its allotted time.

Only rarely will the sports anchor appear in more than one part of a half-hour program. It may happen when there's a major sports story of great local interest that's worth reporting early in a newscast, before the regular sports segment, or when late scores of great local interest call for the sports anchor's reappearance at the end of the program. Experimentation in the day-to-day treatment of sports news is limited. Repetition of the weather forecast at the end of a program is generally accepted, but no one would consider a reprise on the baseball scores. In fact, some stations are experimenting with dropping the sports anchor from their early evening newscasts and letting the news anchors give whatever scores and sports news are deemed important.

At the risk of oversimplifying, it can be argued that sports anchors fall into only two categories—those who work hard to deliver as much sports news as possible for their audience, and those who work hard to establish themselves as television personalities. As a producer, you're almost sure to prefer the former.

Your Day as Producer

For our purposes, assume you are producing the early evening newscast, the one that most stations air adjacent to their network's evening news program. Let's say you come in around 9:30 and work until your 6 o'clock show is off the air.

First off, you need to know how the program is segmented and how much time you have for news. Then you need to know what news is available to you. Next, you decide which stories to use, the order and form in which you'll use them, and how long they'll run.

After that, you'll supervise the writing and editing of the news. In small to medium markets, you may do the lion's share of the writing yourself. You'll be in the control room to oversee production of the show and make any editorial decisions that come up. When the program is over, you'll return to the newsroom for post-mortems and possibly planning discussions for the next day.

The Time You've Got to Fill

It makes sense to determine the size of your news hole as soon as you get to work. Everything else depends on it.

When does your program begin—at what hour and second? When does it end—at what hour and second? How many commercials are scheduled and how long are they? With this information, you can determine how many minutes and seconds you have to fill, and the number of segments you must do it in.

Once you know that (and typically it's around 22 minutes for a half-hour program) you can deduct other known quantities: the weather, the sports, and the format materials which generally are the same program after program. These include the opening, the headlines, the teases, the bumpers, the closing, sometimes even the happy talk or cross talk, although a good many producers feel it is best to budget this chit-chat as they go along, just as if it were a news story. What's left is the news hole, the minutes and seconds available for the news of the day, including whatever management-dictated features are included in your program.

The fact is, most of the time the result of this arithmetic is almost always the same—a news hole in the range of 13 and a half or 14 minutes. Still, it never hurts to double-check.

Moreover, you get to see who your sponsors are, just in case a conflict develops. It can and does happen that you have a fast food commercial the same day you have a story about health authorities in the Pacific Northwest tracing two deaths and 27 hospitalizations to tainted hamburgers sold by the same company. Knowing that enables you to alert the sales department, which might then arrange to reschedule the commercial. That's always better than dropping a story because of a commercial. If you know the commercial can be replaced, you'll feel no pressure one way or the other about the story and you won't wind up using a marginal story just to avoid the appearance of capitulating to a sponsor.

What's Going in the Program?

Of course, you've got the weather and sports, and for the heck of it let's say a brief national/international package is standard for your program.

But what else? Is this doctor day—a required medical segment? Is it orphaned children day, another required segment? Or maybe it's your money day, or consumer complaint day or movie-review day or restaurant-review day or what's-going-on-in-town-this-weekend day?

There's a chance you may personally disdain every one of these segments. More likely, you'll have good feelings about a few, bad feelings about many, and mixed feelings about others. Your feelings make no difference: management has paid for these segments and management is going to be sure they are used. Management may even have sent its sister-in-law to do one of them. You can be sure it's going to be used, if not by you, then by your successor.

Next, you need to know what's making news locally. You find out from the assignment desk, either by visiting with them or by consulting a rundown (often called a daybook or assignment list) that's been left for you, or both ways, usually both.

Generally speaking, the list will give the stories already covered or being covered, and the coverage planned for the rest of the day. Stories are usually listed by slugs, followed by a sentence or two about them and information on who is covering—reporter and camera, or camera only, whether a package is planned or just a voice-over/sound bite, and when the event takes place. The list also might tell you that a remote is already planned on a particular story or that a news maker has already been invited to be a studio guest. And if you are a large enough operation to have bureaus or a Washington D.C. correspondent or news service, the list will tell you what they are offering.

The list may also include information about events taking place that the desk isn't covering, and, perhaps, which reporters and photographers are working on features, series, investigative pieces and so on for future use.

In most shops you'll probably also have a commercial routine from the programming or traffic department that shows where the commercials go and how they are grouped. In these days of 15-second commercials, a lot of sponsors can be heard from before 90 seconds or two minutes are used up. In any event, the commercial lineup establishes the skeleton of your program. Your task is to fill the dead air between commercials.

You can probably block out your program right now—a tentative lineup. You can do it in your head or on paper. In part, that choice depends on when the first news meeting will take place. If it's coming up soon, there's little need to write down a tentative lineup because a lot of questions about stories and plans will be clarified at the meeting and you can do it afterwards. But if it's a couple of hours away, putting a tentative lineup on paper makes sense.

Either way, once you've looked over your commercial log and talked with the assignment desk you'll have a good idea about the important considerations. Is a closer being shot—that is, a good story to end the program? Does one story stand out as a sure lead story? Are any story groupings becoming obvious—crime stories, politics, the city's economy and a new factory, etc. Does a particular story suggest a sidebar that the assignment desk may have overlooked?

Several budget meetings or news meetings or editorial meetings (they can be called any of the three names) are held every day—in the morning, after lunch, in late afternoon and the early evening. Whenever the meetings are held, the cast of characters is basically the same: the news director and/or the assistant ND and/or the executive producer (if you have one), program producers, the anchor or anchors (if they are available), the assignment editor and or/assistant assignment editor, the director or some representative of the technical side, maybe the chief tape editor if your newsroom has one, and a graphics person.

Stations that broadcast a noon news might have a news meeting at 8 or 9 a.m., but stations that don't may hold their first meeting around 10 or 10:30. In our scenario, there is no noon news and the first meeting takes place at 10 a.m. You, the 6 o'clock producer, are there.

As a rule, the news director presides but soon turns the meeting over to whoever has been running the assignment desk. That's because the desk editor is the only person who really knows what's going on and what's coming up, and this meeting is an information and planning session.

If you were a fly on the wall at the meeting, you might be able to tell who really is in charge of news programs at the station. Is it the program producers, the news director, the executive producer, an anchor? You might be able to tell whether reporters are autonomous or members of a team. You might be able to tell whether the assignment editor is a solid, serious journalist or a sycophantic news clerk aiming for the management ranks. The answers to these vital questions might elude you for a time, but the sooner you know, the better job you can do.

Budget meetings can be brutal, or at least they can appear that way to an invisible guest unfamiliar with the culture of newsrooms. You'll hear all manner of unflattering comments about everyone, and you'll wonder what's said about you behind your back.

Someone, even you, may say in reference to a handsome reporter aspiring to become an anchor: "That's a complicated story. Better not let The Profile near it." Or, "Hang on! That story's got foreign names. Goldilocks (your blonde bombshell reporter) will trip all over her tongue." Or maybe, "Look, he may have a perfectly valid proposal, but I think Lard Ass (a portly city councilor) is getting on the news too much and we shouldn't encourage him. Let's just do a liner, not an interview." Or maybe, "Yeah, well...let's cover her (a visiting centerfold model). Sex at six can't hurt."

These meetings can also reveal a much better side of the business and the people in it. You'll hear—or should hear—serious discussion of coverage and the impact of your station's news programs on the community. You'll hear genuine expressions of concern about fairness, good taste, ethics and all the other considerations you discussed in journalism classes or read about in journalism reviews. If these issues never come up at your station, preparing a resume might be in order.

Whether the meeting is dominated by cynicism and wise guy remarks or by idealism, it should produce two important results: A plan will have been drawn up and everyone intimately involved will know whether the day shapes up as difficult or easy.

What will the day be like? Is there a clear lead story, or are we going to have to scramble for something? Is there a closer, or must we still come up with one? Is this one of those rare days when the program practically produces and writes itself, or will it be a bear? Are all three main stories hitting the house after 5:15? When will we know whether they've got the second remote unit running again? Are we going to be short an editor or can we get Annette to come in (again) on her day off?

What will be in the program? Not only will you know what's being covered, you'll also have come to some general agreements about how events will be covered. Have the reporters and photographers been told what is expected of them on the assignment? Will it be a package? If so, how long—one minute, a minute-45? Will it be a VOB (an anchor voice-over plus a sound bite)? Maybe just a plain VO without a bite will do it.

If it strikes you as arbitrary to make these decisions even before the events take place and a reporter lets you know what happened, well—it is. But so long as the decisions are based on experience rather than whim and so long as the decision makers remain flexible, it's the most practical way to go. Assignment editors and producers often take a different view of stories than reporters. That's because they are more familiar than reporters with what's already been used on programs. It's part of their job to keep track. They have a better idea of a day's overall coverage and priorities than individual reporters. That's also part of their job. And they—the producer in particular—know the needs of tonight's 6 o'clock news. Reporters, on the other hand, tend to judge today's news from the rather narrow perspective of stories they covered in the past.

Making these decisions in advance saves a lot of wheel-spinning and allows the assignment editor to use his troops efficiently. A reporter and photographer shouldn't have to put a package-worth of time and effort into a story the producer wants for a 30-second VOB. Nor should they have to pull out of an important story to cover an event the producer sees as worth 15 seconds if it's used at all. On the other hand, when the reporter telephones the desk with the news that what began as a routine little VOB at an elementary school has the potential to be a delightful closing package, the desk and producer need to be flexible enough to listen.

If you met at 10:00, the session probably ended before 11:00 so it's too early to break for lunch. You can hang out by the water cooler or sneak in a phone call to your Significant Other. Or you can do some work.

One worthwhile task is to block out the program on paper as completely as you can, guessing at which stories will hold up and which will fall through, assigning times to devote to each story, figuring which stories might fit with others, and so on. You may do it on a yellow legal pad, like this:

LIVE OPEN	:20
VTR OPEN	:10
COMMERCIAL BREAK	1:00
LIVE LEAD	:30
MURDER TRIAL SOT	1:30
DRUG BUST VOICE-OVER	:40
POLICE BRUTALITY SUIT VOB	:45
ETC.....	

Another thing you may do, or get someone to do for you, is type up as much regular format material as you can. Get the routine stuff out of the way so it won't be in the way when deadline approaches. Format material includes introductions to regular segments, teases before commercials, promos for the late news program, and commercial-break pages. These last may name each sponsor in the commercial break and give the commercials' running times, or they may simply give the total time for all commercials in the break. Knowing the length of the break is important, because it's usually during commercials that you make changes and you need to know how much time is available to do it in.

Unless your station is fully computerized and never uses paper for scripts, you'll type on copybooks of four to ten pages, with carbon paper between the pages.

Copybooks are distinguished by the number of pages in them and the color of the pages. They can have all the way to 10 pages, with thin carbon paper between pages. The pages can be all the same—all white, all blue, all pink, etc., or they can come in a mix of colors (white first page, medium blue second page, canary third, and so on). The first page of either style copybook is a heavier stock than the copies and is often called the "hard copy." It usually goes to the anchors or the TelePrompTer.

Some shops use single-color books, but it's more common to use multi-color copybooks for program scripts. When the copybooks are snapped apart just before air time, the script is assembled according to colors so that in the end you have full scripts in each of the colors in the book. Then, as standard procedure, the white script may go to the teleprompter, the pink to one anchor, canary to the other anchor, medium blue to the director, buff to the assistant director (if you have one), melon to the audio operator, light green to the producer, and so on, depending on how many people are believed to need full scripts. Each gets the same color every day, and people refer to them as "director's script" and "producer's script" rather than the canary copy and the pink copy. In some shops, anchors may get scripts in two colors, one for him or her to read and the other so she or he will know what the other anchor is reading. Otherwise, anchors tell their copy from their co-anchor's the way the pages are marked.

A good trick, by the way, is to keep a supply of single-color books in a color that doesn't appear in the multi-color copybooks. When you're close to deadline and still waiting for some stories to be typed, you can substitute for them with pages of the reserve color on which you've written the story slug and page number. Then you can break down the completed copy books, distribute the scripts, and replace the late pages when they're finished, even after the program starts—just take out the substitute blank page, which will be easy to find because of its color, and slip in the new page.

But back to writing your format pages in advance. Here are examples of what they might be:

OPEN	(TOM) Good Afternoon. I'm Tom Sawyer... (BECKY) and I'm Becky Thatcher ... In the headlines at 6 o'clock ... (The headlines will be typed on the page shortly before air time, when you know what the headlines are.)
TEASE BREAK THREE	(TOM) "Next up, Dr. Denton and news we all need to know about a disease...we thought was wiped out...but now is making a come-back."
GOODBYE	(TOM) Well, that's our early news ... Stay tuned now for NBC Nightly News with Madonna ... I'm Tom Sawyer... (BECKY) And I'm Becky Thatcher ... hoping you'll join us at eleven for the late-breaking edition of etc ...

This is all standard material that's better written early than late. Other format material varies from day to day, according to the structure of the program and the events of the day. You might always slot sports in the same place, but unless you want a generic intro to sports ("It's been a busy day in the sports world. Biff will tell us all about it after this"), you can't write the format page until you know specifically the sports news Biff will be reporting. ("The biggest names in golf squared off in the first round of the Master's this afternoon, but an unknown left-hander is four strokes up. Biff will tell us all about it in a moment.") It's good practice to keep after these format pages and type them as soon as you know what to say. It's better to write them early and have to change later than to let the task pile up to the point that it becomes a last-minute nightmare.

This is also a good time to start thinking about graphics and supers for the program. You can begin a list of lower-third supers, based on what you know of the stories being covered—where the story is taking place, who is being interviewed, who the reporter is, whether you'll need a "file" super, or even a dated file super, etc. You can look ahead to names of people you know will be in the news and start a list of chroma key headshots. You might be able to order a map or a chart. All of this will have to be done sometime; the sooner you get started the easier it is for you and more importantly, the easier it is for the people you depend on to get all this work done by 6 o'clock.

Now it may be time for lunch. Maybe you'll go out. Maybe you'll send out. One thing for sure—long, leisurely lunches are *not* part of a news producer's regimen. You can have them, of course, but usually because you've made it a point to clear the time.

Ordinarily, you're just too bugged by the constant need to make decisions—big decisions, little decisions, decisions other people should have made—and by myriad problems that come up during the working day; phone calls from viewers, phone calls the news director doesn't want and sticks you with, squabbles between the assignment desk and reporters or photographers, the indifference of some reporters and shooters to your requests, disagreements about script content, negotiations with reporters on the length of packages, explanation of exactly what you want in a graphic, and more, much more.

As a rule, producers in small to medium markets have little help in preparing programs, so they become directly involved in more details and writing than producers in major markets who have staffs of writers and associate producers. If you like producing (and if you don't, you shouldn't be doing it), this assures that you'll be in the middle of everything and will have fun. It also means a hectic pace.

Your most important task as producer is to devise the routine or rundown of the program—that is, to decide which stories will be in the program, the order they'll run in, the amount of time given to each (rounding off to the nearest five seconds), and which anchor will read them or introduce them.

You decide on this day that a fire story will lead the program rather than comments the mayor has made on preparing his next budget and the possibility he might ask for a tax increase. You choose the fire because the pictures are truly spectacular and because its aftermath will cause rush-hour traffic detours. The budget and tax story is more important, of course, but it's going to be in the news a lot in the next couple of months and this opening round is speculative. In many respects, it's a trial balloon the mayor is floating.

The fire, on the other hand, is solid hard news. It's also a simple fire uncomplicated by drama, death or serious injury and the traffic snarl will be easy to explain. You put it down for a 15-second lead-in, allow a minute for the reporter's package, and allot 25 seconds to an anchor explanation of the traffic problems. That's 1-40 for the fire story.

You decided to leave the traffic angle out of the reporter's package because it might never materialize or it could turn out worse than expected. If either happened, it's easier to adjust the anchor script than to revise the package. Another choice would be to switch to a live shot on the fire so the reporter could also handle the traffic aspect and be as current as the anchor would have been. This might add 15 or 20 seconds to the fire story because the anchor and the reporter would cross-talk. This gets you up to 1-55 or 2-00 for the fire, and so you opt for the live shot to please management as well as fill a tad more time on what's shaping up as a slow news day.

Still, 1-55 or 2-00 isn't enough for a lead segment. What news to report next? There are stories that will play with the fire—a couple of crime items and two minor residential fires in a new subdivision. Even though you have pictures of the two fires, the most you can get out of them and the two crime stories is 1-15 to 1-30, tops—which added to the fire story gives you up to three and a half minutes, still not enough for an opening segment.

Unfortunately, if you choose to follow these stories with the mayor's tax story, your lead segment might run too long. Let's take a look. You have the mayor's comments at a news conference and a sidebar on reaction from key members of the city council. You also must explain the process by which the mayor's comments may grow into proposals and the route his proposals must travel to become law.

The mayor's comments are still being edited, but based on a rundown from the reporter you've given the mayor a minute and a half and the council members the same. That's 3-00, plus about 45 seconds to explain the processes and introduce the subject—altogether, 3-45 for the tax story. Add that to the live-shot version of the fire, plus the crime stories and residential fires and you have an opening segment that approaches 8-00.

Will that work? Maybe yes but probably no, because 8-00's a very big chunk of the 14-00 or 13-and-a-half minutes you have for news after subtracting sports, weather and commercials from your program's running time of the 28-30. Format material will take a minute. You have a 60-second mandatory national and international news segment, and a 2-00 medical report, leaving you 9 and a half to 10 minutes for the local news of the day. You usually don't want to put the majority of it in one segment containing only two major topics.

And there's another problem. The tax story is mostly talking heads: the anchors talk, the mayor talks, the council members talk. Talk, talk, talk! Less than gripping visually, even if it is important. And less than definitive, because the process has a long way to go.

A partial solution is to order from file footage and fresh photography some "cover" for the mayor. When he talks about more money for the police department, show police scenes; more money for garbage services, show garbage trucks; more money for the zoo, show the monkeys and some children; more money for street repair, show ugly pot holes; and for his trial balloon on raising property taxes, show some residential neighborhoods.

This will help, but it doesn't solve the basic problem of how to structure the opening segment. You might consider splitting the tax story by running the mayor's portion in the first segment after the fire and teasing to the "political process and City Council's reaction to talk of higher taxes after this." That would work in terms of time. But you shouldn't consider this approach for very long because it requires the viewer to hold details of the mayor's comments in mind through a couple of minutes of commercials, and most viewers won't do that. If they don't, the sidebars on reaction and the process lose punch and you communicate less information than you hoped.

How about other approaches? You could make the tax story the program lead, dig up some other government news to pad the segment out, and lead the second segment with the fire. Or you could simply run the fire story, the two police items and the two residential fires for longer than they're really worth—pad them out to four and a half minutes—and save the tax and budget story for the second segment. Or you could get your opening segment down to size by dropping the police and residential fire stories to another segment and leading with the live shot from the fire scene, followed by the budget and tax stories.

Whoops! Here's another solution. Kill the SOT of the council members' reactions—after all, they're only reacting to the mayor's speculations. Replace the SOT with 15 seconds of script that council leaders told your station the mayor might be right. That way you can lead with the fire live shot, plus the police and residential fire stories, plus the mayor, and have all the major local news in your opening segment.

Whoa! Leaders of the city council say the mayor may be right about raising property taxes? Trial balloon or not, that really might add up to a tax increase so taxes is the lead story! Maybe what we need is more on this subject, maybe taxpayers' reaction.

All this is by way of illustrating the kinds of debates you'll have as a producer—debates with yourself, with your news director and sometimes with your anchors. Routining television news programs comes down to judgment—which can be defined as opinion formed by experience. One matter of opinion that needs to be considered is how long should an opening segment normally be?

One theory is that you want all your segments to run more or less the same length. Another theory is that if the segment lengths are consistent the show becomes predictable. Another holds that it's okay to vary the length of segments if you stay away from extremes that result in news segments shorter than the commercial breaks before and after them. Another theory says make sure your opening segment is longer than your rivals' so it will look like you've always got more news than they do, or so viewers will feel they've got so much time invested in your show they won't switch channels during the first commercial break.

A major factor, of course, is how long your half-hour news program really is. If you are producing the 6 o'clock local news and it runs right before you air the direct feed of the network evening news at 6:30, your program likely will run around 28-30 and you'd better finish on time because the upcoming network feed allows no slack.

If you are producing the late evening news program and it is followed by a program on tape that your station controls rather than a direct feed of Jay Leno or David Letterman, you're in an open-ended situation. Station management might sell a couple of extra news commercials and give you another four or five minutes of air time to space out the extra commercials. This half-hour newscast could really run 35 or 36 minutes.

The next factor is how many commercials you have and how they are supposed to run—in four groups, in five, in six? If it's four, you have five program segments. If it's six, you have seven segments. The greater the number of segments in a given period of time, the shorter they will be on average, of course, and the more time you will need to devote to teases.

In any event, your job is to fill the time between commercials with news, weather and sports, and to do it in a way that attracts and holds viewers while still giving the news in a serious, cohesive and fair manner.

The segments that will demand most of your time and attention day after day are the first two segments, especially the first, where you put most of the freshest news, and the last segment, where you have your closer. The weather and sports generally go in the middle segments and are written and produced by the respective anchors. Management-mandated features also usually go in the middle segments. Whether they're canned or locally produced, your involvement is generally limited to integrating them into your program and making sure their lead-ins work.

As the day progresses, your program takes shape. The morning coverage list may turn out to have been the roughest of guides to the news of the day. One story may be much stronger than anticipated. Another may be a semi-bust, usable but no longer the winner it appeared to be on paper at 10 a.m. A scheduled event may never take place. And new stories come up, solid stories. This is the very nature of news.

You may find yourself constantly revising tentative rundowns as old stories die and new ones are born. That's fine. In fact, you want to be working on rundowns, experimenting with the order, length and grouping of stories.

The way stories are grouped is regarded by many professionals as the key to producing a cohesive and unified newscast. If you have two running trial stories and three brand-new crime stories it probably makes sense to run them in the same segment rather than have two new crimes and a trial in one segment and the other trial and new crime in a different segment. If the trials are a rape and a murder and the new crime stories include one of each, it makes sense to spot the new rape next to the rape trial and the new murder next to the murder trial rather than run two trials followed by three new crimes in random order.

Such groupings are natural. They happen with little thought on your part. On the other hand, grouping a criminal trial with a political story can be difficult—unless, for example, they both take place in the state capital or both were highlighted by unexpected developments or stepped-up timetables, giving you a way to link them with the anchor script.

You should look for ways to link unrelated stories so the newscast appears to flow along rather than letting "orphan" stories abruptly alter its direction. But be careful. Make it a point to step back and check your work for artificiality; if your linking is too much of a stretch it will show—not just to you, but to your audience, which may form the opinion that your anchors are trivializing the news.

The menu of stories available to you usually expands during the day. Your own reporters will provide video stories and liners as they cover their assignments. The afternoon paper, if you have one, will provide fresh news and updates on running stories. The Associated Press will break away from its regular transmission of national and international news and features to run several "splits" of regional, state and local news. An active assignment desk, or your assistant producer or writer, if you have one, should provide even more local news and updates by working the telephones.

You've got to keep track of it all, particularly the items you think you might use. Give the stories slugs and file them by slug. Get as many written as possible, even before the program's routine is final. Writing the stories familiarizes the writer (you, the anchor or someone else) with the facts of the stories, so you can rewrite them quickly to specified times and to stress particular angles. It also provides you with a store of "pad" stories to use if you find yourself running short while the program is on the air.

At most shops an afternoon meeting brings together the people who attended the morning meeting as well as those who couldn't make it or might not have been due at work—the anchors, the director, the late evening producer, a technical facilities person. A typical time for this meeting is around 2 o'clock.

Important decisions are made, and you need to be prepared. You should have a rundown ready—giving the video stories you intend to use and the form and length you have in mind. Will it be a package or a VOB? Will it be 45 seconds or a minute and a half? Are the reporters doing what you want? Do they know? Will you have a guest on the set or at a remote? Will you have a reporter live in the newsroom, or live on a real remote? What's the outlook on the purchasing scandal the state capitol bureau is covering? Will it really push your program's deadline? Is it wiser to decide right now to leave that package for the late news, which always needs fresh material, and simply script any newsworthy developments? What should the early news promote for the late news?

All of this can be decided by mutual agreement among producers and the desk. Or the news director or an executive producer can dictate who gets what and how things will be done. The more influence you are able to exert, the better; it's always easier to do a good job when you're doing things your way.

Out of this meeting should come a lineup that will be final or close to it, barring unforseen news developments or disasters in your own coverage and plans.

Unless something pressing comes up, your immediate task will be to turn that rundown into a detailed routine. You should construct each segment in what you expect to be its final form—lead-ins, readers, videos, live shots, graphics, video teases, item-by-item times, which anchor reads which item, and so on—the works. Then get it copied and distributed to everyone who needs it, which usually means everyone in the building who's involved in bringing the program together and broadcasting it.

This can be a handwritten routine, followed by a formal typed routine. The idea is to get the basic information out as soon as possible so people will know what is expected of them. Television news is a team effort. Members must know the game plan.

You can take one of two basic approaches to details in your routine. You can indicate every last detail or you can be a little sketchy. It depends largely on your personality and the size of your operation. If you're in a small market, you won't be overwhelmed with fresh news and you and your anchors will constitute the writing staff. You and they can keep a lot of detail in your heads. In a large market, you'll have more news from day to day, your program will be more complicated and your staff larger. Many people will need detailed information and you'll have to give it to them on paper.

The same is true about timings—you can try to do it with precision, or you can play it loose. Most producers play it loose on their routines, rounding off every entry to the nearest five seconds. An alternative is to mix approximations with accurate timings as items are written and packages completed (creating a bit of a nightmare for all but arithmetic wizards.) You can try to make your routine timings add up to the exact time you have for the program—say 28 minutes 22 seconds—or you can shoot for around 28-15, believing that it's always easier to pad a program than to trim it.

Getting the Show Written

The writing crunch begins after you draw up your final routine. Until then, what you can write is limited because you cannot write the stories in a way that ties them together until you know their order in the program.

As suggested earlier, you can write some format material in the morning and other pages as the requisite information becomes available during the day. You may be able to write leads for canned features, prepare a national/international news segment (if you have one), write simple voice-overs and prepare a stack of liners for pad (to use in case the program runs short). The more you can do, the better. Even if you have to rewrite some material near deadline, as situations and events change, having done it once means you can revise a lot faster than if you were writing from scratch.

In addition, two ongoing tasks will demand some of your time—ordering supers and graphics. Some of these are used frequently enough that they are stored electronically and don't need to be made up every day. Supers for the mayor, the governor, your congressman, your senators, the police chief, your city's political gadflies and activists—scores of people who are in the news regularly—are kept ready to go. So, too, are headshots of these same people and many graphics that are used generically—the state seal, state capitol building, city hall, unemployment, interest rates, gas prices, and so on. Even though these are ready to go, you must mark them on scripts and tell graphics in advance that you are going to use them. Otherwise, they won't be there when you want them.

New supers are needed for all new stories. You get these—mostly the names of people, but also locations, dates, etc.—from reporters or the assignment desk. The easiest way is to type a list on a copy book, indicating by slug the story the supers belong to, and pass it along to graphics. Simply give graphics one of the carbon copies and keep the rest of the book as a "master" to which you add the next batch of supers. Pass supers along several times a day, rather than all at once on deadline. And insofar as possible, try to get all the supers for a story rather than ordering them piecemeal. If your station has adopted the use of underlines that characterize a person's position or explain why they are being interviewed, you need to make those a part of your list—"Likes Punk Rock," "Hates Punk Rock," "Witnessed Accident," "Swallowed 13 Goldfish" and so on. Remember this: Type the supers exactly as you want them; graphics' job is to do what you want, not to correct your mistakes.

You must also order the chroma key art that appears over the anchors' shoulders—the headshots, generics, etc. Some of these are "freeze frames" pulled directly from videotape. One might be a headshot of the defendant in a murder trial. Another might be a stolen painting pulled from file footage. Generics might come from freeze frames or might be created by your graphics people using computer graphics equipment. You should consult with them and make sure they understand what you want. This art often requires names or numbers; it's up to you order them correctly.

You also need to keep up with teases, especially those that require production work, as most do. The purpose of a tease is to tell viewers what's coming up in the hope that they'll be interested and stay with your program rather than switching to a rival. They also serve as buffers—or "bumpers"—between news content and commercial content.

At some stations, the rule is that you tease only what's going to lead the next segment. You might call this a concession to truth in advertising. Other stations have no restrictions. You can tease anything you want so long as it hasn't already been aired. You might call this a clever (albeit hardly respectful) way to keep an audience. If your station's policy is to tease anything rather than only the lead of the next segment, make it your policy use a term like "still ahead" when what you're teasing won't be next, and reserve "next" for what really will be next.

Some stations have it both ways by double-teasing. They do live teases (the anchor on camera) for items that really will lead the next segment, and use pre-produced videotaped teases (sometimes with a live VO or even an SOT) for items that are somewhere ahead in the program but not next. In a dual anchor show, one anchor may do the on-camera and the other the VO.

Pre-produced teases typically incorporate computer graphics with dubbed scenes from the story or feature being promoted by the tease. Your role as producer is to decide which stories to tease, write the necessary copy, and turn the rest of the task over to the graphics or videotape department, leaving it to them to pick the scenes unless you specify particular pictures or a sound bite. Sometimes you'll have an anchor pre-record the voice-over. Some stations even have a staff announcer to handle this chore.

The national/international segment (if you have one) can be put together relatively early, especially at stations in the western U.S., which can take advantage of the fact that Washington, D.C., where so much news is generated, is in the Eastern time zone.

Your video will come from the daily satellite news feeds your station gets from its network, or from independent syndicators such as CNN, Conus and Visnews, which stations buy in addition to network services.

By the time the feeds start in mid-afternoon, you'll know from reading the wires what stories you want to use in your program, and you'll know from feed lists and scripts sent by the syndicators whether you'll have video for those stories. Almost always, you will.

You or someone you designate can take notes on the feeds as they come in, and have a tape editor edit according to the notes. If you have adequate staff, an editorial person can work with the editor and write the stories after they are edited.

Or you can write voice-overs—even without ever seeing the feeds—and have an editor cut tape to go with your script. Just mark any key "hit" times on the script before giving it to the editor. If there are sound bites, you may work briefly with the editor to pick them and get times and outcues.

This is an extremely efficient approach. It works so long as your scripts do not call for many specific scenes and so long as you have a tape editor interested enough in the project to care that the program doesn't show the British prime minister while talking about the French president.

The resulting voice-overs and VOBs are very much "illustrated radio news" and represent a decline from the days when such news scripts were carefully written to match carefully edited news film, but it's the industry standard today and it works. If you keep the pieces short, deficiencies won't be obvious to many viewers.

As the day progresses, reporters will be finishing stories and working up packages or writing voice-overs. In many shops, you'll have a chance to discuss the stories with them—possibly even to the point of helping shape them and determine their angle. Later, you'll get copies of the reporters' scripts and their suggested lead-ins to packages. At a minimum, these lead-ins and voice-overs will have to be retyped on copy books. It's often necessary to do some rewriting as you retype, to maintain a flow the reporter could not have known you wanted. Don't drop basic information from the lead-in until you make sure it's in the script. Do try to work the point of the story into the lead-in to help your viewers and your reporter.

As you and any helpers (anchors, associate producer, writer) write during the day you can put slugs on the pages but not page numbers. Accurate numbering can't be done until you have a final rundown. You can, however, stack the copy books in anticipated order of use so it will be easier to find them and add page numbers when the time comes.

When you have the rundown and know page numbers, you can keep track of the script in a stack or lay it out on a table, inserting single sheets of colored paper for script pages yet to be written. Just write the page number and slug on the paper and pull it when the script is completed.

As the script is being written and assembled, many anchors will rehearse their portions and mark up the TelePrompTer copy—underlining words they want to stress, changing a word here and there, and so on. This is good; you want them to do everything that increases the chance of flawless delivery.

Many anchors write a lot of their copy. Some do it very well, others not at all well. Either way, that copy is your responsibility; as the producer you are also the master editor. You read *everything* before it goes into the program and out over the air.

If you're working with a veteran anchor, perhaps a highly-paid anchor, you should develop tactful ways of rejecting his or her copy. If it's simply inaccurate, you might ask the anchor to double-check the source copy saying something like, "I couldn't figure out whether they meant this (correct) or that (what the anchor wrote). Would you take another look for me, Jim? Thanks."

If it's a lead-in that doesn't work you might commiserate with the anchor for having been given a rotten fill-in. Sometimes you might take the blame yourself. Or you might apologize for not having made clear the way Story B plays out of Story A, and there-fore Story A needs a revised lead-in.

Until you've developed a good working relationship and, you hope, won the trust and respect of the anchor, don't just rewrite the copy and say nothing. Take it back and do your best to appear to be working with the anchor for the anchor's benefit.

Getting On and Off the Air, Smoothly

Once you get your program and yourself to the control room, you have two more responsibilities. You must watch over its production to make sure it goes smoothly and is editorially consistent and correct, and you must get it off the air smoothly and on time.

During the broadcast you listen to what is being said by the anchors and reporters and you keep an eye on the visual information that is put on the screen—identification supers, telephone numbers, charts and graphs, lists, and even sports scores.

In most shops, the sports anchor is more or less autonomous. You will seldom supervise or even look at the sports script. When the anchor says the Dodgers beat the Mets 3 to 2 and the scoreboard you put on the air has it the other way around, Mets 2, Dodgers 3, the fault will belong to someone on the sports staff or in graphics, where the scoreboard is made up. It won't be your fault. Nor will it be the viewer's fault. But the program is your program. You are the producer and it's your responsibility to your viewers to get things right, everything, and to make corrections as quickly as possible after a mistake is made.

In the case of the baseball score, you may be able to get to the sports anchor during a sound on tape or a commercial and point out the discrepancy. Usually, the anchor will know the correct score and can ad-lib a correction. If the anchor doesn't know, you or an assistant may have to call the newsroom or check the sports wire for the score. If sports is over by the time you get the score, a news anchor can make the correction—or, if your format calls for having all anchors, including sports and weather, on the set for final comment, chit-chat and goodnights, the sports anchor can do it then.

If you display a telephone number the police have set up as part of an investigation, or that a charity uses for people who want to donate food, the number must be right and the anchor script and the graphic must agree. If there's a mistake, you must move the same way you did with the baseball score—in fact, faster and more urgently because this is a more serious matter than a baseball score.

When it comes to identification supers, you would probably let a misspelling pass because correcting it verbally is extremely awkward. But if you have supered the victim with the suspect's name and the suspect with the victim's name in a crime story, you must to correct it at the soonest possible moment—there's no choice.

How could a mistake of this magnitude occur? Well, in many shops today it is the practice—or at least, it is permissible—to leave names out of sound-bite setups and rely solely on supers for identification. If the supers of the victim and the suspect are loaded in reverse order, and there's no clue in the lead-in and none in the super underline, mistakes are inevitable.

If the blunder is caught at all, it's likely to be caught by someone who worked on the story—the reporter, photographer or tape editor—and is watching in the newsroom or at home and calls you. (Yes, there are staffers who watch at home and who will call.) This kind of mistake is serious and you must either write correction copy for the anchor or, if the anchor is reliable, verbally provide the anchor with information for an ad lib.

Some mistakes you might let go. If witnesses to a dramatic police rescue are misidentified, you might ignore it for your audience but point out the mistake to the producer of the next program in case the story is used again. However, if one of the witnesses criticizes the cops' handling of the situation, you would do everything reasonably possible to correct a misidentification. You do not want to attribute the criticism to Mr. Trout when, in fact, it came from Mr. Carp. Trout could raise the devil with your station manager.

What should you do when you are in the control room and the program is on the air and the director asks you, "Which guy is this?" or "Is this Carp?" If you know the answer, tell the director so the super can be inserted. If you don't, it's a mistake to guess. No super is better than a misidentification. No super doesn't demand a correction, and no super doesn't hold the potential of a law suit. So, as is true in so many cases—when in doubt, leave it out.

In addition to these details, you are also responsible for getting the program off the air smoothly and on time. There are three ways to accomplish it.

The first is to prepare a perfect program, with exactly the same amount of material as you have time to fill, and then have it produced perfectly.

Your chances of doing this are slim. Tapes often are still being edited while you're on the air and no one will know for sure how long the tape runs until the editor finishes and times it. You've put the story down for 1-30 and it comes out 1-15. Your program is no longer perfect. Or, you have a live shot with your most skilled and experienced reporter interviewing the mayor. You put it down for 1-30 but for some reason on this day your reporter can't shut the mayor up; it runs 1-57 and your perfect program is no longer perfect.

Perfection is rare. Being close to perfection isn't. If you are good enough to be close most of the time, you still face the problem of finishing the program cleanly. You need to "backtime" and there are two methods, the easy way and the hard way.

The hard way works best. The easy way is most popular.

When you first routined the show, you figured it out so the times you allotted to the various segments added up to the air time available. If you had 28-30 of air time, you had, on paper, 28-30 of material—news, sports, weather, commercials. If everything subsequently was written and edited just as you planned, you would go into the control room ready to do that rare perfect show.

But that doesn't happen. You put the package on the fire down for 1-00 and when the editor finished it was 1-13, which you rounded off to 1-15 to make the addition easier. You put the mayor's budget down for 1-30 and it came to 1-45 (rounded off). You put the council members' reaction down for 60 seconds and the blabbermouths took 1-20 (rounded off). This means you're going to be 50 seconds over, unless other times come in shorter than planned. And that happens, too. You thought you'd need 25 seconds for the lead-in to a complicated medical feature, but you did it in 15. Now you're only 40 seconds over. A feature package on a kindergarten class comes in 20 seconds short. You're now only over by 20, and things are beginning to balance out.

Before you go on the air, you update your original rundown to include all the actual times that you have. Depending on your preference, you can use actual "actual times" like 1-17 and 2-09, or you can round them off to 1-15 and 2-10, etc., to make the backtiming math easier. (Just make sure your scripts have times accurate to the second.) If you are lucky, you'll have all the actual times before you go into the control room. If not, if something's still being written or edited, you backtime using the best estimate you can come up with (the original might be best, or maybe the reporter or tape editor has told you the piece will be long or short and you plug in a revised estimate).

Literally, you time backwards when you backtime. You calculate from the bottom and instead of adding you subtract. You start at the clock time you are supposed to be off the air and subtract from it. Let's say that time is 28 minutes and 30 seconds after 6 o'clock. You start backtiming from 28-30. The closing goodbye is going to take 15 seconds. Subtract that from 28-30 and you have 28-15. You jot that down on your copy of the routine. The closer runs 1-10. Subtract that from 28-15 and you have 27-05. You write that on the routine. Go through this process all the way to the very top of the show, the very first page. (You can save a lot of headaches by investing in a specialized pocket calculator that adds and subtracts in minutes and seconds.) Unless it's that rare perfect show, you'll either run out of material before you get to 6 o'clock straight up (6-00:00), meaning you are "short" or "under," or you'll backtime right past 6 p.m. to, say, 5-56:15 before you account for all of your material. This means you are "over" or "long," and that to use all your material you'd have to start the program at 5-56:15 p.m.

You'll find you are over more often than under. You have too much material and you're going to have to cut. What to cut? If you are way over, you'll pull something big out of the program right away. In the 5-56:15 example, you'd need to kill 3-45 of material. But if you're in pretty good shape—say within 30 seconds—you'll wait a bit to see how things are really going to play out. Being over half a minute on paper doesn't mean you'll be over that much in production. Things can happen. Things do happen. The anchor reads a particular story faster than normal. Cross-talk down for 30 seconds in the first segment actually runs 20. The TelePrompTer operator lets the liner that was Page 7 fall on the floor and you lose 15 seconds. Things can happen. Things do happen.

As you go along, you compare real time, the time on the clock in the control room, with the item-by-item backtimes you have written on your copy of the routine. At 6-04:50 on the clock you've just finished Page 8 and your rundown sheet says Page 8 should end at 6-04:35. That's not bad. You're 15 seconds over. The best thing to do right now is nothing; don't cut anything yet. But if you're a full minute over, and the item on Page 12 is marginal news at best, you might decide to drop it. You have to announce this decision to the director in timely manner, so the director can pass the word over the intercom system—usually during the next SOT or commercial. (At some stations, the producer talks directly to the anchor on a telephone from the control room to the set.)

The crew needs time to prepare. The graphics operator needs time to drop the headshot of the person in the story you are killing and get ready with the next graphic on the list. Otherwise, when you get to Page 13 and need a graphic on the economy you may instead get the headshot that was intended for Page 12, the killed page. The teleprompter operator needs to know. Otherwise, Page 12 will stay on the prompter and the anchor is apt to start reading it (the anchor can't just stop talking, waiting for Page 12 to go by and 13 to appear—and unless the anchor has been forewarned she will have no reason to dump Page 12 and go to her hand script for Page 13.) A kill can also mean videotape playback must have a tape ready earlier than expected, so they need to know. Your kill decisions must be announced in time, and you must be decisive about them.

Most days you'll know going in which stories are weak—minor developments in a running story, an unimportant appointment by the governor, a future item you could just as well save until tomorrow. When you have prospects for elimination in mind, you can make faster and better kill decisions when the time comes.

Another way to get off on time without killing too much news is to borrow time from the weather forecaster. Some are very cooperative, and if you ask them for 30 seconds they'll give it to you—just as you might agree one day next week to give them an extra 30 seconds because they want to talk a bit about the history of the harvest moon or the terrible winter of '37.

Other weather forecasters fiercely resist giving up time; they just won't do it. Still others may have the amount of time they are on the air written in their contracts, so that on any regular basis you can't take it and they can't give it. But these are the exceptions. Most forecasters are cooperative, and remarkably facile in cutting or stretching their forecasts on short notice.

So much for the easy way to get off the air smoothly, the piecemeal, ad-lib approach. Now for the hard way, which is the best way because if you do it right you assure yourself of two things—airing the news you really want to air, and ending the program exactly as you planned. The ending is important because viewers remember it: if the ending goes well, they're apt to remember a good program, but if it is obviously sloppy, they'll think the whole half hour was a mess.

To backtime the hard way, you create a segment toward the end of the program that can be shortened or lengthened, a "pad" segment made up of liners or short voice-overs. You plan on using this material and include it in your timing. A good place for this pad is right before the last commercial and soon after an SOT piece. That way, you make your adjustment late in the program so it will hold up, and you spread the word during the SOT piece. If you have that rare perfect show, all of it stays in. If not, you drop as needed. If you provide four or five stories adding up to 60 seconds you'll have plenty of flexibility if you run over and need to cut.

And if you are short—what then? You add copy to the pad segment. Go into the studio with extra stories you have identified by letters rather than numbers—Pad A, Pad B, Pad C, etc. If you need them, distribute them. You can even hand them out to the anchors and TelePrompTer operator before the program, to hold in reserve and use only when told to. Then you need only distribute in the control room if and when the time comes and tell the others on the intercom to "insert Pad B after Page 28."

When you backtime "the hard way" the term "backtime" takes on additional meanings. It will continue to mean the process of backtiming, a verb, but it will also have two meanings as a noun and one as an adjective. As a noun, it will refer to the portion of the program that runs from the end of the pad segment to the end of the program. This will be the "backtime" (also called the "backtime [adjective] package"). Also as a noun, it will mean the time on the clock that you must start the "backtime" in order to end the program exactly as you planned.

This is very important when you have planned the end of the program with precision to preserve a particular effect that will be lost if the material is cut or if extraneous material is added. Your program can be known for its endings as well as its beginnings, so treat the last segment with care.

Finally, you have two other ways to stretch a program and finish on time when you get close to the end and still running significantly short. One is so artificial that viewers notice. You run credits—the names of the people who work on the program—slowly and in great detail. You can run them over music. You can run them over credits footage, stock scenes of your city or scenes cut from one of that evening's stories. Credits once a week, on purpose to publicly recognize the members of your team, is fine. It's a good morale booster. That's why graphics always has credits prepared and ready to go. But if you find yourself using credits several times a week to get off the air on time, it may mean you need a new team, or the team needs a new producer.

A second last-ditch way to fill is to keep your anchors on the set and let them stretch their normal "goodnight, see you tomorrow" for the needed time. Viewers tend to notice this, too, because it isn't what they are accustomed to.

Television news is a business, or part of the larger business of television broadcasting. You don't need to be reminded that the station's income (and yours) comes from commercials. Therefore, you don't adjust the timing of your show by killing a commercial, or the last few seconds of one. Don't do anything that might cause a commercial to be misrolled or upcut. The advertiser will demand and get a "make-good"—that is, the station will run the commercial again, properly, without cost to the advertiser. That squanders forever 30 seconds or a minute of revenue-producing time that might have been sold to another advertiser.

Your station manager will not say "thank you" for losing revenue. If you do it often, what the station manager will say to you, through the news director, is "goodbye."

What a Routine (Rundown) Looks Like

The routine—which serves as the road map of a program—can also be called a rundown, long-sheet or line-up. The amount of information you need to put in it depends largely on two factors: how large your station is—or, at least, how large and spread out its production facilities are—and the degree of detail required by ordinary prudence and, if you have them, union considerations.

At network owned and operated stations and in top ten markets, you're apt to have several studios for news programs. Some may be devoted to major shows, others to cut-ins and overnight casts, and still others to network originations. You're also apt to have videotape playback facilities in several locations, sometimes even on different floors. You could have one kind of graphics capability for one studio and another for another studio. Production crews may rotate frequently, so that you depend on one cast of characters one day and another group the next. They never get to settle in and you never get to really know them. Under these circumstances, it's important to have enough detail in your routine to minimize confusion and errors.

In small and medium markets, you usually work with the same people day after day in the same studio with the same facilities. They know you, you know them, and all of you know what has to be done and how to do it. Under these circumstances, routines can be much less detailed. Your routine could be as simple as the sample that follows. Assume your anchors are Tom and Becky. Your notations may need no more than the Page Number, the studio talent doing the story, the slug of the story, any graphic that may be used, the type of story or video, and the time allotted. In this case, the times are rounded off to simplify addition—zero, one or two seconds become no seconds and three, four or five seconds become five seconds. This usually balances out. Make sure, of course, that times on scripts are exact.

PAGE	TALENT	ITEM	GRAPHIC	VIDEO	AUDIO	TIME
11	T/B	TRIAL	—	T/B/VTR	T/B/SOT	1-45
12	T	JUDGE	JONES	T		15
13	B	COURTS	SCALES	B/VTR	B/SOT	2-00
14	B/T	TEASE #2	—	B/T/VTR	B/T/TVO	15

15			COMMERCIAL BREAK #2		SOT	2-00

On Page 11 above, Tom and Becky will split the introduction, with Tom going first. No graphic will be used before a reporter pack-age called Trial. The whole business, lead-ins and SOT, is slotted for 1-45. Next, Page 12, Tom will read a liner about the appointment of Jones as a state district judge, backed by a headshot of Jones. That's down for 15 seconds. Then, Page 14, Becky will intro a reporter's package about the courts with the scales of justice over her shoulder. The intro and the package are down for 2-00. Next comes the program's second tease, with Becky live on camera promoing one story and Tom doing a V/O behind a videotape snippet from a second story. Then comes the program's second commercial break, 2-00 minutes. A slightly more complicated routine might look like this:

PAGE	ITEM	TIME	CUME TIME	GRAPHIC	VIDEO	AUDIO
11	TRIAL LEDE 1	05	(6-00—6-05)	—	TOM	TOM
12	TRIAL LEDE 2	10	(6-05—6-15)	—	BECKY	BECKY
13	TRIAL	1-30	(6-15—7-45)	—	VTR	SOT
14	JUDGE	15	(7-45—8-00)	JONES	TOM	TOM
15	INTRO COURTS	15	(8-00—8-15)	SCALES	BECKY	BECKY
16	COURTS	1-45	(8-15—10-00)	—	VTR	SOT
17	WATER TEASE	05	(10-00—10-05)	—	BECKY	BECKY
18	BANK TEASE	10	(10-05—10-15)	—	VTR	TOM

COMMERCIAL BREAK #2	SOT	2-00

Here, when Tom and Becky share a story it is treated as two different items with two page numbers. A running or cumulative time has been added, showing at what point in the program any particular item should start and when it should end.

A Note on Supers

It's hardly unknown for a broadcast journalist to have tried to excuse a particular professional weakness—poor spelling—by citing the criticism of some print journalists that broadcasters don't need to know how to spell anyway, because they never ave to do it. The print critic may have said "those stupid broadcasters," but so what? The implication of the criticism, of course, is that television attracts the bottom of the class, the people who couldn't make the grade in print. Well, neither part of that equation is true. Television news attracts top people and yes, they do need to know how to spell. Especially when it comes to supers, which flash on the screen and call attention to themselves—making mistakes much more obvious than those buried deep in a column of newspaper text.

Names are crucial. Get them right. Reporters should give them to you typed if they're in the newsroom. If it's by telephone, you should question every name—even, for example, plain Jane. Me Tarzan, you Jane. Oh—you not Jane? You Jayne! John. Jon. Hillary. Hilary. Andersen. Anderson. And so on. Names are important to their owners, and if a lot of people are able to run around town complaining Channel 7 didn't get my name right, Channel 7 may develop a credibility problem. You can have legal problems, too, when a misspelling results in misidentification—as when you super rape suspect Carl Haines as Karl Haynes, who happens to be your superintendant of schools. Superintendent? Defendent? Defendant? Prosecutor? Prosecuter? Alter boy? Altar boy? Keep a dictionary handy.

Underlines are also important. Get those spellings right, just because mistakes are so obvious. But pay particular attention to abbreviations, which come up often because space is so limited. The following might be clear, but it wouldn't look good, in Chicago or anywhere else: "Ill. Public Health Ass."

Underlines that characterize a person's position on an issue are very helpful to viewers, but only if you get them right. If the edited sound bite says:

> *"This could cost the city several hundred jobs. We can't afford that loss."*

an underline like "Opposes Plan" would seem to be in order. But maybe the bite was edited in haste, as often happens. The possible loss of jobs may well be a necessary part of the story, and there may be nothing whatever wrong with the selection of that bite. But context could have been lost under deadline pressure. The person may have said:

"I'm worried about something that we haven't really addressed yet. This could cost the city several hundred jobs. We can't afford that loss. So until we have a plan to deal with that possibility, I'm on the fence."

In that case, the underline "Opposes Plan" would be wrong. The person who made the comment is on the fence and not in opposition, and would have every right to be upset. And viewers could have been inadvertently but seriously misled if the person were a city councilman holding the swing vote on the question. Suddenly, accidentally, you are telling viewers it's all over but the formal voting.

Underlines that explain an individual's connection with the story, such as "Witnessed Collision" or "Rescued His Grandmother" seldom cause problems, but those that characterize need special attention. Be sure you give it.

A Note on Graphics

In television news, graphics serve two basic purposes. One is to dress up the production, to make a visual medium visual. The other is to reinforce or expand on information being provided verbally, either by the anchorperson over whose shoulder the graphic appears or by a reporter in a package.

As a producer, you want your program to look as good as it possibly can so you're going to make use of graphics. No question about that. As a journalist, you want viewers to understand what you are telling them, so you'll use graphics for that reason, too.

If two corporations merge, a graphic of their corporate logos side by side is helpful. The viewer will know the anchor is reporting something about those two companies. If one logo can be made to blend into another, merger will be suggested. Or the word "Merging" might be added. If a famous actress dies, it helps to have her picture and it's even better to add her name (correctly spelled); if you add dates, "1922-1994," her death will be suggested. If inflation is up by a tenth of a percent, a simple graphic with an arrow or chart, the word "Inflation" and $\frac{1}{10}\%$ will be fine. In fact, except for the time period, it tells the whole story. If the median price of a house in your community rises three-fourths of a percent over a year, a graphic combining a house with an arrow pointing up, a dollar sign and $\frac{3}{4}\%$ will work well. If you can work in the name of your town and dates to mark the period, the graphic will tell the whole story. It will also be a crowded graphic, perhaps too much so.

So you should seek the happy combination that reminds the viewer of the topic and adds or reinforces information without getting so busy that the viewer must study it to understand, or decide to ignore it entirely. You need to put simplicity and clarity first. Start with the basics and add elements only insofar as they contribute to understanding without requiring viewers to scrutinize and interpret.

Keep in mind always that your graphics can have a powerful impact on viewers, especially if they are unusual. As an example, take the 1993 story about reports of soda drinkers finding syringes in cans of Pepsi Cola. You could use just the Pepsi corporate logo, to make clear the story being read is about the Pepsi Cola company. A Pepsi can would be better, because that narrows the subject from the very diverse multi-national company to the soft drink. You could elaborate by displaying a needle and syringe overlaid on a Pepsi can at a rakish angle. Or further, you might add a word or two: "10 Cities" or even "Now 10 Cities." Which of these graphics is best? No question the last is most powerful. But is it too powerful? Would it overwhelm a carefully written script, to the point that viewers might not really notice the anchor is talking about "reports" and "claims" rather than verified instances of product tampering? It very well might, and if it did your use of the graphic would be a disservice to Pepsi Cola and your viewers. You need to be able to step back and consider how you as a viewer in your living room would react to a graphic, rather than think only in terms of how complete and dramatic you can make it as a producer.

How to be a Journalist as Well as a Producer

As a news program producer you are also an editor, putting out your own televised newspaper. The news content of your program is smaller than that of a newspaper, but your influence on the program is much greater than a newspaper editor's on his paper. You will decide what gets on the air and what doesn't. You will decide the play and the time allotted to stories. You may coach and advise reporters, some before they go out on stories, some while they're on the scene, and some while they're back in the shop writing scripts. And far more than any newspaper editor, you'll be intimately involved in the writing—the selection and emphasis of information. In fact, in smaller markets you may even do most of the writing yourself, and you'll read almost everything everyone else has written before it goes on the air. No editor ever gets that close to his or her paper. You'll have plenty of opportunity as a producer to be a journalist. How well you capitalize is entirely up to you. It is going to depend in major degree on how you view yourself—as a whiz kid of video images and frenetic pacing, or as a journalist who happens to be working in television? The answer you choose now will go a long way towards determining which you really are, or turn out to be.

If it's a journalist you want to be, make it a point to converse and consult with your reporters and the assignment desk when you have a chance—especially after your program. Ask what they thought of the play and emphasis? What do they think could be done next with a particular story? Does one story suggest a similar line of inquiry in another area? Let the desk and reporters know you genuinely care about their work, about informing the public, and being a constructive force in the community.

If you have story ideas of your own, propose them. Order them, if it's in your power. Play reporter, even if you're never in the field. But try just as hard to help your colleagues come up with their own ideas. Even when you plant the seed and cultivate it, let them feel the idea is theirs rather than yours. Your harvest is bound to be more bountiful.

Summary of What to Do

1. Wake up, dress, etc. Read the morning paper or papers and watch your station's cut-ins or morning news program. If you think of something you want covered or checked out, call the assignment desk. Just be diplomatic.

2. Get to work on time.

3. Check the assignment desk to find out what's being covered, how it's going, what's coming up.

4. Check program logs (or equivalent) for on and off times, commercial breaks, etc., and calculate your air time.

5. Work out a preliminary routine, on a pad or in your head (a pad's better because writing it down requires more attention and thought).

6. Attend the morning meeting. Listen carefully. Ask questions to clarify. Try to have suggestions on how stories on the list will be covered and on additional stories.

7. Type as much format material as possible.

8. Begin your supers list. If personnel are on hand to make supers, give them your first list.

9. Begin your graphics list—what you know you'll want and some that you think you might want. Order those you know you'll want.

10. Lunch—in station or out.

11. If possible, write more format material.

12. Start writing liners, pad, anything you might possibly use. If you have to rewrite anything for time, emphasis or flow later in the day, that's fine because having written it once you are ahead.

13. Keep after supers and graphics, and stay in touch with the assignment editor.

14. Draw up a routine as complete and close to final as you can and take it to the afternoon meeting.

15. Attend the afternoon meeting. Be sharp. Think. Listen.

16. Draw up your final routine, or a semi-final routine that's a potential final. Distribute as needed, because it's about time everyone on your team had something in writing as a guide to performing or scheduling their work.

17. Begin writing like crazy, and/or get others to do so or to help you, while also keeping in touch with reporters, the desk, tape editing, graphics, etc.

18. Read and edit script, keeping in mind that as the producer you are responsible for every word— every word. Begin stacking pages in order or laying them out on a table in order, even though you won't write numbers on the pages until you have a truly final routine.

19. If you're going to use national and international news, check on satellite feeds from your network or syndicators. Prepare your pieces or segment as quickly as possible.

20. Touch base with persons involved in any remotes that are planned. It may not be up to you to ride herd on these setups, but the last thing you want is an unpleasant surprise 10 minutes before air.

21. Keep updating information on your routine as package and story timings become available, and revise the routine if necessary. Your goal is to go into the control room with the most accurate routine possible.

22. Assemble the script and number the pages once you feel pretty certain you won't have to change the numbers.

23. Rip scripts ("break books") and distribute copies.

24. Make a "routine" check of editing and graphics so you'll be forewarned of impending problems.

25. Enter the control room as the coolest and most collected person in the building. Smile.

26. Check on the status of remotes, if any. Also check editing or graphics or anywhere you know there to have been a budding problem.

27. Watch the program like a hawk, especially for accuracy. Were the supers OK? Did charts match script? Make corrections where necessary and possible.

28. Watch what your crew is doing. If someone heads off a mistake with a nice catch or saves the day with a spectacular recovery, thank him or her, on the spot if possible, or during the next commercial, if that person is in the control room. Do it so others hear you, as a kind of cheerleading. If it's someone outside the control room, seek the per-

son out after the program and say how much you appreciated the help.

29. If you detect a persistent problem in procedure, try to take care of it right after the program when what happened is fresh in everyone's mind.

30. Drop by the newsroom to check with reporters and the assignment desk on the next day. Express your appreciation for jobs well done—to reporters, photographers, tape editors, writers.

31. Remember that the golden words are "Please" and "Thank You." Use them. Mean them.

32. Remember, you are the producer and you are responsible for *everything* in the program—responsible to your station, your bosses and your audience. Never forget it!

Glossary

AC Adapter: See transformer.

Actuality: A radio term meaning the recorded voice of a newsmaker or the sound of the event, usually incorporated in a "spot" but sometimes used alone with lead-in by the anchor. In television, an actuality is a "sound bite," "bite" or "NAT SOT" (natural sound on tape).

AFTRA: An acronym for American Federation of Television and Radio Artists, a nearly all-inclusive union for people who perform on network and major market television (and radio)—actors, dancers, singers, jugglers, talk show hosts, reporters, anchors.

Ambient Light: See available light.

Ambient Sound (Audio): See natural sound.

Ambush Interview: An interview in which the subject is caught by surprise, often after declining formal requests for interviews. The news crew may lie in wait for the subject or burst unannounced into the subject's office. This style was made famous but not originated by "60 Minutes."

Anchor: The person in the radio or television studio who delivers the news and introduces stories from field reporters. Many television news programs use dual anchors, typically a man

254 | Professional's TV News Handbook

and a woman. The terms "sports anchor" and even "weather anchor" are also used.

Angle: Editorially, the approach taken by a reporter to a story, the way the reporter "plays" the story.

Aperture: The adjustable opening inside a lens that controls the amount of light passing through the lens to the pickup tubes or film in the body of a camera.

A-roll/B-roll: This is editing with two source tapes rather than one. The two tapes are fed through a switcher or a controller with a built-in switcher, and edits are made by dissolving or wiping from one to the other, rather than by making a direct cut (as in "cuts only" editing with a single source machine). In the same way, other effects as well as writing and graphics may be introduced to the package tape. Some stations also do VOBs with what are called A and B rolls, putting the voice-over material on the A roll and the sound bite on the B. The VO tape is edited with ample pad and the sound bite is rolled off the script, reducing the chance of upcutting.

ASCAP: An acronym for American Society of Composers, Authors and Publishers; with BMI, it is one of the two major music-licensing organizations.

Aspect Ratio: The ratio of picture width to picture height, which in television is 4 to 3—four units wide by three high.

Assemble Editing: As opposed to insert editing, assemble editing erases control track on the editing tape and lays down new track, with the result that you cannot change existing sound while preserving existing picture, and vice versa. You can't edit a package in assemble edit.

Assignment Editor: The person who determines which news and features will be covered and assigns reporters and photographers to the coverage. Assignment editors can have more influence than anyone in the newsroom in shaping a station's news product, or they can be no more important than a news clerk, all depending on their inclinations, on how much autonomy the news director gives them, and the extent to which they are empowered to direct the way reporters cover individual stories.

Audio: Sound.

Audio Mixer: An electronic device for controlling audio. In the studio, the mixer allows its operator to set levels for a variety of audio sources and choose which signal or combination of signals to put on the air. In the editing bay, a mixer allows the editor to set levels, choose sources and combine two or more sound sources into one "mixed" signal. In the field, portable mixers make it possible to monitor and control the levels of several microphones as they are fed into a recorder.

Audio Perspective (Presence): The impression that the sound a viewer hears is distant or nearby, in keeping with the apparent proximity of the video subject to the camera.

Audio Track: The portion of a videotape on which sound is recorded. Most equipment provides for two "channels" or tracks of audio on a tape, usually along the lower edge. Sony Beta provides up to four audio tracks.

Available Light: The light at the scene of a shoot, whether indoors or outdoors, that is "available" to the photographer without adding light.

Backlight: Light behind the subject. Backlight is a standard part of studio lighting setups, usually mounted so it shines down at a 45-degree angle between the anchor and the background, and makes the anchor stand out from the background of the set. Ambient backlight in the field can be troublesome when it is stronger than the light on the subject—for example, when an interview subject is at a desk in front of an uncurtained window on a bright summer day.

Backtime: The clock time or real time at which you intend to start the "backtime package."

Backtime Package: Material at the end of a program, more or less the last segment, that you want to use intact in order to end the program neatly and with a particular, planned feeling. The idea is to make cuts or additions before reaching the backtime package.

Backtiming: The process of timing a news program item by item, backwards from the end to the beginning. This provides a comparison of the program's timetable on paper with what is actually happening as the program is being broadcast, so that adjustments can be made to end the program smoothly and on time.

Barn Doors: Hinged flaps on the perimeter of a studio or portable television light which can be adjusted to control the spread of the light. Usually there are four flaps per light head.

Bars: See color bars.

Beat: A reporter's area of specialization: police beat, city hall beat, financial beat, etc. A reporter or station scores a "beat" by getting a story first. Also, a deliberate pause in narration to create an effect or emphasize natural sound or music.

Beta: The half-inch video format developed and manufactured by Sony.

Billboard: A short announcement—in audio, video or both—telling what is coming up on a news program or, sometimes, acknowledging a sponsor.

Bite: Same as sound bite.

Black: A video source with sync signal but no picture. Video switchers have controls to turn "black" into any color for use as a background for text and other graphics. Also the darkest tone in the gray scale.

Black Balance: Adjustment of a camera's black (pedestal) level.

Blacking: Recording uninterrupted control track to prepare a tape for insert editing. This wipes out any material already on the tape.

BMI: Broadcast Music Incorporated, with ASCAP, one of the two major music-licensing organizations.

Boom: A device for holding a microphone near a speaker but out of sight; usually made of telescoping metal tubing. Also used to refer to the microphone attached to the boom—a "boom" or "boom mic."

Bridge: A reporter or anchor's narration between two sound bites.

Briefs: Short news stories, but not as short as headlines. They may average around 10 seconds in radio and a little longer in television news. Some TV news producers regularly include a package of four or five briefs with videotape in their shows.

Bulk Eraser: A device for erasing all the material recorded on an audio cassette or video cassette without running the tape through a recorder across an erase head. The bulk eraser creates a magnetic field strong enough to penetrate plastic cassettes and erase the tape in 30 seconds to a minute. Place the cassette on its side and move it around on the surface of the bulk eraser for about 30 seconds. Then turn the cassette over and manipulate it the same way to erase the other half of the tape.

Bumper: A brief item between the end of a news segment and a commercial, used to advertise what is coming up in the program and to clearly distinguish news material from commercials. Most bumpers are pre-taped on videotape.

Bump Up: To re-record a videotape to a larger format, such as from half-inch to three-quarter.

Bus: A row of buttons on a switcher, often called "video bus." Also, "effects bus," the bank of buttons for dissolves, wipes, keys, etc.

Cans: Headphones worn by the director and studio crew through which the director communicates and commands. "Split cans" provide two audio systems—for example, production audio (the director, etc). in one ear, and program audio in the other.

Cardioid Microphone: A directional or unidirectional microphone with a more-or-less heart-shaped pickup pattern, as compared with the spherical pickup pattern of an omnidirectional mic. Cardioid mics must be pointed at the wanted sound source. Because their pickup pattern is smaller than an omnidirectional mic's, they pickup less unwanted background noise.

Character Generator: An electronic machine for creating text, primarily lower-third supers ("CGs") to identify people, places, etc. on the television screen.

Chroma: The purity of color. Also short for chroma key.

Chroma Key: A method for combining the image from one video source with the image from another video source so they look like one. In news, "to key" means putting a still or graphic over the shoulder of an anchor, or running videotape or the shot from a live remote over the anchor's shoulder.

Chyron: A brand name of a character generator/graphics machine.

Close: The close can refer to the final portion of a script but usually it means the final picture or picture sequence. The close, whether picture or script, should be as strong as possible. Many reporters and photographers begin looking for a close as soon as they start coverage.

Closer: The closing item in a program, often chosen for that spot because it is light, amusing, pretty, whimsical, ironic, etc.

Close-Up: A shot in which a single object fills all or most of the frame; close-up of a face, close-up of the nose on the face, etc.

Color Bars: An electronically-generated test signal used as a standard for adjusting color in television cameras and monitors. Cameras and switchers generate "bars" as a series of six vertical bands of color. From the left, they are yellow, cyan (a hue between blue and green), green, magenta, red and blue.

Condenser Microphone: See electret condenser microphone.

Connectors: Fittings used at the ends of audio or video cables to connect them to terminals or other cables. One connector, the "male," fits into the other, the "female." Varieties in audio are mini (also called Sony), phono (also RCA), phone (also quarter-inch) and XLR (also Canon). In video they are BNC, UHF and RF.

Control Room: The room, effectively a command post, from which the director and other technicians put a program on the air (or commit it to tape). It's usually adjacent to the studio, often separated by a glass panel so the director can see what people in the studio are doing.

Control Track: Electronic pulses on videotape, analogous in some ways to sprocket holes in film. Videotape machines count control track pulses to play tape at the right speed and to synchronize signals in editing. Pulses can be put on the tape by video cameras and switchers.

Copy: News text for a newspaper or broadcast. Part of a news program script. "Hard copy" refers to the first sheet of a multisheet copybook or multi-sheet wire machine paper; it's of heavier stock and easier to read and handle than the copies. "Hand copy" is an anchor's paper script.

Countdown: Signals given either by hand or voice to cue the talent, or count the talent into a videotape, out of a voice-over, or out of a program.

Countdown Leader: See leader.

Cover: Footage used to "cover" narration or sound bites, it can be generic file footage rather than footage shot for a particular story. Similar to but less specific than "layover" footage, which is usually shot specifically for the story being covered.

Crawl: Words that move horizontally across the screen, usually at the bottom. Used, for example, for weather bulletins while allowing viewers to continue to watch the program on the air.

Cross Fade: Simultaneously bringing in a new audio source while fading another out. In video, it's a dissolve.

Crosstalk: Undesired leakage of one signal into another, creating "noise" which undermines clarity. Crosstalk can be audio or video. Also, a live, on-air Q & A discussion between an anchor and a field reporter about the reporter's story. The reporter can be on remote or in the studio.

Cue: To give verbal or hand signals to anchors, telling them when to start something and when to stop. Outcues, the final words of an audio track, are written to prompt audio-board operators to switch audio sources. Videotapes are "cued" to be ready to play.

Cume Time: The minutes and seconds of air time used to reach a particular point in the program, the "accumulated" time of all the program elements up to this point. Cume time or "running time" is an essential part of most news program routines.

Cut: In editing script or a program, to cut is to shorten. In editing videotape, to cut is to switch from one scene to another directly, without a dissolve, wipe or other effect; it can also mean to shorten a tape. Cutting or direct cutting is the preferred picture editing technique. Cut also means to stop, or sometimes to pause.

Cutaway: A cutaway is a scene that cuts away from the basic scene. Most commonly refers to a shot of a reporter listening to an interviewee, or an audience listening to a speaker, inserted so that the audio can be edited without a jump cut.

Cut-In: In videotape or film editing, an insert scene. In programming, the term usually refers to the five-minute news programs local stations broadcast when they cut into the network morning news programs at 25 minutes past the hour.

Daybook: A list of the day's scheduled news events—meetings, news conferences, speeches, trials, etc.

Depth of Field: In photography, the area between the closest and the most distant objects in focus. It can be measured but seldom is. Depth is a function of the focal length of a lens and available light. The smaller the lens opening, the greater the depth of field (and the more light needed). For most work, photographers want almost everything in focus, which requires deep depth of field.

DGA: Directors Guild of America, a union for directors, assistant directors and floor managers.

Directional Microphone: See cardioid microphone. Confusingly, also called unidirectional microphone.

Director: The person who brings together all the technical elements of a program; the one who is in charge and gives the commands in the control room.

Dissolve: Video signals "dissolve" when one fades away while another replaces it. A studio and theatrical technique increasingly used in news editing for a softer effect than using cutaways, or to disguise jump cuts and lack of cutaways. The time it takes to dissolve can be controlled to produce a variety of effects.

Dolly: A platform or frame with wheels or casters on which a studio camera's tripod or pedestal is mounted, so the camera may move around smoothly. Also, any wheeled device used in the field so a cameraman can be pushed or pulled while shooting. Also used as a verb, "to dolly," and to describe a "dolly shot" in which the camera is moving on a dolly, and as a studio command for moving toward or away from the talent, "dolly in" or "dolly out."

Dope Sheet: Usually a photographer's general description and/or notes on what he or she shot. Sometimes an editor's scene-by-scene breakdown of an edited newstape (also called "shot list" or "spotsheet").

Dropout: The temporary loss of picture signal or sound level.

Dry Run: A studio rehearsal.

Dub: A copy of an audio or videotape, or to make a copy.

Dump Out: To leave a videotape before it is finished, an emergency measure taken when a program is running too long.

Dynamic Microphone: A microphone with a permanent magnet and coil that turn sound waves into electrical impulses. Generally heavier and sturdier than battery-operated electret condenser mics.

Echo Effect: When a reporter's lead-in to an actuality or sound bite uses practically the same words as the start of the bite, producing an undesirable "echo." Also used when an anchor's lead-in echoes the start of a reporter's package.

Electret Condenser Microphone: A battery-operated microphone using a condenser rather than a magnet and coil to turn sound waves into electrical impulses. Most small, clip-on mics are electrets.

End Cue: Same as outcue.

Equalizer: Electronic device allowing the manipulation of audio signals, often used to "clean up" deficient audio.

Erase Heads: Magnetic heads that remove whatever signal may be on a videotape just before new material is recorded on the tape. It is better to "black" a tape before re-using it than to rely exclusively on erase heads. A "flying erase head" makes insert editing possible.

Establisher: The opening shot in a news story, or the first shot in a sequence within a story, that establishes what's being seen and orients the viewer as to location, principal persons, time period, etc.

Eyewash: See wallpaper.

Fade: To gradually increase or decrease a video or audio signal; to fade up from black, fade down to black, fade up from silence or low volume, or fade down to background volume or silence.

Fader: A control bar or handle on a video switcher for fading video up or down.

Feed: An incoming signal, usually referring to news stories from a station's network or syndicated supplier, or from a station's live remote unit, usually fed via satellite or microwave.

Feedback: When an audio or video signal feeds into itself as the result of a technical mistake or equipment malfunction, the result is feedback—a random pattern in video and a shriek or whine in audio. Audio feedback can be created intentionally to produce an echo or reverberation.

Field Producer: The person in charge of producing material outside the studio. In news, field producers may develop stories, do the reporting, oversee the shooting and editing, and write the script for a correspondent, anchor or narrator.

Field Production: Production outside the studio. In news, shooting the story.

Fill, Fill Light: Light used to eliminate shadows, primarily on faces. Usually artificial light bounced or reflected rather than shined directly on the subject. Sunlight can be used as fill by reflecting it from a large sheet of white pasteboard.

Filler: Second- or third-rank news items written to pad out a program that otherwise might run short, or to have on hand in case the program unexpectedly runs short. Also called pad.

Filter: An electronic device used to improve the legibility of audio signals by eliminating undesired frequencies that are the source of the problem. Also, a piece of glass or plastic placed in front of a lens to correct the color temperature of incoming light. Most video cameras have a built-in filter wheel providing filters for the most commonly encountered light problems.

Flash: A news bulletin.

Flash Frame: Material from a previous recording that remains on a tape when a new edit misses by a frame or two. It "flashes" so briefly the viewer sees something but doesn't know what.

Fluff: A mistake made by an anchor or reporter reading copy. Also a light, newsless news item.

Follow Focus: To change focus in order to keep a moving subject in forcus, to prevent it from getting out of the depth of field. The ability to "follow focus" can be important in covering fast-moving events, such as a football game, or staying relatively tight on a reporter doing a long, walking standupper towards or away from the camera.

Format: A word with many uses in broadcasting. It can refer to the structure of a radio or television news program—the length, number of commercial breaks, time between commercials, etc., or to material regularly used in the program, such as the opening video, the listing of headlines, the billboards, etc. It also refers to a type of program—Q & A format, dual-anchor format. It is used to describe the various ENG systems—U-Matic, Betamax, VHS and Super-8 formats, etc.

Frame: A single frame of picture. Also, the way a shot is framed.

Frame Storer: A digital device which holds still shots, freeze-frames and graphics in readiness for airing. They can be called up instantly by address number, and used over and over again.

Freeze Frame: A single frame of picture electronically "frozen" so it can be used as a still, either over an anchor's shoulder or full screen. Freeze frames can be stored on tape or video disk. Many news rooms routinely collect freeze frames, particularly head shots, from each day's coverage to have them available for future stories involving the same people or subject.

Fresnel: A thick glass lens with concentric rings or ridges to diffuse the light from studio or field lights.

Frezzi: Specifically refers to a hand-held, battery-powered light made by the Frezzolini company, but also a fairly generic term for such a light. "Sun Gun" is used similarly.

From the Top: To do something from the very beginning, often to start all over after a botched pre-taping or rehearsal.

Full Screen: Using the entire television screen.

Futures, Futures File: Information and reminders about stories to be covered in the future, usually kept in chronological order— anything from a simple list of scheduled events and possible follow-ups to pages of material about a single story.

Gaffer: The member of a studio or field crew who is in charge of lighting. Also called an electrician.

Gaffer's Tape: Special adhesive tape used by gaffers to temporarily hold light heads and wires in place on furniture, walls, etc., or to cover wires strung across the floor so people won't trip over them. Most gaffer's tape is gray and looks like duct tape, but it holds more firmly, is stronger and contains no metal fibers.

Gain: The signal amplification (or apparent loudness or brightness) of audio and video signals. In video, raising the gain makes it possible to take pictures in lower than optimal light (at the cost of some graininess and loss of definition).

Gang Bang: An impromptu and indecorous interview or news conference involving large numbers of reporters and photographers from all media, often characterized by shouting and shoving.

Gel: A sheet of colored gelatin or plastic, placed in front of a studio or portable light to change its color and alter the color of the scene accordingly.

Generation: Each dub or copy away from the original videotape is a "generation." A package created from field tapes is second generation videotape, although sometimes it is inconsistently referred to as the first generation of the story, or of a one-hour documentary, or a commercial. Video quality is somewhat reduced with each dub.

Gopher, Go-fer: A person whose job is to go get things.

Happy Talk: Exchange of pleasantries between anchors or anchors and reporters, often used as a transition from, for example, news to sports. Defended by some as a way to humanize news-people, criticized by others as wasting valuable air time on inanities.

Hard Copy: See copy.

Head: The beginning of a tape or package.

Headlines: A rundown of the major news or features (most commonly three)in a news program, announced by anchors at the beginning of the program often as short voice-overs with scenes from the stories.

Head Room: Usually refers to the space between an anchor or subject's head and the top of the television screen. The term also refers to the space between any object, with or without a head, and the top of the screen.

Hit: A point or points at which script and scenes in a videotape coincide by design; as the anchor says "the secretary of state" the viewer sees the secretary of state.

Hot: Videotape or film that is overexposed is "hot."

IATSE: International Association of Theatrical and Stage Employees, a technical and craft union found in broadcasting and elsewhere.

IBEW: International Brotherhood of Electrical Workers, similar to IATSE.

IFB: Interrupted Feedback, an audio system allowing an anchor or remote reporter (or remote interview guest) to hear program audio and the director's instructions through an earpiece.

Incue: The words in a speech, interview, song, etc., on which a sound bite begins; the pickup point.

Insert: A close-up shot of the preceding scene.

Insert Editing: Editing videotape without erasing control track on the package tape, so that video can be re-edited while the audio remains unchanged, or vice versa. Cutaways or layover would be impossible without insert editing.

Intercom: An audio system enabling the director and members of a studio crew to talk with each other. Each person wears a headset with a microphone.

Intercut: A series of sound bites edited so as to create an apparent "debate" between opponents on an issue or in an election. Intercutting is regarded as an unethical practice by some journalists, unless the bites come from a real debate between the individuals.

Intro: See lead-in.

Iris: The adjustable mechanism which increases or decreases the aperture of a lens, thereby controlling the amount of light that enters a camera.

Item: See slug.

Jump Cut: A jarring edit, usually in interviews, that should have been covered with a cutaway. An interviewee may have a cigarette dangling from the mouth in the first cut, but it miraculously vanishes in the second cut to which it is directly butted; or a person may go from a smiley face to a frown, or from looking right to looking left, without benefit of intervening movement.

Kelvin: A scale used to measure the color temperature of light, after physicist and mathematician William Thompson Kelvin.

Keying: See chroma key.

Key Light: The principal source of light in a lighting setup.

Kicker: Similar to closer, the term is more common in radio than television.

Lavaliere: A small, unobtrusive microphone that is usually clipped to the clothes of the person using it. Lavalieres are almost always used by anchors and in studio and field interviews. Most "lavs" are electret condenser, battery-powered omnidirectional mics.

Lead: In a program, the first story. Theoretically, it's the day's most important story, or it's the freshest major story at the time of broadcast. In a story, the lead is the first sentence or two. Also a verb, to lead (with).

Leader: A second-by-second countdown from ten to zero that is dubbed at the head of a newstape or commercial and used to cue the tape before putting it on the air.

Lead-In: An anchor's introduction to a tape package, sound bite, live interview or reporter at a remote location. Usually not used in reference to the copy preceding an anchor's live voice-over.

Legs: A tripod.

Level: The strength of an audio or video signal, as measured by its magnitude above a reference value.

Limbo: A picture or other visual, put on the air by taping or tacking it to a wall and shooting it with a studio camera. Practically extinct.

Line Level: An amplified audio signal, usable in editing/mixing and capable of driving a loud speaker. Line level produces distorted sound if fed into a mic level input.

Liner: See reader.

Line-Up: See routine.

Lip Flap: When the mouth or lips move but no words are heard. This was a big problem in editing 16 mm news film, because the sound and picture were recorded 28 frames, or nearly a minute apart, on the film. It's not a factor in videotape.

Lip Sync: Sound on tape of a person talking with lips and words synchronized. "Out of sync" means the lips and words noticeably don't match.

Localize: To add local information, local people or a local angle to a national story, or the local example of a national problem or trend.

Long Lens: Same as telephoto lens.

Long Sheet: See routine.

Long Shot: See wide shot.

Loop: A continuous piece of audio or videotape or film that plays over and over. Sometimes created on audiotape to use as a sound bed.

Lower Thirds: Supers—names, locations, telephone numbers, logos, etc.—appearing in the lower third of a television picture.

Master Control: The room that is the electronic hub of a television facility, where distribution of audio and video feeds into, within and out of the facility is controlled.

Master Shot: The shot, usually wide or long, that is used as a master reference in an editing sequence.

Match Cut: An edit that matches the action in two scenes so well that it appears to have been shot with two cameras when, in fact, it is two takes shot from different angles with one camera.

Medium Shot: Imprecise; a shot halfway between wide and close-up. In interviews, the subject from mid-chest up.

Mic Level: A weak audio signal directly from a microphone. It must be amplified before being mixed or aired.

Microwave: Transmission of video or audio signals by line of sight from a remote location to the station or to a receiver which relays the material to the station. Used for live shots and sending raw tape for editing.

Mix, Mixer: See Audio Mixer.

Monitor: A television set for viewing the output of a video or program source. A true monitor is a high definition set with extra electronics for diagnosis of picture problems and for looping audio and video out to another video machine.

Montage: Different shots of the same or similar subjects, edited together to produce an impression rather than illustrate an action.

MOS: A series of "man on the street" interviews in a random, unscientific sampling of public opinion. See Vox Pop.

Mult, Mult Box, Repeater: An electronic device that multiplies the number of feeds available—one feed in, many feeds out, so that several news crews may share the same line-level audio and/or video feed. Mults are often provided at speeches, news conferences, hearings and trials.

NABET: An acronym for National Association of Broadcast Employees and Technicians, a union primarily composed of technicians but including writers, editors and producers in some shops. The union is usually found only at the major-market or network level.

NAT SOT: Script or rundown notation for "natural sound on tape." In film days, it was "NAT SOF."

Natural Sound: The naturally occurring sound at a shoot—noises at a fire, chatter at a party, the music of a marching band, factory clatter, a bubbling brook, chirping birds, the crack of the bat, etc.

Newsclip: Edited tape of a news event; usually a short VO or VOB.

Noise: Random unwanted audio or video signals that interfere with the desired output.

NPPA: National Press Photographers Association, the professional organization for news photographers working with stills, video and film.

NTSC: National Television Systems Committee, sets technical standards for American television.

Omnidirectional Microphone: An all-purpose microphone with a spherical pickup pattern; it picks up sound from all directions.

One-man Band: A reporter/photographer/editor who covers a story alone, who does it all. Managements like the money-saving opportunities offered by one-person coverage. Most reporters and photographers say quality is unavoidably reduced, especially when attempting to cover fast-moving events under deadline pressure. Some people in the industry look to a day when a one-man band, using a few battery-powered digital devices the size of cigarette packages, is able to do a live wraparound from Times Square or the Brazilian rain forest on a moment's notice.

Open: The beginning of something, the first item in a program.

Outcue: The words on which a sound bite ends; the end cue.

Out of Sync: When lips and words don't match in a sound bite. Also slang, with a pejorative meaning similar to "out to lunch."

Outtakes: Unused, leftover scenes. In film days, they were what wound up on the cutting room floor.

Pacing: The rhythm, speed and "feel" of a program, from beginning to end and also within segments, determined by length, visual appeal and type of material. Exciting fire footage, a dull but important speech, a baby contest, a concert rehearsal, a racial confrontation, a recitation of statistics, more readers than voice-overs, etc.—all of these affect pacing.

Package: A reporter's story "packaged" or edited into SOT or sound on tape. In radio, a "spot." Also, a group of stories "packaged" together—today's financial news, today's state capital news, etc.

Pad: Extra picture at the beginning and end of a videotape as a guard against inadvertently going to black. Also, extra news copy that can be eliminated if the program is running long. Also, resistance placed in an audio circuit to match impedances.

Paint: Same as wallpaper, eyewash, etc.

Paint Box: Brand name of a computerized graphics machine.

Pan: Lateral camera movement giving a panoramic view.

Patch: To plug in or connect a line, usually an audio or video source. A "patch panel" is an audio or video routing system somewhat like a switchboard.

Pedestal: Support for a studio camera; more elaborate than a tripod, some pedestals are mechanized and can move the camera and the camera operator up or down. Also, the black level is set for a camera with a waveform monitor.

Pickup: The word with which a sound bite begins.

Playback: To play or playback an audio or videotape; also machines that playback only and do not record.

Pool: In running stories, particularly trials, networks and local stations take turns providing video coverage which is then shared as a means of cutting expenses and minimizing disruption of the event. Also, in political campaigns and presidential trips one "pool reporter" and one "pool camera" may be allowed to ride on the candidate's or president's plane or be in the car directly behind the president's limousine, etc., and provide coverage for all media. Most of the video from political conventions and space shots is pooled.

Portable: Shooting without a tripod, to "go portable" or "on the brace" or "on the shoulder."

Post Production: The editing of field tapes, etc. into the finished product— a news package, a documentary, a sit-com.

Pot: The knob or sliding control used to set audio and video levels. Abbreviation for potentiometer.

Pre-production: The planning process, before field and/or studio production.

Presence: Indistinct background sound sometimes added in preference to absolute silence.

Preview Monitor: Monitors showing the output of the various video sources available to the director before being punched up and put on the air.

Production: Shooting the program or segment in the field or studio (or both). Also, refers to the program or segment itself.

Promo: An in-house commercial promoting a station's or network's programs, service, etc. Also the promotion within a program of a part of that program—to promo the weather, to promo the investigative reporter.

Prompter: A system for displaying a script directly in front of studio cameras so that anchors can appear to be in nearly continuous eye contact with viewers while reading the script. Eye contact is lost when anchors refer to hand scripts. In a prompter system, pages of typed script move on a conveyor belt under a camera whose output is displayed directly in front of studio camera lenses on a sort of one-way mirror. The script is not picked up by the cameras. TelePrompTer is a trademark name for this device.

PSA: Public service announcement. A commercial or promo for a non-profit organization that is broadcast without charge.

Punch, Punch Up: To push the button that puts a video or audio source on the air.

Push: To move closer; can mean by moving the camera or by moving the zoom lens part way in.

Rack Focus: To change focus so that the part of the scene that was in focus is thrown out of focus and another part of the same scene is brought into focus—something either closer or further from the camera than the starting scene. Often used as a transition. Also called throw focus.

Ratio: See Shooting Ratio.

Reaction Shot: A cutaway which shows the reaction of a reporter, bystanders or other audience.

Reader: A news item delivered by the anchor, with or without an over-the-shoulder visual but without videotape. Also a liner. Used also to refer unflatteringly to an anchor who delivers the news but isn't much of a journalist.

Remote: A live broadcast location away from the anchor desk, as close as the newsroom or as far as Kuala Lumpur or a space station.

Repeater: See mult.

Reverse: A cutaway of a reporter in an interview, silently listening or, in sound, asking a question.

Rip and Read: The practice of ripping radio news copy from the wire machine and reading it on the air without rehearsal or editing. Pejorative.

Roll Cue: A director's order to roll (start) a videotape playback machine or film chain, and the point (word) in the script the director has determined to be the right time to give the order.

Rough Cut: The preliminary edited version of a videotape or package.

Routine: The "map" of a television news program, a list showing chronologically, page by page, what is seen and what is heard, at what time and for how long. The routine includes both editorial and production information. Also called line-up, long sheet and rundown.

RTNDA: Radio-Television News Directors Association. It is the major professional organization in broadcast news, with a broad range of membership categories, not just NDs.

Rundown: See routine.

Running Time: The length of a tape or story. Also "cume" time.

Run-Through: A tape or film edited so that somewhere in the middle the director punches up the anchor while the tape or film keeps running, and then goes back to the tape or film for voice-over or a sound bite. Also, a practice session.

Scene: A "shot."

Scoop: A large, old-fashioned "scoop-shaped" or semi-spherical studio light used to illuminate large areas. Editorially, to beat your opposition on a story.

Screen Direction: the direction of movement, left to right or right to left, in a video sequence.

Scrim: A piece of wire screening placed inches in front of the bulb in a light head. It diffuses and softens the light, minimizing harsh shadows on the subject being lit.

Segment: Another of television's imprecise terms. Segment refers to the portions of a program between commercials. Segments are usually assigned designations like opening, first, second, last, closing, sports, weather. It also refers to portions of these segments, as in "the medical segment is in the third segment." It is also used as a synonym for sequence.

Segue: In a general sense, this means to continue without interruption from one element of a program to the next. With specific reference to sound sources, it means to begin one immediately after the other ends, without overlap. Often, one source is faded down and the other faded up.

Self-Standing: A report by a television or radio reporter containing all five W's and enough additional information that it could be used without a lead-in and still be understood; it stands on its own.

Sequence: A series of scenes with a common theme.

Shooter: A video photographer.

Shooting Ratio: The amount of tape shot compared to the amount actually used. If you use up a 30-minute cassette on a story that runs two minutes on the air the shooting ratio is 15 to 1.

Shot: A scene that has been or will be photographed.

Shotgun Microphone: A long, cylindrical cardioid microphone primarily used to isolate and pickup sync sound at a distance. Shotguns can be camera-mounted, hand-held or attached to a boom.

Shouter: An anchor (or reporter) with a strident delivery. Pejorative.

Show: A program.

Sidebar: A story that complements, helps explain or elaborates on the main story. The governor picks your town's mayor for a high state house position. That's the main story. The sidebar is a recap of your mayor's career, or the reaction of townsfolk to his appointment.

SIL: A notation on a script or routine indicating tape with no sound, silent tape. This notation tells the audio director to keep the pot down and not to look for sound on a piece of tape.

Skew: Adjustment of the tape tension in a VCR for optimum playback.

Slant: Editorially, sometimes a synonym for "angle" but also a pejorative term indicating bias.

Slug: The name given to a story and generally used throughout the day to identify it. The assignment desk would list "Axe Murder" in the day's coverage, the photographer would label his tape "Axe Murder," the reporter would title his script "Axe Murder," the tape editor would edit the "Axe Murder" package, the writer would order supers for "Axe Murder," and the producer would slot the story in his routine as "Axe Murder." The purpose is to avoid confusion and misidentification.

SMPTE: Society of Motion Picture and Television Engineers. SMPTE time code shows hours, minutes, seconds and frames.

Snow: White spots in a television picture, resulting from a high "noise" level.

Soft: Out of focus but still recognizable.

SOT: A script or rundown notation for Sound on Tape (videotape). In film days, SOF.

Sound Bed: Music or effects, usually very simple and even repetitious, run behind a program element or added to other sound during post production.

Sound Effect: Non-musical, non-speech sound that is added in post production and was not recorded on the scene as part of the original field production. Effects usually come from commercial collections of sounds on tapes, records or CDs.

Sound Under: When natural sound (or effects) is kept low so that a narration can be clearly heard. A "voice-over" is the same as a "sound under" if there is sound on the tape. The notation "fade sound under" means to drop the sound from normal to very low level.

Split Screen: When the screen is filled with video from two sources, half from one source and half from the other, usually left and right split rather than top and bottom.

Spot: In news, this is primarily a radio term meaning the same as "package" in television. TV often refers to commercials as spots.

Spot Sheet: A tape editor's scene-by-scene breakdown of a story, giving the time of each shot and a description as an aid for the writer. Sometimes called "dope sheet" or "shot list."

Squeezer, Squeeze: An electronic device that squeezes or reduces the size of a video picture, allowing the director to use it in combination with an entirely different full-screen visual. For example, when a reporter at a remote location is seen in small size over the shoulder of the anchor who is introducing the story the reporter will do.

Stacker: A producer who gives little thought to the order and relationship of stories in a news program and instead merely "stacks" the show. Pejorative.

Standupper: A reporter on camera delivering part of the narration of a story. Sometimes the reporter may actually sit down, or walk while delivering the "standupper." Standuppers are often used when the reporter has no pictures for part of a story, or when the reporter is providing analysis or commentary on the story.

Steadicam: Trade name for a camera-mounting system that allows a photographer to go portable while getting close to tripod-like smoothness.

Sticks: A tripod. Originally it referred to tripods with wooden legs. Also called "legs."

Stop Down: To reduce the aperture of a lens so less light gets in the camera. Lenses have standard "f-stops"—f-8, f-11, f-16, f-22, etc. The higher the number, the smaller the aperture. Therefore, confusingly, to "stop *down*" (and reduce the light) you move to a *higher* number.

Stretch: To reduce reading speed. Done on-camera (with script or ad lib) to use more time if the program is running short, and done during voice-overs in order to hit a sound bite rather than run short.

Stringer: A reporter or photographer who works by the story rather than receiving a regular paycheck. Some stringers receive small but regular retainers in addition to per-story pay.

Sun Gun: A battery-operated light that can be hand-held or mounted on an ENG camera. Sun Gun is a brand name that is used generically.

Super: A name or other identification or information superimposed on the screen.

S-VHS: Super-VHS, the high end version of the Video Home System video format. S-VHS is used in industrial and educational video and by some broadcasters.

Sweetening: The final fine editing, usually in reference to audio, in highly-produced programs or segments.

Switcher: The electronic device used to choose between and combine (to switch) the various video sources available in the production of a program. Also, the person who operates the switcher. Video switchers are sometimes called video mixers.

Sync Generator: A device, usually incorporated in a switcher, that provides horizontal and vertical sync pulses. These are then used to synchronize the various cameras and other video sources used in a production.

Tag: Additional information added by an anchor, on camera, at the end of a newsclip, package or live report.

Tail: The end of a tape or package.

Take: As a command, to "take" the output of an audio or video source and put it on the air. Also, one of several versions of a shot, sequence or segment.

Talent: In general, anyone who appears on the air; more often refers to anchors than reporters. Sometimes used sarcastically.

Talking Head: Any person (but usually an interview subject) in sync sound, talking, talking, talking. Regarded by some producers as dull and therefore to be avoided.

Tally, Tally Light: In the studio, a red light on the top front of a camera that comes on when the camera is put on the air by the director. The light tells the anchor which camera to look at. It also appears in the camera viewfinder to tell the camera operator not to move unless directed to do so. ENG cameras also have tally lights, as well as a tally indicator in the viewfinder to tell the photographer a recording is being made.

Tease: A line or two read by the anchor, sometimes on-camera, sometimes voice-over, promoting an upcoming story.

Technical Director (TD): A person responsible for various technical aspects of program production; often refers to the person who operates the switcher.

Telephoto Lens: A lens with a long focal length and narrow angle of view. It magnifies and permits you to photograph distant scenes so they appear to be close. Also called long lens.

TelePrompTer: See prompter.

Three-Shot: Three people in a scene, most often three people who are going to be interviewed at the same time or three talents on the studio set.

Throwaway: A news item or lines of script that are dispensable.

Tight: A close-up shot of a person or object, or a program with so much material there's a strong chance of running over. Also used to refer to anything that seems rushed or a package that seems to have too much information.

Tilt: Motion of a camera, up or down from a pivot point.

Time Base Corrector (TBC): An electronic device that corrects timing errors in the video signal of a tape as it is being played on the air or into an editing system.

Tracking: Adjustment on a VCR which controls the way the machine's video heads line up with the tracks of video information on the videotape. They must be correctly aligned to get the best picture the tape can deliver.

Transformer: Device that converts alternating current (AC) to the direct current (DC) on which most portable video equipment operates. The photographer plugs the transformer (also called the AC Adapter) into an ordinary household outlet and uses a line from the transformer to run the camera and save batteries.

Truck: Lateral movement of a studio camera. Compare with dolly in and dolly out.

TV Cutoff: The part of the picture that is "lost" between being photographed and received on the home screen, for lack of uniformity in cameras and TV sets. Many ENG cameras record more of a scene than shows in the viewfinder. Some viewfinders include lines suggesting the area you can count on as being seen at home. The trick is to avoid putting important material in the margins of the picture.

Two-Shot: When two people, usually an interviewer and interviewee, are in the same shot.

U-Matic: The video format used in three-quarter-inch machines.

Upcut: When the beginning or end of a sound bite or anchor script are lost because of a technical error. Sometimes done deliberately in editing to wipe out an unwanted syllable or two.

Update: To report new information about a previously-recorded story.

VCR: Video Cassette Recorder.

VHS: Video Home System, the half-inch video format used by all manufacturers except Sony.

Video: The picture portion of a television signal.

Video Switcher: See switcher.

Viewfinder: The tiny television monitor on an ENG camera that shows what the camera is seeing or recording.

Visual(s): Pictures, something other than a "talking head."

VOB: A voice-over followed by a (sound) bite. Variations are a bite followed by a voice-over, or a bite between two voice-overs, etc.

Voice-Over (VO): A narration, live or recorded, behind silent or "sound under" news videotape. The term is also used in reference to commercials.

Voicer: A radio reporter's report without actuality. The television equivalent is a "standup report."

Vox Pop: See MOS. From Latin, *vox populi* or voice of the people.

VTR: Video Tape Recording.

VU Meter: Volume Unit meter which indicates the level of an audio signal, roughly equivalent to volume.

Walking Shot: When the photographer walks while shooting. Sometimes refers to a standupper in which the reporter walks.

Wallpaper: Generic file footage used in VOs and as cover and lay-over. You might "wallpaper" a story about lumber prices with footage from old spotted owl or home-construction stories, or a story about the Florida economy with sunbathers in bikinis. Wallpapering is a common technique that sometimes misleads viewers because it wasn't shot the day of the story, it isn't necessarily exactly what the story is about, and it may be remembered by some viewers as belonging to a different story. Also called "eyewash," "wash," and "paint."

WGA: Writers Guild of America, a union primarily for entertainment and documentary writers.

White Balance: An adjustment that provides a camera's electronics with a white to use as a reference in setting other colors. Photographers must "white balance" every time they change locations or when there's a change in light while they are shooting at a location.

Wide-angle Lens: A lens with a short focal length and wide angle of view.

Wide-eye Lens: Television version of a fish-eye 180-degree lens, it provides a very wide angle of view while providing a rectangular scene rather than a fish-eye's circular scene.

Wide Shot: In general, the whole scene rather than a close-up of part of it.

Wild Sound (Track): Natural or ambient non-synchronous sound, recorded on videotape or audiotape for later mixing into a video production.

Wind Screen: A foam cover for the head of a microphone to minimize the noise caused by wind blowing across the grille of the mic.

Wing, Wing It: To go on the air (or record a program or segment) without rehearsal or a great deal of preparation.

Wipe: A video effect in which one picture replaces another, seeming to push the old picture out of the way. Wipes can be done horizontally, vertically and diagonally, in one direction or two, starting anywhere in the frame.

Wireless Mic: A microphone with a pocket-sized transmitter to send its output to a receiver and recorder up to several hundred yards away. This eliminates inconvenient and unsightly microphone wires. Wireless mics are used for walking interviews, standuppers, situations in which featured people may go about their activities while explaining how they do what they do, etc., and for surreptitious recording.

Workprint: An exact copy of original video or film, used in place of the original for screening and making editing decisions to avoid damage to the original.

Wrap: The end of something—a wrap, it's finished.

Wraparound: A news story in which a reporter's narration precedes and follows—or "wraps around"—an actuality or sound bite. Primarily a radio term.

Zoom: A lens movement from a starting shot to a closer shot. Also "zoom in" and the reverse, "zoom out" or "pullback."

Zoom Lens: A variable focus lens, from wide-angle to telephoto, which enables you to get close and distant views of a scene without changing position.

Index

About the Author

Charles Coates has spent more than 35 years teaching and working as a writer, reporter, editor and producer. He served as a producer for NBC news shows in New York ("Today," "Huntley-Brinkley," and the "NBC Nightly News") and reported for the *New York Times.* He shares an Emmy as a television news producer and now teaches at the University of New Mexico.